MICHAEL
FIELD'S
COOKING
SCHOOL

MICHAEL FIELD'S COOKING SCHOOL

a selection of great recipes demonstrating
the pleasures and principles of fine cooking

DRAWINGS BY RODERICK WELLS

HOLT, RINEHART AND WINSTON

NEW YORK

Library of Congress Cataloging in Publication Data

Field, Michael, 1915–1971.
  Michael Field's Cooking school.

  Includes index.
  1. Cookery, International. I. Title. II. Title:
Cooking school.
TX725.A1F5 1977   641.5′9   77–1943

ISBN: 0-03-018476-2

Originally published by M. Barrows and Company, New York
First Holt edition: 1977

Printed in the United States of America
1   3   5   7   9   10   8   6   4   2

to Frances and Jonathan

Contents

Introduction

THIS BOOK is based on my years of experience as a teacher of cooking. The disparate backgrounds of my students, their likes and dislikes, abilities or the lack of them, have led me to include here those recipes that proved most useful to their varied family and social needs. At the same time I have concentrated on recipes that have particular value for demonstrating basic culinary principles. And, each recipe is an example of fine cooking at its best, chosen to give you, the cook, the pleasure of setting on your table a dish of true excellence—whether it be simple or intricate, of humble origin or in the great classic tradition.

Here is the place to set forth without equivocation a personal prejudice: There is no such thing as gourmet cooking. You will not find the word again in these pages. Having started as a perfectly respectable part of the French language, it has been abused to serve as a label for the worst eccentricities and superficial elaborations of modern American cooking. Unfortunately, it commonly serves to label the best, too. The contradiction has left the word without any justifiable meaning. Tradition, taste, technical skill, and respect for ingredients are the standards of good cooks everywhere. It is to these that this book is devoted.

These recipes have been taught by me innumerable times and the method of presentation here follows closely that of my classes. There, the cooking is done by myself and my assistant so that each completed dish is an ideal example of its kind. Students may participate in the cooking to a point if they wish, but by and large they prefer to take voluminous notes on every aspect of the recipe, taste the dish when it is done, then return home to duplicate it in the privacy of their own kitchens. Because this method works so well for them, I have every reason to believe that this carefully transcribed version of my classes will serve a similar function for you.

The repertory of dishes offered here is ample and well balanced for planning many and varied menus (see p. 347), but the total number of recipes is nevertheless not large, and with good reason: Each recipe is explored in depth and is almost wholly self-contained, with a minimum of cross references to other recipes; every process is described as it occurs in the particular dish you are making at the moment, no matter where else the same procedure may also be applied.

✱ *You will, however, find the descriptions of certain important processes italicized and indented as is this paragraph. Whenever necessary, the same instructions are repeated again and again in other recipes, but sometimes in abbreviated form; therefore they are there accompanied by page references so that you may turn to this more complete description if you wish. Moreover, all these procedures are listed in the index, as they are repeatedly useful whether you are cooking from this book or from another.*

At the beginning of each chapter I have written a summary of important things to be learned in that chapter, be they techniques, definitions of classic terms, or notes on the theory or background of certain dishes. And at the end of each recipe I have listed AFTERTHOUGHTS—additional information concerning variations on the dish, possible short cuts, different ways of garnishing and serving, and other helpful miscellany. These details are appended in this way in order not to interrupt the primary sequence of the recipe.

Cooking a new dish can be an exciting adventure but it might be well, particularly if you haven't cooked much before, to temper your courage with a few precautions. Choose a recipe that suits your particular purpose, but make sure you have the correct ingredients and equipment, or adequate substitutes, and, most importantly, the time to prepare and cook the dish properly. Short cuts, unless they reproduce almost exactly the original intention, have no place in really fine cooking. And certain dishes cannot be hurried. There are a sufficient number of simple, and important, dishes in this book that can be made easily and quickly when you are pressed for time.

I cannot emphasize enough the need to follow these recipes precisely, especially the first few times you make them. Departures are all well and good provided you know exactly what it is you are departing from. But if you remember that great classical dishes should retain the characteristics that made them great, you are less likely to want to tamper with them. Concentrate on learning the techniques these recipes require first; in time, you will be able to apply the same principles to all manner of interesting improvisations of your own because you will understand precisely how they work and what they accomplish.

For advanced cooks who may have found these introductory notes unnecessary, I hope that some of the unfamiliar recipes in this book will be new discoveries and that my detailed exposition of the familiar classics will contain an insight or two of value. Perhaps you will learn here why some of your favorite dishes have not been turning out exactly as they should, or for that matter discover just why they have been turning out perfectly.

For the beginner, it might be noted that these cooking lessons by no means cover all the complex territory of fine cooking. But whenever possible I have chosen generic recipes; more often than not, mastering just one of them will enable you to read between the lines of any good conventionally written recipe of a related type. Should you eventually master them all, you will be able to tackle confidently a very considerable part of culinary literature, so much of which unreasonably assumes that the reader has a "reasonable" knowledge of cooking.

I feel strongly that one must understand the reasons for culinary processes, or cooking becomes an arbitrary and uncertain affair indeed. Here, as in my classes, I stress the predictability of good cooking. In this lies another of the pleasures of cooking, and every means is presented to achieve it. As a teacher, I have little patience with the concept of cooking as a mysterious art available only to the talented few. And, as a concert pianist, I have too long been confronted with the imponderables of art not to be grateful for the certainties of cooking. After all, cooking, no matter to what heights it may soar, in the end depends upon cause and effect. Given a love for fine food, a palate of some sensibility, and sound instructions, anyone, I am convinced, can learn to cook well.

M.F.

MICHAEL FIELD'S COOKING SCHOOL

CHAPTER I

Hors d'Oeuvres

Mushroom Croustades
Blini with Butter, Caviar, and Sour Cream
Spiedino alla Romana
Chicken Liver Pâté
Marinated Anchovies with Herbs,
    Pimientos, and Olives
Gougère Bourguignonne
Cheese Beignets
Bagna Cauda
Cheese Fondue Jurassienne
Cold Mixed Vegetables à la Grecque

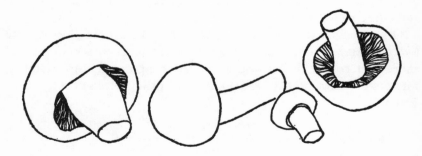

THE TERM hors d'oeuvre originally meant a variety of delicacies served hot or cold as the first course of luncheon or dinner. But the phrase is now used in this country mostly to describe any kind of food served with cocktails. And this can cover quite a range— anything from salted peanuts to elaborate canapés; the so-called "finger foods"; or any savory dish presented more or less in miniature at the cocktail table. This last category, which Americans tend to use to replace a first course, can be troublesome if it requires the use of a plate and fork. As anyone who has tried it knows, manipulating a plate with one hand and a glass with the other away from a dining table requires more dexterity than most of us are capable of. And, if the dish is a particularly fine and subtle one, what a waste of good food!—it should not be served with hard liquor at all but presented with a good wine at table as it was meant to be in the first place.

This chapter contains an international sampling of both cocktail and first-course hors d'oeuvres, some of which can be served in a variety of ways. Among the recipes you will come across several basic processes that recur throughout culinary literature: the bread cases used for MUSHROOM CROUSTADES and the mushroom *duxelles* used in their filling; and *pâte à chou,* the classic paste with which both GOUGÈRE BOURGUIGNONNE and CHEESE BEIGNETS are made. *Pâte à chou* is used again for PROFITEROLES in the chapter on desserts (see page 342).

Other recipes that can be adapted for cocktail hors d'oeuvre are SWEDISH MEAT BALLS, BROILED SHRIMP, and VITELLO TONNATO; and more first course dishes appear in the chapter on fish—notably, FILLETS OF MACKEREL EN ESCABECHE and CLAMS ROCKEFELLER (see Index).

*

*

MUSHROOM CROUSTADES

CROUSTADES are little bread cases made with round slices of soft white bread that are pressed into tiny muffin tins and slowly toasted so they hold their cuplike shape. Filled with a creamy, herb-flavored mixture based on the classic mushroom *duxelles,* they most successfully solve the ever-present problem of how to serve an elegant cocktail hors d'oeuvre with very little labor.

] To serve six or eight [

CROUSTADES:

24 slices fresh, thin-sliced white bread
2 tablespoons very soft butter

MUSHROOM DUXELLES FILLING:

4 tablespoons butter
3 tablespoons finely chopped shallots
½ pound mushrooms, finely chopped

2 level tablespoons flour
1 cup heavy cream
½ teaspoon salt
⅛ teaspoon cayenne
1 tablespoon finely chopped parsley
1½ tablespoons finely chopped chives
½ teaspoon lemon juice

2 tablespoons grated Parmesan cheese
Butter

* *For 24 croustades, you need a 3-inch plain or fluted cooky cutter and 24 tiny muffin tins, each about 2 inches wide at the*

4

top. You can buy them, usually combined in panels of twelve, in most hardware stores.

With a pastry brush, coat the inside of the tins heavily with the 2 tablespoons of soft butter. Cut a 3-inch round from each slice of bread. Carefully fit these into the muffin tins, pushing the center of the bread into the well and gently molding it around the bottom of the tin with the tip of your finger; if you have a small wooden pestle or small round bottle slightly smaller than the bottom of the muffin tin, use this to force the bread in, but don't be rough or the bread will tear. Each bread round, however you mold it, should form a perfect little cup.

Preheat the oven to **400° F.** *and bake the* croustades *for about 10 minutes, or until they brown lightly on the rims and on the outsides. Remove them from the tins and let them cool.*

✳ *The mushroom* duxelles *for the filling is made as follows: Chop the shallots and mushrooms very, very fine. In a heavy 10-inch frying pan, slowly melt the 4 tablespoons of butter and, before the foam subsides, add the shallots. Stir them almost constantly, over moderate heat, for about 4 minutes without letting them brown; then stir in the mushrooms. Mix them well into the butter and see that they are thoroughly coated before leaving them on their own. In a few minutes they will begin to give off a good deal of moisture. Stir them now from time to time, and continue to cook until all the moisture has evaporated—10 to 15 minutes. Then remove the pan from the heat.*

To finish the filling, sprinkle 2 level tablespoons of flour over the mushrooms and stir thoroughly together until not a trace of flour is visible. Immediately pour over this 1 cup of heavy cream and, stirring continuously, bring the mixture to a boil. It will thicken heavily; turn down the heat to the barest simmer, and cook a minute or two longer to remove any taste of raw flour. Remove the pan from the heat and stir in the seasonings and herbs: salt, cayenne, parsley, chives, and lemon juice. Taste, transfer the filling

5

to a bowl, and let it cool; then cover it with Saran wrap and refrigerate until you are ready to use it.

———————

Use a small spoon to fill the *croustades* and mound the filling slightly. Sprinkle each one with a few grains of cheese, dot with a speck of butter, and arrange them on a cooky sheet or jelly-roll pan. Preheat the oven to **350° F.** Ten minutes or so before you want to serve them, heat the *croustades* for 10 minutes in the oven, then briefly under the broiler, but watch them carefully as they burn easily.

AFTERTHOUGHTS:

✳ Like all breads, the unfilled *croustades* freeze wonderfully well. Without defrosting them, fill them with the creamed *duxelles* and heat as described above. If you want to double the recipe for a larger party, freezing the *croustades* ahead is by all means the most convenient.

✳ Other fillings, of course, may be used in *croustades*. It must be made clear, however, that the filling must never be too liquid or the bread cases will get soggy and even fall apart. A custard type of filling or anything combined with an averagely thin sauce will not do, for example.

BLINI WITH BUTTER, CAVIAR
AND SOUR CREAM

To DESCRIBE blini as small Russian pancakes tells only part of their story, for their distinction lies not so much in what they are as in what accompanies them. It would be unthinkable to serve blini to a Russian without butter, caviar, and sour cream; as well offer griddle cakes to an American without butter and syrup! But apart from the trimmings, the difference between the two pancakes is not very great. Mainly, blini are made with yeast which gives them their characteristic flavor, whereas griddle cakes are leavened only with eggs and, sometimes, baking powder. The cooking techniques are exactly the same.

Because of their size, blini make perfect hors d'oeuvres and may be served with cocktails, with a dry champagne or white wine, or, more traditionally, with small glasses of chilled vodka.

] To serve eight or ten [

BLINI BATTER:

½ cup warm water
1 envelope dry granular yeast
1 cup milk, at room temperature
1½ cups sifted flour
3 egg yolks
½ teaspoon salt
¼ teaspoon sugar
6 tablespoons butter, melted and cooled
3 egg whites
Salt

Butter for frying

½ pound butter, clarified and warm
1 pint sour cream
1 large jar caviar, red or black (at least 8 ounces)

The batter for the blini may be made either in an electric blender or by hand. However you make it, time the procedures fairly accurately, for the yeast, if it rises too long, will overferment and give the blini an unpleasant flavor. Moreover, remember that blini cannot be cooked ahead and reheated; they must be eaten directly as they are cooked or they are hardly worth eating at all.

Prepare the batter about 2½ hours before you plan to serve the blini: Stir into ½ cup of warm—not hot—water 1 envelope of dry granular yeast and let it stand until it dissolves, or about 5 minutes. Pour this into the blender jar and add the milk, flour, egg yolks, salt, sugar, and melted butter. Blend at high speed for about 40 seconds; turn off the machine and, with a rubber spatula, scrape down the flour clinging to the sides of the jar. Blend a few seconds longer, then pour the batter into a mixing bowl and cover it loosely with a kitchen towel. Let it rest for 2 hours at room temperature, preferably on the warm side. If your kitchen seems cool, place the bowl near a warm stove or radiator.

To make the batter by hand, sift the flour into a large mixing bowl and, with a large spoon, rub into it the 3 egg yolks and the salt and sugar. Beat in, a few drops at a time, the dissolved yeast and the milk, and continue to beat until the mixture becomes a fairly smooth cream. Strain this through a fine-meshed sieve, rubbing any undissolved bits of flour through with the back of the spoon. Cover the bowl loosely with a towel and let the batter rise as above.

At the end of 2 hours the batter, however you made it, will have risen considerably and bubbled at the top. Now beat the egg whites, with a pinch of salt, until they are stiff, then gently but thoroughly fold them into the batter. (If you are in doubt about how to "fold," take a look at page 337.) The finished batter may be used immediately, or you may let it stand for 15 to 20 minutes without it coming to any harm.

The most reliable way to cook blini is on an automatic electric griddle. Not only is it large enough to cook at least a dozen blini simultaneously but, because the temperature remains constant, each batch is entirely predictable. Moreover, you can set up the griddle directly in the living room and make the cooking of the blini as dramatic a production as you like. If you do this, make sure all your accessories are within easy reach. On one side of the griddle arrange the bowl of batter, a small dish of softened butter, a pastry brush, a small ladle, and a large metal spatula; on the other a bowl of warm clarified butter, one of sour cream, and another of caviar, each with its own serving spoon. Try to have your plates hot, or at least warm.

Preheat the griddle to **400° F.**, then brush it lightly with a little butter. Ladle out enough batter to make blini about 3 inches in diameter, leaving enough space between them so that they can be turned easily. Cook until lightly browned on each side, turning them only once. To serve, arrange three blini on each plate, and bathe them with a little of the clarified butter. Drop a small mound of sour cream on each pancake and top with spoonfuls of caviar. Serve at once.

If you don't own an electric griddle, there are alternatives. The Scandinavians cook their pancakes in an ingenious utensil called a *plett* pan. Made of cast iron and divided into six or seven circular sections, it insures almost the same predictable results as the electric griddle and each time produces blini of exactly the same size. Slowly preheat the pan, then butter each circle lightly before you pour in the batter. (Russians also frequently brush a little butter on the uncooked sides of the blini before turning them over.)

Blini made on a simple cast-iron griddle or in a frying pan are cooked in exactly the same way, but you will need to keep them warm as they are done, in a very slow oven, until you have accumulated a sufficient number to serve.

AFTERTHOUGHTS:

✻ If you don't know how to clarify butter, see page 81.

✻ It isn't at all necessary to limit yourself to caviar. Do as the Russians do and serve the blini with a variety of smoked fish as well, such as whitefish, herring, and/or salmon.

✻ If red caviar is a bit salty for your taste, put it in a sieve and run cold water through it. Spread the eggs out on a paper towel and gently pat them dry. They break easily, so be careful.

✻ Blini are frequently made with buckwheat flour or a combination of buckwheat and white flours. The buckwheat tends to produce a heavier pancake but, if you like it, it may be substituted all or in part for the white.

*

SPIEDINO ALLA ROMANA

THE ITALIANS have all sorts of fanciful names for their celebrated bread-and-cheese dishes and perhaps the most colorful is *mozzarella in carrozza* or, literally, mozzarella in a carriage. A slice of mozzarella is enclosed between two slices of bread, soaked and sealed in a batter of milk, eggs, and bread crumbs, and fried until the cheese melts. When you string together a number of these sandwiches on a *spiedino,* or small skewer, and cook them as a loaf, they become a *spiedino alla romana.* Served with a sauce of anchovies, capers, parsley, lemon, and butter, this is an original and spectacular dish. It does equally well at luncheon, supper, or as a first course for dinner.

] To serve four [

SAUCE:

½ pound unsalted butter
8 flat anchovy fillets, finely chopped
1 tablespoon lemon juice
1 tablespoon capers, coarsely chopped
2 tablespoons finely chopped parsley

2 loaves of French or Italian bread about 12 inches
    long
1 pound mozzarella cheese
1 cup milk
1 cup dry bread crumbs
4 eggs
¼ cup heavy cream
Oil for half-deep frying (vegetable oil, or olive oil,
    or a combination of both)

Make the sauce ahead, as early as you wish. In a small saucepan, slowly melt ½ pound of unsalted butter, but don't let it brown.

10

Stir in the chopped anchovies and keep stirring over low heat until they dissolve. Add the lemon juice, capers, and parsley, and put the pan aside until the *spiedini* are ready to serve.

Slice about 1½ inches off the ends of the two loaves of French or Italian bread, and cut the loaves in half crosswise. Each piece should be about 5 inches long. Stand them upright on a board and, with a sharp knife, carefully cut away all but the bottom crusts; then trim the bread into long narrow "bricks" about 3 inches wide and 2 inches high. Don't fuss too much with this if the bread tends to crumble. Cut each piece into six or seven slices about half an inch thick, cutting down to, but not through the bottom crust. Fanlike, spread the slices apart, and in each space place a slice of mozzarella about a quarter inch thick, trimmed to fit so that no cheese protrudes above or at the sides of the bread. Firmly press bread and cheese together like an accordion, and insert a 6- to 8-inch skewer lengthwise all the way through each one.

Then dip each *spiedino* briefly in milk, but don't let the bread get too soggy or it may fall apart. When the bread is moist and pliable, gently press it into a small compact loaf. Lay the *spiedini* on a strip of waxed paper, sprinkle each one generously with the dry crumbs, and pat the crumbs on with the flat of a knife or a spatula to make them stick. Beat the 4 eggs and ¼ cup of cream together only long enough to combine them, and in this dip the *spiedini*, one by one, coating them thoroughly on all sides.

For obvious reasons, don't attempt to fry the *spiedini* in a pan smaller in diameter than the length of your skewer. If you have one, a 10-inch sauté pan about 2½ inches deep works best. Whatever the pan, fill it with oil to a depth of 1½ inches and heat it to a temperature of **360°F.** (use a deep-frying thermometer). At the same time, preheat the oven to **250°F.**

Carefully lower the *spiedini* into the hot oil, one or two at a time, depending on the size of the pan. Let each side get golden brown before turning them gently with two large spoons. As the *spiedini* are done, use a large spatula to transfer them to a baking dish lined with a paper towel (this to absorb the excess oil), and keep them warm on the middle shelf of the oven. You may leave the finished *spiedini* in the oven for about 10 minutes, but no longer. If the cheese overcooks, it becomes dry and stringy.

———————

In the meantime, reheat the sauce without letting it boil. Serve the *spiedini* on a large heated platter, or individual hot plates, with a generous helping of the sauce poured over and around each one. Remove the skewers or not, as you will.

AFTERTHOUGHTS:

❋ If you feel 5-inch *spiedini* are too large for individual servings, make them smaller. The large ones may, of course, be cut in half after they are cooked.

❋ The Japanese make attractive and durable bamboo skewers about 8 inches long. Find some if you can. Metal skewers, however, are available at any housewares store.

❋ There are different types of mozzarella available, some with higher butter-fat content than others. Most stores, supermarkets particularly, carry only the skim-milk variety but the richer mozzarellas, if you can find them, are worth experimenting with. In any case, avoid the packaged so-called pizza cheese, a rubbery mozzarella with little if any quality or flavor.

❋ For a more substantial *spiedino,* add a thin slice of ham, preferably a mild *prosciutto,* along with each piece of cheese before soaking and frying the *spiedino.*

❋ Although the *spiedini* cannot be cooked ahead and reheated, they may be assembled, crumbed, and dipped in the egg, then covered with waxed paper and refrigerated for an hour or two before they are fried.

CHICKEN LIVER PÂTÉ

IF RICHNESS and velvety smoothness are the criteria, this pâté of chicken livers is one of the closest approximations of a Strasbourg *pâté de foie gras* ever devised. Comparisons aside, it has a quality

12

and distinction all its own. Moreover, it is easy to make, keeps well, and may be frozen quite successfully.

] To make approximately three cups [

3 tablespoons butter
½ cup finely chopped onions
2 tablespoons finely chopped shallots
1 small tart apple, peeled, cored, and chopped coarsely (about ¼ cup)

3 tablespoons butter
1 pound chicken livers, cut in halves
¼ cup Calvados or applejack
2–4 tablespoons heavy cream

10 tablespoons butter (1 stick plus 2 tablespoons)
1 teaspoon lemon juice
1½ teaspoons salt
¼ teaspoon freshly ground black pepper
Optional: 1–2 tablespoons finely chopped truffles
¼ pound butter, clarified

To spare you unnecessary arithmetical speculation, the first three separate amounts of butter in the list of ingredients add up to one half pound, precisely. Divide it into the amounts specified, and in a small bowl put aside 10 tablespoons of it to soften to room temperature. Clean the chicken livers carefully, cutting away any green or brown spots, then wash them quickly under cold running water, and pat them dry with paper towels. Now cut them each in half.

In a large heavy frying pan, melt the first 3 tablespoons of butter. Add the chopped onions and shallots and cook over moderate heat for 5 to 7 minutes, stirring every now and then, until the onions are soft and lightly colored. Mix in the chopped apple, and cook 3 or 4 minutes longer. When it is soft enough to mash with a spoon, transfer the whole mixture to the container of an electric blender.

In the same frying pan, melt the second 3 tablespoons of butter, this time over rather brisk heat. As the butter foam subsides, add the chicken livers. Over high heat, turn them in the sputtering butter with a wooden spoon for about 3 or 4 minutes. When the livers are quite brown on the outsides and still pink within (cut into one to make sure), remove the pan from the heat and flame them with ¼ cup of warmed Calvados or applejack; if you need advice on how to do this, look at page 115. Let the alcohol burn itself out completely.

Now add the livers and all their juices to the onion-apple mixture in the blender. Moisten this with 2 tablespoons of cream and blend at high speed, pouring in a little additional cream if the blender clogs. It doesn't matter if the liver mixture finally becomes somewhat fluid but it *must* be smooth. With a rubber spatula, scrape it out into a fairly fine mesh sieve set over a mixing bowl. Rub the paste through with the back of a large spoon, and let it cool completely.

In the meantime, cream the 10 tablespoons of, by now, softened butter by beating, mixing, and mashing it against the sides of the bowl until it is absolutely smooth. When the liver paste is cool— and no sooner—beat it, little by little, into the butter; if the liver is too warm, the butter will melt and give the finished pâté an oily texture. Stir in thoroughly the teaspoon of lemon juice, 1½ teaspoons of salt (or less if your butter was salted), and a few grindings of black pepper. Fold in the chopped truffles, if you have them, and taste the pâté now for seasonings. Don't be over-cautious about the salt; since cold deadens flavor, the pâté will be surprisingly less salty than you thought after it is refrigerated.

Pack the soft pâté into a couple of small earthenware crocks or *terrines* if you have them; if not, any attractive quart-size glass or pottery dish will do. Smooth the top of the pâté with a spatula, and pour over it enough clarified butter to cover it completely. This will not only prevent the pâté from changing color as it chills but will make an almost airtight covering that lessens the possibility of spoilage. (If you do not use the clarified butter, cover the crocks

14

with Saran wrap.) Refrigerate at least 3 or 4 hours, or until the pâté is firm, before serving it with French bread, pumpernickel, or homemade Melba toast.

AFTERTHOUGHTS:

✳ If you don't know how to clarify butter, see page 81.

✳ To make the pâté by hand, instead of puréing the onion-apple-liver mixture in the blender, do this in a food mill. Then rub it through a fine sieve. Combine it with the creamed butter as described above.

✳ This pâté may be made quite successfully with frozen chicken livers. Defrost the livers. After they are browned in butter, you must remove them from the pan and drain off, or almost completely reduce by hard boiling, the excessive amount of liquid they will have thrown off.

✳ The pâté with its seal of clarified butter will keep at least a week under constant refrigeration. If you must keep it longer, freeze it, and let it thaw to refrigerator temperature before serving.

✳ To present the pâté more colorfully, sprinkle a narrow ring of finely chopped parsley around the edge of the chilled butter seal and decorate the center with a truffle cut-out.

MARINATED ANCHOVIES
WITH HERBS, PIMIENTOS, AND OLIVES

FOR THE AVERAGE palate, canned, flat anchovies are too insistent and forthright in flavor to be served as they are. Marinated in the Mediterranean fashion, they are something else again. And arranged on a platter, strewn with fresh herbs, and garnished with pimiento and black olives, they look almost as impressive as they taste.

］ To serve six ［

2 two-ounce cans flat anchovies in olive oil
1 tablespoon lemon juice
1 tablespoon olive oil

15

1 tablespoon finely chopped shallot
1/4 teaspoon finely chopped garlic
Freshly ground black pepper
1 tablespoon finely chopped fresh dill
    or 1 teaspoon crumbled dried dill weed
1 tablespoon finely chopped parsley
1 teaspoon finely chopped chives
1 four-ounce can whole pimientos
12 black olives, Greek or Italian if possible
Buttered toast

Choose flat anchovies of superior quality; too often the supermarket bargains are too highly salted, pulpy, or crudely filleted. Open the cans and drain all their oil into a small mixing bowl. Add to it the lemon juice, olive oil, shallot, garlic, and a little freshly ground black pepper. Beat these together thoroughly with a fork, then stir in the dill, parsley, and chives. The mixture should be thick but still fluid; if it seems too dense, thin it with a little more olive oil.

In the center of 10- or 12-inch circular platter place a whole pimiento. Cut the rest of the pimientos into narrow, 2-inch-long strips. Separate the anchovies, and arrange them alternating with strips of pimiento like the spokes of a wheel all around the whole pimiento. Spread the herbed marinade over the wheel and garnish the edge of the platter with the black olives. Cover the platter loosely with waxed paper and let the anchovies marinate for at least an hour at room temperature before serving with hot buttered toast. Cocktail napkins are a necessity with these.

AFTERTHOUGHTS:

✻ Make the buttered toast ahead of time and reheat it on a cooky sheet in a **250° F.** oven just before serving.

✻ Substitute minced onions for the shallots, if you must, but in that case omit the chives.

✻ If you must refrigerate the anchovies after preparing them, be sure to let them return to room temperature before serving.

✳

GOUGÈRE BOURGUIGNONNE

Pâte à chou, a simple paste of water, butter, flour, and eggs is perhaps the most versatile of all French doughs and is certainly the easiest to make. Used as it is in America almost exclusively as a cream-puff base (see page 341), we know too little about the culinary miracles the French accomplish with it. And the Burgundian *gougère* is one of them. The basic *pâte à chou* is combined with cheese and seasonings, piped into a ring, sprinkled with more cheese, and baked until it puffs quite incredibly into an impressive hollow crown. Served hot, warm, or cold, the *gougère* makes a delectable hors d'oeuvre; but it also does well at lunch, with a salad, or eaten at any time of the day, as the Burgundians eat it, accompanied by a glass of red wine.

] To serve eight or ten [

Pâte à Chou:

¼ pound butter, cut in small pieces
1 cup water
1 cup unsifted flour
4 large eggs

1 teaspoon Dijon mustard
½ teaspoon dry mustard
1½ teaspoons salt
1½ cups coarsely grated imported Swiss cheese

1 tablespoon soft butter
¼ cup flour

1 egg yolk mixed with 1 tablespoon heavy cream

✳ *The classic* pâte à chou *is always made the same way, no matter to what use it is finally put. Cut the butter into small*

17

pieces and add it to the cup of water in a 2-quart saucepan. Bring the water to a rolling boil, and when the butter is completely melted, remove the pan from the heat and dump in the cup of flour. With a large wooden spoon, quickly mix the flour and water together to the consistency of mashed potatoes, then return the pan to the stove. Over moderate heat, beat and mix the paste vigorously for a minute or two until it becomes a smooth, doughy mass that moves all together with the spoon. Now remove the pan again from the heat.

With the back of the spoon, make a small indentation in the center of the paste before it begins to cool; break an egg into it and quickly begin to beat. After the first few strokes, the paste will separate into moist doughy strands. Continue to beat vigorously until the strands come together again and form a solid mass. At that point, make another indentation in the paste and add another egg. Beat together as before, and proceed in the same fashion to add the third and fourth eggs.

After the last egg is beaten in, the paste should be smooth and shiny and should fall lazily off the lifted spoon back into the pan. If the paste is too firm and resistant, break another egg into a dish, stir it lightly with a fork, then beat from a quarter to a half of it into the paste to give it the proper consistency.

This procedure of adding the eggs requires somewhat less energy if you own an electric mixer equipped with a pastry-arm attachment: Transfer the hot dough to the mixing bowl and, with the mixer set at medium speed, beat in the eggs one at a time. But don't attempt this with an ordinary beater attachment; the paste is much too dense.

For *gougères,* beat the seasonings into the *pâte à chou*—the salt and the Dijon and dry mustards—and follow with 1¼ cups of the grated cheese, reserving the remaining ¼ cup until later. Taste the *chou* paste and adjust the seasonings any way you like.

18

Preheat the oven to **450° F.** Meanwhile, prepare a large cooky sheet or jelly-roll pan: First grease it evenly with a tablespoon of soft butter; then carelessly scatter ¼ cup of flour over this, tilt the pan so the flour spreads over the whole buttered surface, then shake off the excess flour by holding the pan upright on its side and rapping it sharply on the table. This operation will be considerably less messy if you do it over a long strip of waxed paper which can then be rolled up and thrown away.

Using a 7-inch cake pan or flan ring, press the outlines of two circles on the floured surface of the pan or cooky sheet, spacing them about 2 inches apart. If there isn't room, make smaller circles or use a second pan. Scoop up the *pâte à chou* a tablespoon at a time and place the spoonfuls one next to the other in a ring just inside the outline of each circle. Then, with a spatula, join and shape the dough into smooth, 2-inch-thick rings about an inch high.

A more professional way to do this is with a pastry bag fitted with a number 6 or 8 plain tip. Fill the bag no more than two thirds full of paste at a time. Fold the top opening firmly over itself so that no paste can escape, and press out an even 2-inch-thick ring inside each circle as above.

However you make the rings, paint them lightly with a pastry brush dipped into the egg yolk and cream mixture; make sure the egg doesn't drip down the sides of the *gougères* and stick to the pan —this could make them rise unevenly. Sprinkle the reserved ¼ cup of cheese over the surface of the rings, and slide the cooky sheet onto the center shelf of the preheated oven. In about 10 minutes the *gougères* will have begun to expand; turn the heat down to **350° F.** Bake them at this temperature for 10 more minutes, then reduce the heat further, to **325° F.,** at which temperature the *gougères* will bake another 20 minutes—and which makes about 40 minutes baking time in all

The finished *gougères* should be well puffed, attractively brown, and crisp and dry on the outsides. If you don't intend to serve them at once—and prefer them warm—let them rest in the turned-off oven with the door slightly ajar. They can stay this way a good half hour before they begin to cool. It's a good idea, if you do this, also to pierce the sides of the *gougères* with the point of a sharp knife in three or four places to let out the steam; otherwise the insides will get soggy and the *gougères* may collapse as they wait.

At the last minute, cut into generous pieces and serve immediately.

AFTERTHOUGHTS:

✳ You may use more cheese than is specified if you like, but the *gougères* will be heavier in texture and less spectacularly puffed.

✳ For many tastes a *gougère* is at its best served hot, although, surprisingly, the Burgundians themselves prefer it cold.

✳ Although it is hardly traditional, there is no reason why you can't substitute freshly grated Parmesan cheese for half the Swiss cheese.

CHEESE BEIGNETS

THESE CHEESE *beignets,* or fritters, as we call them, are really *beignets soufflés.* They puff up to spectacular proportions and are light and delicate as any soufflé. Apart from the dramatic effect they create, what makes them technically interesting is their close kinship with the preceding GOUGÈRE BOURGUIGNONNE; in fact, the cheese-flavored *pâte à chou* used in both is exactly the same. The only difference is the manner in which they are cooked—the *beignets* being deep fried instead of baked in a ring. They are excellent served with cocktails.

] To serve eight [

For enough *beignets* to serve eight people generously, make half the amount of seasoned *pâte à chou* in the preceding recipe for GOUGÈRE BOURGUIGNONNE. In place of the Swiss cheese use freshly grated Parmesan cheese, if you like; or try a combination of both. Although the *pâte à chou* may be made hours ahead, the *beignets* themselves should not be fried until you are ready to serve them. They are at their best very hot.

Whatever deep-frying pan you use (there is a discussion of deep-frying technique on page 136), make sure the fat or oil is at least 2½ inches deep. The *beignets* will swell as they cook and will most assuredly stick to the bottom of the frying basket if they are crowded. Slowly heat the fat to **365°** **F.** and, at the same time, preheat the oven to **250°** **F.** Line a baking dish with a double thickness of paper towels.

Scoop up a heaping teaspoon of *chou* paste and drop it into the hot fat, pushing it off the spoon with the tip of your finger or with another small spoon. Don't cook too many *beignets* at once or the temperature of the fat will drop. As they slowly brown and puff up, they will take on all kinds of fanciful shapes, and, theoretically, when they are half done, they should turn over of their own accord. But frequently, they don't; with a wooden spoon, help the recalcitrant ones along. Try to get them as evenly brown as possible, without burning them, before transferring them to the baking dish to drain. Keep them warm in the oven where they may remain for at least a half hour without coming to any harm.

To serve, arrange the *beignets* on a doily-lined platter and sprinkle them generously with finely grated Parmesan or Swiss cheese.

BAGNA CAUDA

ONLY THE ITALIANS with their love of the dramatic and the unexpected could devise so original a dish as *bagna cauda.* A specialty of the province of Piedmont in northern Italy, it consists of a hot anchovy and garlic cream sauce—*bagna cauda* literally means "hot bath"—into which icy cold vegetables are dipped. It may be served as an hors d'oeuvre with cocktails or as part of an *antipasto* at lunch or dinner.

] To serve six [

VEGETABLES*:

1 sweet red pepper
1 green pepper
2 medium carrots, scraped
1 cucumber, peeled and seeded
4 stalks celery
1 bunch young scallions

SAUCE:

2 cups heavy cream
4 tablespoons unsalted butter
8 flat canned anchovy fillets, finely chopped
1 teaspoon finely chopped garlic
1 canned white truffle, finely chopped
⅛ teaspoon cayenne

Italian bread sticks

* See also AFTERTHOUGHTS at the end of this recipe.

Before making the *bagna cauda,* clean all the vegetables and cut them up, all except the scallions, into 2- or 3-inch lengths about one half inch wide. Soak them in a bowl of ice water for at least an hour. When they are crisp and icy cold, dry them with paper towels, arrange them on a platter in as colorful a fashion as you can, and refrigerate them, covered, until the sauce is ready.

First reduce the 2 cups of cream by bringing it to a boil in a small heavy saucepan. Let the cream boil rather briskly until it shows signs of thickening, then turn down the heat to moderate and, with a wooden spoon, stir the hot cream almost constantly until it measures just 1 cupful. Pour it into a cup or small bowl and let it cool.

Meanwhile, in a clean saucepan, melt 4 tablespoons of unsalted butter over low heat, and add to it the chopped anchovies and garlic. In no circumstances must the butter be allowed to brown. Stir in the reduced cream, the chopped truffle and cayenne, and heat the sauce almost to the boiling point, but don't let it boil.

The most satisfactory and attractive dish in which to serve the *bagna cauda* is in a small earthenware or enamel casserole which can be kept hot, without boiling, over a candle warmer, spirit lamp, electric hot tray, or any such source of heat that can be controlled. Whatever your choice, present the *bagna cauda* with the platter of cold vegetables and plenty of napkins. If, as the sauce stands, it gets too thick, add a few tablespoons of hot cream. Serve bread sticks for a more substantial dish, and suggest to your guests that they dip these also in the sauce.

AFTERTHOUGHTS:

✻ The variety of vegetables you may serve with the *bagna cauda* is almost endless. Try, among others, raw broccoli or cauliflower flowerettes, raw white turnip, small raw mushrooms, endive leaves, raw asparagus tips, strips of white radish, or whole red radishes.

✻ If you object to the texture and taste of chopped garlic, use thin slices or whole cloves of garlic when you first make the sauce and fish them out later. Or, for the mildest garlic flavor, cook 5 whole, unpeeled cloves of garlic with the cream as you reduce it, and remove them when you make the sauce.

✻ White truffles are available in most good Italian food stores. In the small cans they come usually one to the can. If you have never tasted or smelled a white truffle, don't be alarmed at its almost excessively gamey aroma. In the sauce, its character changes completely and its contribution to this dish is an important one.

✳

CHEESE FONDUE JURASSIENNE

THERE ARE many versions of the classic cheese fondue which, when all is said and done, is simply a fragrant melted cheese flavored with wine and spirits. Although the Swiss fondue is the best known, it has, to some of us at least, a certain sharp crudity, the result of melting the cheese in heated but uncooked wine. In the following French version of this dish, the wine is first reduced before being mixed with the cheese. The addition of a little butter, cream, and Kirsch refines it even further and produces a fondue of great delicacy.

] To serve eight or ten [

1¾ cups dry white wine (Riesling, Traminer, or
      Chablis)
2 cloves garlic, cut up coarsely
¾ pound imported Switzerland Swiss cheese, grated
      (about 3 cups)
2 level tablespoons flour
2 tablespoons butter
2–6 tablespoons heavy cream
Salt and freshly ground pepper
3 tablespoons Kirsch

French or Italian bread

Traditionally, a cheese fondue is made in an earthenware dish which is kept hot over an alcohol burner at the table. Use this if you have one; if not, a 1½- or 2-quart chafing dish will do as well if not better, particularly if it has a lower pan which can be filled with hot water.

_____

A successful fondue must be cooked at the last minute, so have all your ingredients prepared and at hand when you start to make it. Earlier in the day, or whenever you like, reduce the 1¾ cups

24

of wine: Bring it to a boil, with the cut-up garlic, in an enamel or Pyrex pot; cook it briskly until it has boiled down to about 1 1/3 cups. Strain out the garlic and put the wine aside, covered with waxed paper or Saran wrap.

The easiest way to grate the cheese is in an electric blender; cut the cheese into half-inch chunks (no larger, or it will clog the blades) and pulverize it a handful at a time. If you don't own a blender, a hand grater gives similar results for the price of a little extra exertion. In a small bowl mix the grated cheese thoroughly with the 2 tablespoons of flour, and cover it with Saran wrap so that it doesn't dry out. Cut the bread into 1-inch slices; cut each slice into 1-inch cubes, and make sure each cube has at least one side of crust. Wrap the bread and put it aside.

When you are ready to make the fondue, light the flame under your chafing dish and fill the lower pan with hot water. Place it where you intend to serve the finished fondue and adjust the flame so that the water barely simmers. In the kitchen, pour the reduced wine into the cooking pan of the chafing dish and bring it to a boil on the stove. Lower the heat at once so the wine simmers slowly. Now throw in the cheese a handful at a time, stirring constantly with a fork until you have used all the cheese and the mixture is a smooth, creamy mass. Don't at any point allow this to boil; if it looks as if it might, lift the pan off the heat from time to time, stirring, however, all the while.

When the cheese has melted completely, mix in the 2 tablespoons of butter and then 2 tablespoons of the cream. Add more cream, a tablespoon at a time, if you think the mixture is too thick. The fondue should be thick enough to coat the spoon heavily but not so thick that it clings to the spoon solidly. Season it lightly with salt and a few grinds of the pepper mill. Stir in the 3 tablespoons of Kirsch—imported, if possible; the domestic variety is too raw—and serve the fondue at once.

Provide each of your guests with a fork. There are special long fondue forks available in restaurant-supply houses but they are not essential; any dinner fork will do. To start the ball rolling, spear a cube of bread on the end of your fork and dip it into the hot fondue. Twirl the bread around until it is thoroughly coated with the hot cheese and pop it into your mouth. Your guests may need a little inducement to follow your lead. If, at any point during this charmingly informal procedure, the fondue seems to be getting unmanageably thick (be prepared for it to thicken somewhat), add a little more heated cream.

AFTERTHOUGHTS:

✳ You *must* use imported Swiss cheese, not only for its far superior flavor but because the domestic imitations are much more likely to produce a fondue that becomes rubbery and stringy. Let's face it, however, the best imported-Swiss fondue may get a little stringy, too. Do not be dismayed, the flavor is not affected. Attack the problem directly: Have at hand a pair of scissors to cut off the stubborn strands that trail off your morsel of bread after it has been dipped in the fondue.

COLD MIXED VEGETABLES À LA GRECQUE

THE MEDITERRANEAN method of preparing cold vegetables is original, simple, and effective: The vegetables are cooked in a lemon-flavored, water and oil based marinade, then served cold with the reduced marinade. But for some tastes the classic marinade is a trifle pallid, the vegetables often emerging from their aromatic bath with too little spice to have much distinction. In the following version, chicken stock and white wine take the place of the water in the original recipe. The result, you will find, more than justifies the elaboration.

Technically, the essential point in this recipe is that the vegetables are each cooked separately so that each can be timed to the right degree of tenderness.

And this, by the way, is a first-course hors d'oeuvre which is best eaten at table. These vegetables are good, also, served with a cold BEEF À LA MODE (see Index).

26

VEGETABLES À LA GRECQUE

] To serve ten or twelve [

MARINADE:

3 cups chicken stock, fresh or canned
1 cup dry white wine, or dry vermouth
1 cup olive oil
10 coriander seeds, slightly bruised
10 peppercorns, slightly bruised
2 large cloves garlic, thinly sliced
3 teaspoons salt
½ teaspoon thyme
4 sprigs parsley
1 large bay leaf
2 stalks fennel, thinly sliced (if available)
½ cup lemon juice

VEGETABLES:

20 small white onions, about 1 inch in diameter
3 zucchini, sliced 1 inch thick
3 yellow squash, sliced 1 inch thick
4 peppers (2 sweet red ones and 2 green), cut lengthwise into ½-inch-wide strips

2 tablespoons finely chopped parsley
Lemon slices

Make your own chicken stock (see page 34) for the marinade if
you can, and skim off all the fat. Apart from its superior flavor,
a strong homemade stock will give the cooked vegetables an attractive thin glaze of gelatine when they are cold. Of course, canned
stock will do, and nicely; but for this recipe, chill the cans first,
then remove all the congealed fat from the stock before you use it.
And, if you like, give it the treatment suggested on page 37.

Plan to cook the vegetables in the marinade at least a day before you serve them. The preparation of the marinade is simplicity itself: Merely combine all the listed ingredients in a shallow 3- or 4-quart pan and bring them to a boil. Then cover the pan tightly, reduce the heat, and simmer very slowly for about 45 minutes. Strain the cooked marinade through a fine sieve into a mixing bowl and, with a large spoon, press down hard on the vegetables to extract their juices before throwing them away. Pour the marinade back into the saucepan and taste for salt; it should be quite salty and the 3 teaspoons suggested may very well not be enough. (Most marinades should be somewhat overseasoned if they are to affect to any perceptible degree the foods that are cooked in them. A delicate marinade is suspect and usually doesn't do its job.)

A fine way to peel small white onions easily is to drop them into a pan of boiling water for a minute or so. Drain at once and, when they are cool enough to handle, peel them carefully. Don't, however, peel the zucchini and squash; just wash and scrub them with a small brush under cold running water. Trim off the ends and slice the vegetables crosswise into 1-inch pieces. Cut away the white inside ribs of the peppers before you slice them lengthwise into strips.

Cook the onions first. Start the marinade boiling, drop the onions in, and cover the pan. Reduce the heat to moderate, and let them boil for 30 minutes or so, depending on their size. Test them from time to time with the point of a small sharp knife; when you can pierce them easily and they still hold their shape, the onions are done. Undercook rather than overcook them, for they will continue to cook as they cool. With a slotted spoon, transfer the onions to a large shallow baking dish.

Next, toss into the boiling marinade the squash and zucchini. Cover the pan again, and this time cook the vegetables rather slowly for about 15 minutes. The best way to test them is to lift out one piece with a slotted spoon, let it cool a couple of seconds, then

28

pinch it gently. If it feels pliable and yet has some resistance, it is done. Place the zucchini and squash alongside the onions in the baking dish.

Bring the marinade to a boil for the last time and add the peppers. Cook them briskly with the pan uncovered for about 8 minutes. They should be *al dente,* or firm to the teeth, and the best way to test them is to taste one. Remember they will get softer as they cool. Now pour both the peppers and the marinade over the vegetables in the baking dish, and arrange them so that each piece is at least partially immersed in the hot liquid. Cool, then cover the dish with Saran wrap or waxed paper, and refrigerate overnight or longer.

To serve, arrange the vegetables on a large round platter, with the white onions in the center, the green zucchini and the yellow squash in two circles around them, and finally the red and green pepper strips alternated around the edge like a garland. Moisten the vegetables with a few spoonfuls of the marinade, sprinkle them liberally with finely chopped parsley, and finish the display with the lemon slices.

AFTERTHOUGHTS:

✳ If you have any left-over marinade, use it as a base for the GAZPACHO on page 39. Supplement it with cold chicken stock.

✳ If you have used a good fresh chicken stock, the marinade will probably jell when it is cold. Let it come to room temperature before you spoon it over the finished platter.

✳ Other vegetables may be prepared *à la grecque.* Experiment with them until you find the ones you like best; cooking times will, of course, be different for each one.

✳ A variety of fresh herbs may be used with or instead of parsley. Chives and dill are particularly good.

CHAPTER II

Soups

Fresh Chicken Stock
Fresh Brown Beef Stock
Improving Canned Broths

COLD SOUPS

Gazpacho
Cold Cream of Chicken Soup Senegalese
Chilled Lemon Soup with Mint
Vichyssoise
Chlodnik

HOT SOUPS

Consommé Belleview
Spinach Soup with Spring Onions
Veal Soup, with Pasta, Bagration
Crème du Barry
S'chee

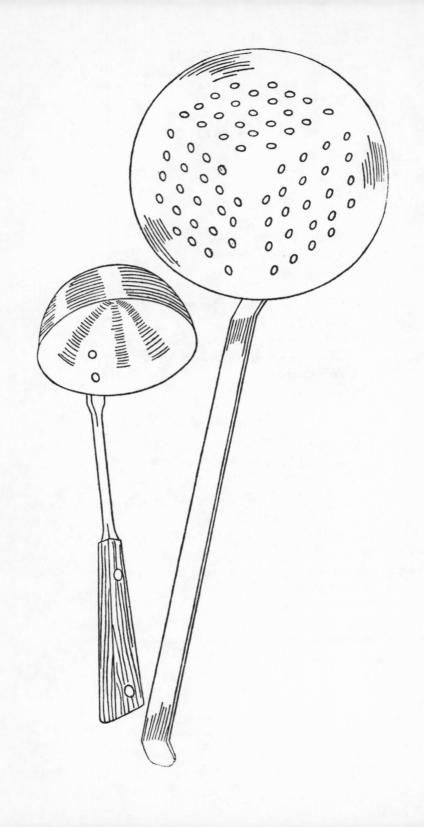

✳

BASIC recipes for stocks appear in this soup chapter because the most satisfying and sustaining soups are those made with a rich chicken- or meat-stock base. Although the preparation of a good stock is one of the least demanding culinary procedures, it does take time, which is doubtless why well-made soups appear so seldom on our tables.

But stocks are also fundamental to all good cooking—and not only to *haute cuisine*. If you are doing a great deal of cooking, you will quickly learn how convenient it is to have stock on hand in the refrigerator or, especially, in the freezer. Making a large batch of stock may seem like a great deal of work, but your reward will be enough stock to prepare any number of dishes at their best instead of second best. And, in fact, you will be spared the bother of doctoring a small quantity of canned stock each time you need it. However, the instructions given, also, for improving canned stocks or broths, though they might evoke a condescending smile from a good chef, are useful for lesser mortals.

The chicken or beef used in making homemade stocks need not go to waste; suggestions are given in the AFTERTHOUGHTS for using them.

Two variations of a classic procedure appear in this chapter— the *veloutés* in the recipes for VEAL SOUP BAGRATION and for CRÈME DU BARRY; these *veloutés* differ only in proportions of ingredients from the *veloutés* that are used to make sauces rather than soups; you will find the term recurring often in the chapters on fish, poultry, and meats. The same recipes describe also the standard method for thickening soups with egg yolks and cream.

The AFTERTHOUGHTS for GAZPACHO describe useful techniques for preparing vegetables. And note the instructions on page 47 for chilling cold soups quickly when you wish to serve them shortly after they are made.

✳

*

FRESH CHICKEN STOCK

] To make about three quarts [

4- to 5-pound fowl, washed and trussed
Optional: 1 veal knuckle, cut up and cracked
2 medium onions, peeled and halved
1 large carrot, cut into 3-inch chunks
3 stalks celery and their leaves
Optional: one 2-inch slice each of turnip and parsnip
2 cloves unpeeled garlic
2 large leeks, white part only
A bouquet consisting of 6 sprigs parsley and a small
      bay leaf, tied together
10 whole peppercorns
1 tablespoon salt
4 quarts cold water, approximately
1 teaspoon thyme

In a large stock pot, combine all the above ingredients except the thyme. Add the 4 quarts of water last and, if the fowl isn't quite covered, add a little more. Over high heat, bring the water to a boil and, with a slotted spoon or skimmer, thoroughly skim off all the scum as it rises to the surface. Reduce the heat so that the liquid barely moves, add the thyme, and simmer, half covered, for at least 4 hours.

Remove the chicken and the veal bones, and strain the finished stock through a fine sieve. If it is to be used at once, let it rest a few moments, then with a large spoon skim off as much of the surface fat as you can. If the flavor of the stock isn't intense enough at this point, return it to the heat and boil it rapidly until it becomes more concentrated. Refrigerate it uncovered.

AFTERTHOUGHTS:

* This stock will keep in the refrigerator about three days, possibly

34

four; at that point, either bring it to a boil and refrigerate it again for the same length of time, or freeze it in small batches to be used as you need it.

✳ To shorten the cooking time of the stock somewhat, have the fowl cut up before cooking.

✳ Make it a practice when you are sautéing a cut-up chicken to save and freeze bits of the uncooked chicken such as the wing tips, gizzard, heart, and neck. For added flavor add them, without defrosting, to the stock pot.

✳ For a brown chicken stock, to use in dishes such as COQ AU VIN (see page 109), first brown the trussed fowl and the carrots and onions in a large frying pan in a little combined butter and vegetable oil. Put the chicken and vegetables in the stock pot, then deglaze the frying pan with a little cold water, bring this to a boil, and scrape up all the brown sediment. Pour this liquid into the pot with the other ingredients, and proceed as described before.

✳ If you plan to use the cooked fowl for another purpose, remove it from the stock when it has simmered for 2½ to 3 hours; it should be thoroughly cooked but not falling apart. Continue to cook the veal knuckle and vegetables, however, for as long thereafter as you wish; and the longer the better.

✳ See the recipe for CHICKEN CURRY on page 128 for using the meat of the cooked fowl. Boned and skinned, the meat may also be served cold with a highly seasoned mayonnaise (possibly the AÏOLI on page 88) and a green salad.

✳ To serve the chicken hot, as a fricassee, follow the directions for making a thickened *velouté* on page 182 in the recipe for BLANQUETTE DE VEAU, starting the sauce with 2 cups of the fresh chicken stock. Serve the chicken carved, masked with the sauce, sprinkled with chopped parsley, and accompanied, if you wish, by little white onions cooked *à blanc* (see page 181) and boiled rice.

✳ Hot poached chicken is also delicious with AVGOLEMONO SAUCE; see page 210.

✳ A good fresh chicken stock is, of course, an ideal base for a clarified aspic. The directions for fish aspic on page 94 can be followed exactly for chicken aspic, substituting 4 cups of strong chicken stock for the 4 cups of reduced fish *court-bouillon,* and omitting the saffron.

35

*

FRESH BROWN BEEF STOCK

] To make three to four quarts [

2 pounds fresh brisket of beef
1½ pounds shin of beef
3 pounds beef bones, split
1 veal knuckle, cut up and cracked
2 whole medium onions, peeled
3 medium carrots, scraped and cut into 3-inch chunks
Optional: one 2-inch slice each of turnip and parsnip
3 cloves garlic, unpeeled

4–5 quarts cold water
2 large leeks, white parts only
A bouquet consisting of 8 sprigs parsley, a large bay
    leaf, and 3 celery tops, all tied together
½ teaspoon thyme

Preheat the oven to **475° F.** Place the brisket and shin of beef in a large shallow roasting pan and surround them with the bones, onions, carrots, turnip, parsnip, and garlic, arranged in one layer if possible. Roast, uncovered, on the center shelf of the oven for about 30 minutes; turn the meat and vegetables from time to time until they are well colored all over. Watch them carefully; they must not burn. Transfer the entire contents of the pan to a large (1½- to 2-gallon) stock pot.

On the top of the stove, deglaze the roasting pan by adding to it 2 quarts of water and bringing it to a boil, meanwhile scraping into it every particle of brown sediment you can dislodge from the bottom and sides of the pan. Pour this into the stock pot and augment it with 2 more quarts of water; if the liquid doesn't quite cover the meat, add another quart of water, but no more than that.

Now, over high heat, bring the liquid almost to the boil, skimming off all the scum (there will be lots of it) as it rises to the surface. Just before the stock reaches an actual boil, add the leeks, the tied bouquet, salt, peppercorns, and thyme, turn the heat down to the barest simmer, and half cover the pot. Allow the stock to simmer undisturbed for a minimum of 4 hours; skim it again periodically for the first half hour or so.

If at the end of 4 hours the stock has not yet achieved a full flavor, cook it an hour or so longer. Strain it then through a fine sieve, first removing the meat and larger bones, and refrigerate it uncovered. You may degrease the stock at any time, but the task will be easier if you first allow the fat to solidify in the refrigerator.

AFTERTHOUGHTS:

❋ This stock will keep in the refrigerator for at least three days, possibly four; at that point, either bring it to a boil and refrigerate for the same length of time, or freeze it in small batches to be used as you need it.

❋ For a lightly colored stock, omit the browning process altogether, but the flavor of the stock won't be quite as intense.

❋ To shorten the cooking time of the stock, have the brisket and shin cut into 3-inch chunks.

❋ If you do not have the meats cut up, remove the brisket when it is tender but not falling apart (in 3 hours or more). Use it cold for a BEEF SALAD VINAIGRETTE (page 305). Or serve it hot as is the boiled beef in the recipe for s'CHEE (page 65). Once the meat is removed, the stock may continue to cook for hours with the shin, bones, and vegetables.

❋ To make a clarified aspic with fresh beef stock, see the directions on page 94 for making fish aspic; merely substitute 4 cups of strong beef stock for the 4 cups of reduced fish *court-bouillon,* and omit the saffron. Beef stock is used in the special aspic for cold BEEF À LA MODE on page 169.

IMPROVING CANNED BROTHS

CANNED broths or dehydrated stock bases are too often unconvincing substitutes for the real thing. The preservatives used in them produce a synthetic flavor impossible to conceal. Fortunately for the busy cook, canned chicken broths today fall into another category altogether. Some of the better brands are good enough, in a pinch, to be used directly from the can, though most varieties should be given some preliminary treatment before going into an important soup or sauce. Simmering the canned broth for half an hour or so with odds and ends of vegetables and bits of cooked or uncooked poultry almost completely masks the "canned" taste and approximates surprisingly well the quality of a freshly made stock.

Regrettably, this is not usually true of the overcaramelized canned brown beef bouillons and consommés. To be sure, a preliminary simmering with some dry wine and vegetables helps somewhat. But the cloying sweetness of the bouillon and, particularly, of the consommé persists and can't be wholly camouflaged. When they are used in any appreciable quantity, this flavor takes over so assertively as to make any culinary subtleties in your soup or sauce superfluous. If you must use canned beef stock, far better is the natural-color canned beef broth now becoming more available than it once was. Simmering this with a few onions and carrots first browned in butter improves its pallid color, and further cooking for even a short time with wine, herbs, and seasonings gives it a more distinctive flavor.

Chicken Stock:

4 cups canned, undiluted chicken stock, all surface fat
    removed
½ cup sliced onions
¼ cup sliced carrots
¼ cup coarsely chopped celery
1 leek, white part only, thinly sliced
4 sprigs parsley
½ small bay leaf
¼ teaspoon thyme
Salt
Optional: A few mushroom parings and stems, if available
    Cooked or uncooked bits of chicken and chicken
    bones; cut-up gizzards, wings, hearts, necks

Combine all the ingredients in a heavy 2-quart saucepan, bring the stock to a boil, then reduce the heat to the barest simmer and cook, half covered, for at least half an hour. Skim when necessary. Strain the stock through a fine sieve before using.

BEEF STOCK OR BOUILLON:

4 cups undiluted canned beef broth or bouillon
2 tablespoons butter
2 small onions, peeled and quartered
Three 2-inch pieces of carrot
¾ cup dry white wine
2 cloves garlic, peeled
A bouquet consisting of 4 sprigs of parsley, 2 celery
    tops, 1 leek (white part only), and a small bay
    leaf, all tied together
½ teaspoon thyme

Melt the butter in a heavy saucepan. When the foam subsides, quickly and lightly brown in it the quartered onions and pieces of carrot. Then pour in the wine, bring it to a boil, and let it boil rapidly until it is reduced to about half a cup. Stir in the undiluted stock and all the other ingredients. Bring to a boil once more, then reduce the heat to the barest simmer and half cover the pan. Cook for at least half an hour.

✳

GAZPACHO

ORIGINALLY a crude and vigorous peasant soup, *gazpacho* has by now undergone so many transformations that it is virtually impossible to give a definitive recipe for it. When you order *gazpacho* in Seville, Madrid, Málaga, or Córdoba, you can be sure of only

39

one thing: it will be a cold soup with uncooked vegetables. From there on out, it will be edible or not, depending on the skill of the cook. At its best, it is likely to be a masterpiece.

] To serve eight or ten [

2 cups dry white wine
1 teaspoon coriander seeds, bruised
½ teaspoon black peppercorns, bruised
1 tablespoon chopped fresh basil
    or 1 teaspoon dried basil
2 large bay leaves
½ teaspoon finely chopped garlic

6 cups chicken stock, fresh or canned
2 teaspoons lemon juice
2 pounds ripe tomatoes, peeled, seeded, and cut into strips
2 small cucumbers, peeled, seeded, and diced (1½ cups)
1/3 cup finely chopped celery
2 small green peppers, chopped (¾ cup)
4 tablespoons chopped scallions
2 tablespoons finely chopped parsley
2 tablespoons finely chopped fresh dill
    or 1 tablespoon dried dill weed
Salt and freshly ground pepper

2/3 cup olive oil

GARLIC CROUTONS:

2 cups ½-inch cubes of bread
½ cup oil (vegetable oil, olive oil, or a combination of both)
1 teaspoon finely chopped garlic

40

If you don't intend to make your own stock (ideally, you should), the only active cooking required in this recipe is the reduction of the wine and the browning of the croutons. And you could be spared part even of that: The croutons are available commercially, but they won't taste anything like the ones you can so easily make yourself.

Reduce the wine first so that it can cool while you prepare the vegetables: In a small saucepan, combine the 2 cups of wine with the bruised coriander seeds and peppercorns, the bay leaves, basil, and garlic, and cook the mixture over moderate heat until it comes to a boil. Stir it, lower the heat, and simmer slowly until the wine has reduced to about 1 cup. This will take anywhere from 15 minutes to a half hour (depending on the size of the pan and the intensity of the heat). Let the wine cool to room temperature, then strain it through a fine sieve.

Remove every trace of fat from the 6 cups of chicken broth, then pour the broth into a 4-quart stainless-steel or glass mixing bowl. Stir in the reduced wine, the lemon juice, and, in whatever order you like, the previously prepared vegetables. Season with a good deal of salt and a few grindings of black pepper.

The 2/3 cup of olive oil may be added now, but it is more practical to chill the soup first and stir in the oil later—about a half hour before you serve it. In this way you will prevent the oil from congealing as the soup chills. (The oil in left-over *gazpacho* will inevitably congeal after being in the refrigerator for any length of time. In that event, merely let the soup rest in a cool place for 15 or 20 minutes so that the flaked oil can dissolve, then stir the soup thoroughly before serving it.)

The quality of the soup will gain immeasurably from being served in really chilled cups. Pass a bowl of croutons separately or float a few on the surface of each cupful.

✳ *The best croutons are made with one- or two-day-old Italian or French bread, though plain white bread will do if it*

41

must. Cut the bread into fairly uniform half-inch squares, with crusts removed first if you prefer. Cover the bottom of a large, heavy (it must be heavy) frying pan with a thin film of oil less than an eighth of an inch deep and, over high heat, bring it almost to the smoking point. Toss in the bread squares. Turn them rapidly in the oil with a large wooden spoon until they begin to brown. By then they will probably have absorbed all the oil, so add a bit more. Lower the heat and cook a moment or two longer.

Now, turn off the heat, and stir in the chopped garlic; it will cook with the heat of the pan and will begin to brown almost at once. Stir until most of the garlic adheres in small brown particles to the bread. The trick is to add the garlic to the pan only a minute or two before the croutons are done and not to let it burn.

For those of you who object to the taste and texture of minced garlic, slowly fry 3 or 4 whole peeled cloves of garlic in the oil until they color lightly, then scoop them out with a slotted spoon, and brown the croutons afterwards in the garlic-flavored oil. However you flavor them (the first method is by far the best), turn the croutons out of the pan into a bowl lined with a double thickness of paper toweling when they are done. Let them drain and cool before serving.

AFTERTHOUGHTS:

✻ The care with which you prepare the individual ingredients for your *gazpacho* will determine the final quality of the soup. To bruise the coriander seeds and peppercorns, lay them on one end of a kitchen towel, cover them with the other end, and run a heavy rolling pin over them a few times. Or pound them lightly with the bottom of a beer or milk bottle until the seeds split open.

The garlic, herbs, and celery should be chopped as finely as possible; for the celery, use the hearts or the inside stalks.

The cucumbers should first be peeled and sliced in half lengthwise. Scoop the seeds out by running the tip of a teaspoon down the centers. Then dice them by cutting the halves into julienne strips an eighth of an inch thick, bunching the strips together on the chopping board, and then slicing these crosswise, at intervals of an eighth of an inch so that the bunches fall into small dice as you proceed.

Before you chop the green peppers (not too finely), be certain that all the white inside membranes have been cut away.

The tomatoes require the most attention if they are not to end up as shapeless, ragged shreds. Peel them in the usual fashion by first dropping them into boiling water, counting to ten slowly, then plunging them into cold water before slipping off their skins. Put the tomatoes on a chopping board and cut each one lengthwise into quarters. Run a small, sharp knife under the pulp of each quarter and cut it out in one piece, leaving only the thin outer shell of tomato meat. Slice the shells lengthwise in eighth-of-an-inch strips, then crosswise in half-inch pieces. Use only these julienned strips in the soup.

COLD CREAM OF CHICKEN SOUP SENEGALESE

THE INTENSITY of curry lends itself particularly well to a chilled, velvety cream soup, intriguing the palate with the unexpected. Delicately flavored with leeks, apple, and lemon, and given substance with julienned breast of chicken, this soup makes an original and memorable beginning for a festive summer meal.

] To serve eight or ten [

6 tablespoons butter
1 medium onion, finely chopped (about ½ cup)
2 medium leeks, finely chopped (about 1/3 cup)
¼ cup finely chopped carrots
¼ cup finely chopped celery
1 small tart apple, peeled, cored, and coarsely
    chopped
2 tablespoons flour

43

2 tablespoons curry powder

6 cups chicken stock, fresh or canned

3 egg yolks
1 cup heavy cream

½ teaspoon lemon juice
Salt
1 cup julienned cooked breast of chicken
2 tablespoons finely chopped parsley

For this soup, as for any curried dish, an imported Madras powder is desirable if you can get it, otherwise a good domestic brand, provided it is fresh, will do.

In a large, heavy frying pan, melt the 6 tablespoons of butter. Add the chopped onions, leeks, carrots, and celery, and cook over low heat, without letting them brown, for about 15 minutes, stirring from time to time with a wooden spoon. Mix in the chopped apple and cook very slowly until the pieces soften and can be mashed easily with the back of your spoon.

Meanwhile, mix together in a small bowl 2 tablespoons each of flour and curry powder. Sprinkle this over the cooked vegetables in the frying pan, remove the pan from the heat and, with the back of the spoon, mix and mash everything together until you have a smooth, pliable paste.

Slowly stir into this the 6 cups of chicken stock and place the pan over moderate heat; the soup will be quite lumpy at this point but will smooth out as it cooks. Beat it constantly with a wire whisk, and as it begins to boil and thicken, lower the heat to the barest simmer and partially cover the pan. Simmer the soup for about 30 minutes. From time to time, carefully skim off the fat and scum which will persistently rise to the surface. If you have the time, cook it longer; even an hour is not too much, but be sure the soup barely moves as it simmers.

When it is done, strain the soup through a fine sieve into a 3-quart saucepan and, with a large spoon, press down hard on the vegetables to extract all their juice before throwing them away.

In a small mixing bowl, beat together with a wire whisk—but only long enough to combine them—the 3 egg yolks and 1 cup of heavy cream. Stir into this, a tablespoon at a time, about a cup of the hot strained soup. Now reverse the process and slowly pour and stir the heated cream-and-egg mixture back into the pan of hot soup.

Stirring constantly over moderate heat, bring the soup almost to the boil, but don't tempt fate by letting it actually boil even though the flour in the soup should prevent the eggs from curdling. Heat it only long enough for the eggs to thicken so that the soup clings lightly to the back of your spoon; it will thicken more as it cools. Remove the pan from the heat at once, and strain the soup once more through a fine sieve into a large stainless-steel or glass mixing bowl.

_____

Stir in the ½ teaspoon of lemon juice and whatever salt you think the soup needs, and cool it to room temperature, stirring every now and then to prevent a crust from forming on top. Cover with Saran wrap or waxed paper and refrigerate until icy cold. If you want to cool and serve the soup immediately after making it, see page 48.

To serve, place in the bottom of each chilled soup cup, four or five strips of cold julienned breast of chicken. Pour in the soup and garnish with a little finely chopped parsley.

AFTERTHOUGHTS:

✳ For the cold chicken, use any left-overs breast of roast or poached chicken you may have; or canned breast of chicken; or 1 small fresh chicken breast brought to a boil in cold salted water or stock to cover, then simmered for about 20 minutes and cooled in its own broth. Whatever chicken you use, it should be free of all skin, bone, and cartilege, and cut into julienned strips half an inch long and an eighth of an inch wide.

✳ If the soup is too thick for your taste after it is chilled (and it will be quite thick if you have used a good fresh stock), thin it with a little light or heavy cream. Amplify the flavor, then, with a touch more lemon juice, salt, and possibly a pinch of cayenne.

CHILLED LEMON SOUP WITH MINT

THIS IS a chilled version of the famous Greek lemon soup known as *avgolemono*. Tapioca, instead of the traditional rice, lightly thickens the chicken broth which is then flavored with lemon and given a velvetlike consistency with egg yolks and heavy cream.

The garnish of fresh mint mingling its fragrance with the lemon is as soothing a balm as one could possibly wish for on a sweltering summer day.

] To serve six [

4 cups chicken stock, fresh or canned
2 tablespoons tapioca
3 egg yolks
2 tablespoons lemon juice
1 tablespoon grated lemon rind
½ teaspoon salt
⅛ teaspoon cayenne
1 cup heavy cream
2 tablespoons fresh mint, finely cut with scissors
½–1 cup light cream, if necessary

This soup is always at its best served as cold as possible. Compensate for the deadening effect of the cold on its flavor, however, by using as strong a chicken stock as you can get your hands on. Naturally, that means your own, made according to the recipe on page 34. If you haven't the time, canned broth will do, but then give it the treatment suggested on page 38. If you *really* haven't the time, the stock may be used directly from the can; the results will be unspectacular, but edible.

In a heavy 2-quart saucepan, bring the 4 cups of stock to a boil, and sprinkle in slowly 2 level tablespoons of tapioca. Cook rapidly for 2 or 3 minutes, then lower the heat and simmer, partially covered, for about 5 minutes.

Meanwhile, with a wire whisk or a fork, beat together in a small bowl the 3 egg yolks and the lemon juice, grated rind, salt, and cayenne. When they are just about combined, mix in the cup of heavy cream. Now, tablespoonful by tablespoonful, add the simmering stock to the cream mixture, stirring well after each addition. At about the tenth spoonful, reverse the process and pour the now heated cream back into the saucepan all at once, stirring constantly.

The next step, always fraught with potential disaster, is to cook the soup until it thickens to a smooth, light custard. But don't bother doing this in a double boiler, a wearisome, unnecessary process. Be more daring and professional and cook it over direct heat instead. If you are really careful not to let the soup get too hot (to say nothing of letting it boil), it won't curdle.

Place the saucepan over moderate heat and, stirring deeply and around the sides of the pan with a wooden spoon, cook the soup until it begins to thicken and you feel a barely perceptible resistance to the spoon. Still stirring, lift the pan above the heat to cool it a bit, then return it to the heat once more. Continue to cook, lifting the pan from time to time, until the soup has thickened enough to coat the back of the spoon lightly. Don't worry if the soup seems thin; it will thicken more as it cools. Pour it at once into a cold bowl, preferably stainless steel, and allow the soup to come to room temperature before covering it tightly with Saran wrap or waxed paper. Place in the refrigerator and chill until icy cold.

✻ *If you want to serve the still hot soup directly after making it, embed the bowl in another larger bowl filled with ice cubes or, better still, crushed ice. Stir the soup constantly with a large metal spoon until it cools. When it is really cold—and this will take less time than you would suppose—taste for seasoning, then pour into soup cups first chilled for a half hour or so in the freezer.*

Garnish each cup with some finely cut mint and sprinkle a little grated lemon rind on top if you wish. Serve at once.

AFTERTHOUGHTS:

✻ If you have made the soup with fresh stock, it will probably thicken to a jelly when it is cold. Thin it with light cream, sour cream, or yoghurt if you like its flavor. Adjust the seasonings accordingly, adding even more lemon juice if necessary.

✻ Although fresh mint is by far the best garnish, other fresh herbs will do almost as well. Try minced dill, tarragon, chervil, parsley, or shredded water cress.

VICHYSSOISE

PERHAPS the most popular cold soup in America today is Vichyssoise, to judge by its periodic appearance on almost every restaurant menu in the country during the summer months. Although Vichyssoise, despite its name, originated here and not in France, it remains, nonetheless, another version of the classic *potage Parmentier*, or leek and potato soup, so beloved by the French.

The following recipe is somewhat richer and more sophisticated than its country cousin—which is as it should be; a cold soup tends to be pallid and should be pampered a bit with good stock and thick cream if it is to make any impression on the palate at all.

] To serve four or six [

4 cups chicken stock, fresh or canned

4 tablespoons butter
2 large leeks, white parts only, finely chopped (about
    1 cup)
1 small onion, chopped (about 1/3 cup)
1 small stalk celery, finely chopped (about ¼ cup)
1½ pints potatoes sliced about ¼ inch thick

Salt
White pepper
1 cup heavy cream
2 tablespoons finely cut chives

The old adage, "the soup is only as good as the stock," applies particularly to Vichyssoise. Potatoes, apart from their wonderful texture, have little actual flavor when hot, and when cold, even less. If your stock has no character to begin with, your Vichyssoise will be an uninteresting brew indeed. So make your own stock if you can, but if you can't, use canned stock and follow the procedures on page 38 for improving it. Now for the soup:

Melt the 4 tablespoons of butter very slowly in a large, heavy frying pan. As soon as it dissolves, mix into it the chopped onion, celery, and the carefully washed and chopped leeks. Cook slowly for about 20 minutes, stirring every now and then and adjusting the heat so that the vegetables barely color.

When they are soft and translucent, with a rubber spatula transfer them to a 3- or 4-quart saucepan. Pour in the stock, add the sliced potatoes, and bring it all to a boil. Reduce the heat at once, partially cover the pan, and simmer until the potatoes are soft and crumble easily when pierced with a fork.

Now, be firm and avoid the temptation to purée the soup in an electric blender. One of the characteristics of a good Vichyssoise

49

is its slightly grainy texture. The blender, no matter how carefully controlled, will reduce the soup to an irretrievable, bland cream. Use a food mill, instead, if you have one; if not, a fairly coarse sieve and the back of a large spoon will do. Whatever implement you use, set it over a large mixing bowl and force the soup through, potatoes, vegetables, and all.

If the purée at this point, seems too coarse in texture, as it may well be if the sieve openings were large ones, force it again through a sieve, this time a finer one. Stir in the seasonings, the white pepper discreetly and the salt liberally; use much more than you would ordinarily, for the cold will dull the soup's flavor later.

Cover the bowl and refrigerate until thoroughly chilled. Or, if you want to serve the soup immediately after making it, see page 48.

Before serving the soup, in chilled cups, stir into it 1 cup of heavy cream, and taste again for salt. If the Vichyssoise seems too thick for your taste, thin it with more cream, heavy or light, and adjust the seasonings accordingly. Garnish each cup with a scant teaspoon of finely cut fresh chives.

AFTERTHOUGHTS:

✳ Fresh dill, finely cut, makes an interesting departure from the usual chives, or combine equal parts of both. If you can't get either, shred very finely the green stems of scallions, but use them sparingly; the flavor is quite strong.

✳ A tablespoon or so of good curry powder mixed into the sautéed vegetables before they are cooked in the stock, will give you a curried Vichyssoise. Try a little apple grated into each cup before garnishing with the chives.

✳ If, before you add the cupful of cream, the potato purée seems thin, for whatever reason, whip the cream lightly and fold it into the soup just before serving.

*

CHLODNIK

A POEM of an iced Russian soup—and, like most poems in another language, almost impossible to translate. If the following *chlodnik* isn't exactly what you might get in Moscow, it still stands up wonderfully well on its own. And lest you lift an incredulous eyebrow at the combination of sour cream, sauerkraut juice, and buttermilk, be assured that together they approximate to a surprising degree the characteristic tart and invigorating flavor of the original, in which Russian *kvas*, a fermented barley liquor, is the key ingredient.

] To serve ten [

½ pound cooked shelled shrimp
2 medium cucumbers, peeled, seeded, and diced
    (about 1½ cups)

2 cups sour cream
5 cups buttermilk
½ cup sauerkraut juice
2 cloves garlic, chopped
Salt
White pepper

3 tablespoons finely chopped fresh dill
    or 2 tablespoons dried dill weed
½ cup finely chopped fresh fennel
    or 1 teaspoon powdered fennel seed
½ cup finely chopped scallions, including some of
    the green tops
2 hard-cooked eggs, finely chopped

For flavor and appearance, the tiny Alaskan shrimp are best for this soup; if you can't get them, any of the larger varieties will do but cut them into half-inch slices before adding them to the soup. In any case, cook the shrimp ever so briefly in boiling, salted water for 3 to 5 minutes, depending on their size, and let them cool in the hot liquid. When they are cool enough to handle, shell them. You can remove the black vein running down the back if you like but, if the shrimp are small, this is definitely a chore and not really necessary. Though they won't be quite as good, use canned shrimp when you're pressed for time; the small Icelandic shrimp, packed so beautifully in glass jars, are especially good but very expensive.

If you don't know precisely how to peel, seed, and dice a cucumber, look at the AFTERTHOUGHTS at the end of the GAZPACHO recipe on page 42. In *chlodnik,* however, the cucumbers, after they are diced, should be marinated in salt to draw off their excess moisture. Mix them with a teaspoon of salt in a small bowl and let them rest for at least half an hour. Before adding them to the soup, drain them in a fine sieve.

The preparation of the soup itself couldn't be easier: First, combine in a 4-quart stainless-steel or glass bowl the sour cream, buttermilk, sauerkraut juice, garlic, salt, and pepper, and beat them together with a wire whisk until smooth. Then, put everything else in the bowl—the shrimp, cucumbers, dill, fennel, and scallions —all but the chopped hard-cooked eggs. Stir the soup gently but thoroughly with a large wooden spoon and chill it in the refrigerator for at least 4 hours, but preferably overnight. Before serving, sprinkle each portion with a teaspoon or so of the chopped hard-cooked egg.

AFTERTHOUGHTS:

✳ In Russian, *chlodnik* means "icehouse," and icy is the way the soup tastes best. Actually, in Poland and Russia, *chlodnik* and all its endless variations are served with a chunk of ice in each plate. Authentic as this procedure is, it is not recommended here for the ice, as it melts turns the soup quite watery. Instead, chill the soup plates or cups in the freezer for about an hour before you fill them.

*

CONSOMMÉ BELLEVIEW

EVERY so often an inspired cook will throw together a couple of unlikely ingredients and the result will be a culinary triumph. Such a triumph is consommé Belleview. Originally a mixture of clear chicken stock and clam broth, the following version is given a Mediterranean accent with a touch of garlic, lemon rind, and parsley. It makes a fine beginning for an elaborate formal dinner.

] To serve eight [

4 cups clear, strong chicken stock, fresh or canned
2 cups clam broth or bottled clam juice
1 teaspoon minced garlic
⅛ teaspoon cayenne
1 teaspoon grated lemon rind and 2 tablespoons
    chopped parsley, combined

Ideally, consommé Belleview should be made with freshly prepared chicken stock and fresh clam broth. For those of you who have neither the time nor the inclination to begin from scratch, all the suggestions at the beginning of this chapter on how to improve canned chicken stock are again applicable here.

As for the clam broth, if you intend to make your own: Scrub a dozen clams, cover them with a couple of cups of cold water, add a few sprigs of parsley and a celery top and, with the pan tightly covered, steam them slowly until they open. Strain the broth through a couple of thicknesses of cheesecloth. Naturally, this broth will have a flavor quite unlike the bottled variety; but it does take some effort and the bottled juice will do nicely if it must. The bottled clam juice may be heightened in flavor by simmering it with a small can of minced clams for about 10 minutes, then straining it through cheesecloth.

However you arrive at the broths, making the soup is simplicity itself: Combine the 4 cups of chicken stock and the 2 cups of clam broth in a 2-quart pan. Add the minced garlic and cayenne and bring the soup almost to the boil. (If you prefer a more delicate garlic flavor, substitute two cloves of unpeeled garlic for the minced garlic.) Reduce the heat, half cover the pan, and simmer slowly for about 15 minutes. Because of the saltiness of the clam broth, it is unlikely that the soup will need any salt, but taste it to make sure. When ready to serve, strain the consommé into bouillon cups and sprinkle each cup with half a teaspoon of the lemon-parsley mixture.

SPINACH SOUP WITH SPRING ONIONS

QUITE simply, this soup is exactly what it says it is, and no more. However, the list of familiar ingredients in the recipe gives little indication of the soup's extraordinary flavor and the delight it arouses when it is served.

] To serve six [

1 package frozen chopped spinach
½ cup chicken stock, fresh or canned
4 tablespoons butter
½ cup spring onions (scallions), thinly sliced,
    including 2 or 3 inches of the green tops
½ teaspoon finely chopped garlic
5 cups chicken broth, fresh or canned
Salt
Freshly ground black pepper
A few gratings of nutmeg

Frozen chopped spinach, ordinarily not to be mentioned in the same breath with fresh spinach, is fortunately suited to the preparation of this soup. Cook it briskly, uncovered, with ½ cup of chicken stock until the spinach is thoroughly separated and the ice particles dissolved. Strain it through a fine sieve set over a small bowl. With the back of a large spoon press down hard on the pulp and extract as much of its moisture as you can. Save every drop of this green broth.

Slowly melt 4 tablespoons of butter in a large heavy frying pan. Add the thinly sliced scallions and chopped garlic and, over low heat, cook them for about 10 minutes, stirring frequently and making sure the scallions don't brown. When they are soft and translucent, stir into them the pressed spinach. Turn the heat up high. Mixing constantly with a spatula or large wooden spoon, sauté the spinach for about 3 minutes, but don't let it color perceptibly. Pour in the green broth you saved earlier, give everything a turn or two with the spatula or spoon, then transfer the spinach, broth and all, to a deep 2- or 3-quart saucepan. Add 5 cups of good, strong chicken stock. Grind in a little black pepper and make sure the soup has enough salt; there is nothing more disappointing than undersalted soup.

Without covering the pan, bring the soup to a boil, then reduce the heat and simmer it, still uncovered, for 15 or 20 minutes. Shortly before it is done, grate in a few specks of nutmeg if you like it, and serve the soup as hot as possible.

AFTERTHOUGHTS:

✳ If you prefer your soup thinner, add another ½ cup of stock.

✳ For variety, add to the soup ½ cup of cooked pasta—vermicelli, spaghettini, any of the small forms. In this case, passing freshly grated Parmesan cheese with the soup wouldn't be amiss.

✳ Naturally, you may make this soup with fresh spinach; its flavor will be incomparable. You will need about 1 pound. Make sure it is entirely free of sand and cook it with a minimum of water until it is barely wilted. Chop it coarsely and proceed with the recipe.

✳ This soup does not do well as a leftover. If you have enough for another meal, strain it, and serve it either as a clear broth or with cooked pasta mixed into it.

✳

VEAL SOUP, WITH PASTA, BAGRATION

LEGEND has it that this extraordinary soup was invented by the great chef Carême for his employer, Prince Bagration, one of the celebrated *gourmands* of his time. And it is, indeed, an elegant creation. It is based, like so many of the great French cream soups, on the classic *sauce velouté*—stock thickened with a *roux* of butter and flour and cooked to a velvetlike smoothness. In this, pieces of sautéed veal are slowly simmered. The whole is then puréed, enriched with eggs and cream, and finally garnished with pasta and grated cheese.

] To serve six [

4 tablespoons butter
½ cup flour
8 cups chicken stock, fresh or canned

2 tablespoons butter
½ pound veal cutlet, free of tendons and fat, cut
    into ½-inch cubes

3 egg yolks
¾ cup heavy cream

Salt
White pepper or cayenne
1 cup cooked *tubetti* or small macaroni
Freshly grated Parmesan cheese

To insure the success of this soup, your *velouté* must be above reproach; and that means starting with the best possible chicken stock, one you have made yourself according to the recipe on page 34. However, if you must use the canned, follow the suggestions on page 38 for improving it.

56

✳ *For the* velouté *begin by preparing the pale* roux *which is its base: In a 3- or 4-quart saucepan, slowly melt the 4 table-spoons of butter without letting it foam. When it is thorough-ly dissolved, remove the pan from the heat and, with a wooden spoon, stir ½ cup of flour into the butter. Mix this to a smooth paste, return the pan to the heat and, stirring constantly, cook the* roux *slowly for about 2 minutes. Don't let it color.*

Now pour over it the 8 cups of hot or cold chicken stock. Raise the heat to moderate and, with a wire whisk, beat the mixture vigorously. The roux *will soon dissolve and the sauce will smooth out and begin to thicken lightly. Reaching down to the bottom and sides of the pan with the whisk, continue to beat and stir until the sauce begins to boil, at which point immediately lower the heat.*

Simmer for about half an hour, and from time to time skim the barely moving surface of all fat and scum which, it is well to remember, will continue to rise persistently. The more of it you remove, the better your sauce will be.

In the meantime, over moderate heat melt the 2 tablespoons of butter in a small heavy frying pan. When the foam subsides and the fat begins to splutter, add the cubed veal cutlet. Shaking the pan occasionally or stirring with a wooden spoon, cook the veal briskly for 5 minutes or so until it is lightly colored, then, with a slotted spoon, transfer it to the simmering *velouté.*

Now cover the saucepan partially and, skimming as frequently as before, simmer the soup for another hour. By that time the veal will be soft enough to purée in the electric blender if you have one. If you don't, you can rub it through a sieve with the help of a large spoon. The purée won't be quite as smooth but will still do nicely. If you use the blender, scoop the cooked veal out of the soup with a slotted spoon, put it in the blender jar, pour in enough soup to fill the jar, blend at high speed for a couple of minutes, and return this to the saucepan.

✻ *Now bring the soup to a boil again, stirring it with a whisk to smooth it out. Let it simmer slowly while you mix together in a small bowl the 3 egg yolks and the ¾ cup of heavy cream. When they are well combined, stir in, a tablespoon at a time, 1 cup of the hot soup. Now reverse the process, and in a thin, even stream pour the heated cream mixture back into the saucepan, stirring all the while. Continuing to stir, cook the soup slowly, but without letting it actually boil, until the eggs thicken it to a smooth, golden cream.*

Taste for salt and pepper, then add the cooked and carefully drained *tubetti* or macaroni. When the pasta is heated through, serve immediately and pass separately a bowl of freshly grated Parmesan cheese. Sprinkle the soup, if you like, with a little finely chopped parsley.

AFTERTHOUGHTS:

✻ A remarkable version of this soup can be made by using in place of the chicken stock an equal amount of the stock in which a VITELLO TON-NATO (page 201) was cooked.

✻ Stirring into the finished soup (off the heat), a couple of tablespoons of softened butter, may sound like gilding the lily, but this is standard procedure for soups of this kind. If you can bring yourself to do it, try it.

✻ Equal parts of Parmesan and Swiss cheese may be used instead of the Parmesan alone. Buy the imported cheeses if you can, and grate them yourself just before serving.

✻ *Tubetti* are small tubes of pasta but any pasta that is small enough may be used in its place.

*

CRÈME DU BARRY

IN THIS soup, the simple cauliflower reaches such elegant heights that its two-hundred-year alliance with the glamorous name of Madame du Barry is easily understandable. Like the preceding recipe for VEAL SOUP BAGRATION, the base is the classic *velouté*. After simmering together, the cauliflower and *velouté* are transformed into a delicate purée that is again enriched with egg yolks and cream.

] To serve eight [

1 large or 2 small cauliflowers

4 tablespoons butter
4 level tablespoons flour
6 cups chicken stock, fresh or canned

1 teaspoon lemon juice
Salt

½ cup milk
3 egg yolks
¾ cup heavy cream

Salt
White pepper or cayenne
¼ teaspoon lemon juice
2 tablespoons minced fresh chives, chervil, or
    parsley
Optional: 1 cup butter-fried croutons

Choose a cauliflower with white, closely packed flowerettes; a speckled or mottled surface indicates a vegetable that is not quite fresh and may have a strong cabbagy flavor. To prepare the cauliflower, cut away the thick stem at its base and tear off the green surrounding leaves. Carefully separate the cauliflower into small flowerettes, wash them well under cold running water, then put aside about 16 small flowerettes to be used as a garnish later. Slice the remaining cauliflower into pieces one quarter of an inch thick.

In a 4-quart saucepan, slowly melt the 4 tablespoons of butter without letting it brown. Remove from the heat and, with a wooden spoon, stir into it the 4 level tablespoons of flour, mixing them together thoroughly. Cook this *roux* over moderate heat for about 30 seconds, stirring all the while; don't let it color. Remove the pan from the heat again and pour in the hot or cold chicken stock, all at once. Beat together vigorously with a wire whisk, then cook over moderate heat, continuing to beat until the sauce thickens slightly and becomes perfectly smooth.

Reduce the heat to as low as you can get it, and simmer the *velouté* for about 15 minutes, skimming the surface of all scum every 5 minutes. Now add the sliced cauliflower and bring the soup to a boil. Reduce the heat again, half cover the pan, and simmer the cauliflower until it is soft enough to mash against the sides of the pan.

Meanwhile cover the 16 reserved flowerettes with with cold water, add a little salt and the teaspoon of lemon juice, and cook the flowerettes, uncovered and rather briskly, until they are soft yet slightly resistant to the touch. Drain them at once, run cold water over them to stop their cooking, and put them aside in a small bowl.

When the cauliflower in the *velouté* is tender—this may take anywhere from 20 minutes to half an hour—purée it. Pour the soup, cauliflower and all, a couple of ladlefuls at a time, into a not-too-fine sieve set over a large mixing bowl. Rub the cauliflower through with the back of a large spoon. Or, if you prefer, use a food mill first, then rub the purée through a fine sieve. However you do it, return the purée to the saucepan, stir in the ½ cup of milk, and heat thoroughly, stirring from time to time.

In a small bowl, combine the 3 egg yolks and the ¾ cup of heavy cream, adding the cream to the eggs a little at a time and beating slowly with a fork or a wire whisk. Stir a ladleful of the hot soup

60

into the egg yolks and cream. Stir in another ladleful, then reverse the process and pour the cream mixture back into the remaining soup in the saucepan, continuing to stir as you pour.

Cook over moderate heat until the soup almost reaches the boiling point, then reduce at once to a simmer. Mix in the seasonings —salt, pepper, and ¼ teaspoon of lemon juice. Shortly before serving, put the reserved flowerettes into the soup to heat them through.

Serve the soup in cups, apportioning a couple of flowerettes to each one and sprinkling the surface with ¼ teaspoon of minced fresh chives, chervil, or parsley. You may float a few croutons in each cup, pass them separately, or omit them altogether.

AFTERTHOUGHTS:

✷ If the soup is too thick for your taste, thin it with a little cream, milk, or stock.

✷ You may use light cream or milk, instead of heavy cream at the end, but there will be a corresponding loss in the smooth, rich texture that makes this soup so exceptional.

✷ This soup can very well be made with fresh broccoli.

✷ The electric blender, although it eliminates the tiresome task of puréeing the cauliflower by hand, also destroys much of the soup's character. No matter what speed the blender is set for, it invariably makes the purée much too smooth and consequently uninteresting.

S'CHEE

A RUSSIAN can live by bread alone—that is, provided the bread is black and a bowl of s'chee is thrown in with it. And, in effect, this is how the Russian peasant has lived for countless generations. That s'chee, even now, is still the most popular soup in Russia is the true measure of its quality.

In all its endless regional forms, s'chee is essentially a cabbage soup, its composition determined more often than not by whatever ingredients happen to be at hand. The following version, a particularly hearty one, is striking because it combines fresh cabbage and sauerkraut. Like so many long-cooking soups, *s'chee* may be made well in advance; in fact, Russians insist that it improves with each reheating. True or not, this isn't important, as *s'chee* is almost unsurpassably good to begin with.

] To serve eight [

3 pounds fresh brisket of beef
  or boneless chuck *or* shin of beef
3 pounds beef marrow bones, cracked
1 large onion
2 carrots
1 parsnip
1 turnip

8 cups boiling water

3 pounds fresh tomatoes, peeled and coarsely chopped
  or 1 large can solid-pack tomatoes, drained
1½ tablespoons tomato paste
Herb bouquet: 5 sprigs parsley, 2 leeks (white parts
  only), 2 celery tops, 2 bay leaves, 5 sprigs fresh
  dill, all tied together
2 tablespoons salt

1 cup finely chopped onions
½ cup finely chopped celery
½ cup finely chopped carrots
1 teaspoon finely chopped garlic
1 pound sauerkraut, fresh or canned
7 cups shredded cabbage (about 2 pounds)

4 tablespoons sugar
3 tablespoons strained lemon juice
¼ cup finely chopped fresh dill
1 pint sour cream

Russians traditionally serve the meat cooked in the *s'chee* as a separate course after the soup. If you intend to do this, use fresh brisket; its flavor and texture are incomparable and stand up well under long, slow cooking. Have the meat securely tied so that it keeps its shape while cooking. If you plan to serve the soup only, a more economical cut like chuck or shin will do quite as well.

Preheat the oven to **500° F.** In a large, shallow roasting pan arrange, in one layer if possible, the meat, bones, and (all peeled but left whole) the onion, carrots, parsnip, and turnip. Roast for 20 minutes on the middle shelf of the oven, turning the meat and vegetables from time to time so that their surfaces brown on all sides. Then, piece by piece, transfer everything to a large soup kettle and, into a small bowl, pour off all the fat left in the roasting pan. Save it.

Into the roasting pan pour the 8 cups of boiling water. With a metal spatula or large spoon, vigorously scrape up and mix into the water all the brown particles and every bit of sediment clinging to the bottom and sides of the pan. Empty it into the soup kettle. If the meat and vegetables aren't quite covered, add a little more water, but not much if you want the soup to have character.

Start the kettle cooking over moderate heat and, with a slotted spoon or skimmer, remove the foam and scum that will persistently rise to the surface for quite a while. When the stock reaches the boil, turn the heat down to the barest simmer. Skim once more, then add the fresh or canned tomatoes, the tomato paste, herb bouquet, and salt. Partially cover the pot and simmer very, very slowly for about 2 hours, skimming whenever necessary.

In the meantime, get out your largest and heaviest frying pan, and in it heat 6 tablespoons of the beef fat you put aside earlier. Add the chopped onions, celery, carrots, and garlic, and fry them over low heat, stirring occasionally until they barely color—about 15 minutes.

The sauerkraut goes into this pan next, but first wash it in a sieve under cold running water; the brine is very strong and if it isn't washed away, it will obliterate the flavor of everything else in the *s'chee*. After squeezing the washed kraut dry, handful by handful, chop it coarsely and add it to the frying pan. Cook briskly for a minute or two, then lower the heat and mix in the shredded cabbage. Carefully stir all the vegetables together and cook over moderate heat until the cabbage begins to wilt. At that point, reduce the heat again and half cover the pan. Add a spoonful of stock from the soup kettle every 8 minutes or so to moisten the vegetables, and let them slowly braise for about a half hour. Remove the pan from the heat and put it aside, half covered.

When the soup in the kettle has cooked for about 2 hours, with a slotted spoon remove all the vegetables and the bouquet and throw them away; they have served their purpose. In their place, add to the soup the waiting braised cabbage and vegetables. Stir in the sugar and lemon juice, bring the soup to a boil, then reduce the heat to the barest simmer. Cook, partially covered, for another hour and a half.

By then the *s'chee* should have reached its full flavor, and the meat should be tender but not falling apart. If, at any point before this, the meat seems in danger of overcooking (the brisket, that is— the other cuts don't matter), remove it from the pot and let the soup continue on its own.

When the soup is done, turn off the heat and remove all the bones, but don't throw them away until you have dislodged every bit of their marrow and added it to the soup. Let the soup rest awhile so that the fat will rise to the top. Skim off as much of it as you can and reheat the soup again before serving.

To serve the soup most effectively, pour it into a large, heated tureen and sprinkle over it the 1/4 cup of chopped fresh dill. At the table, ladle the *s'chee* into large soup plates—no cups for this!— and float a tablespoon of sour cream on each serving. Black bread or pumpernickel and sweet butter are indispensable accompaniments.

AFTERTHOUGHTS:

✳ To serve the meat as a second course, heat it in the soup, then carve it into thin, even slices. Sprinkle each slice with a little chopped dill, and serve with plain boiled potatoes or the more traditional STEAMED KASHA or buckwheat groats (see page 290). Pass a tray of pickles, mustards, and, if you like it, a small bowl of freshly grated horseradish. Ice-cold beer would be a fitting beverage.

✳ For a substantial meal-in-one, the meat may be cut into small chunks and served directly in the soup.

CHAPTER III

Fish & Shellfish

Fillets of Mackerel en Escabeche
Clams Rockefeller
Broiled Shrimp with Tarragon and Garlic
Broiled Swordfish with Cold Cucumber and Dill Sauce
Sautéed Sea Squabs (or Scallops or Frogs' Legs)
    Provençale with Tomato Fondue
Halibut Mousse with Shrimp Sauce
Bourride of Sole with Aïoli Sauce
Cold Striped Bass in Mayonnaise Collée with Saffron Aspic
Lobster à l'Américaine

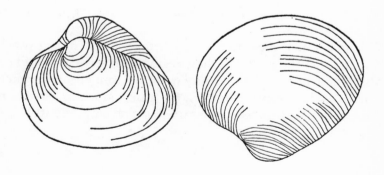

YOU WILL FIND eight kitchen procedures from classic cooking in these recipes. The first is the method for clarifying butter in SAU-TÉED SEA SQUABS PROVENÇALE; here it is later browned and seasoned with garlic, which is a separate process. The tomato fondue in this dish is common in many recipes not necessarily from Provence. The *aïoli* mayonnaise, which is added to the sauce for the BOUR-RIDE OF SOLE, is also a legitimate sauce on its own that Provençal peasants serve with steamed salt codfish and boiled vegetables. In addition, the sole for this *bourride* is poached in a fish stock, or *fumet de poisson,* in which fish for a whole repertory of dishes are cooked when a sauce is subsequently to be made with the cooking liquid. The same stock, for instance, is used for the shrimp sauce for HALIBUT MOUSSE, after the intermediary step of being made into a fish *velouté.*

In the great tradition is the classic sequence of the *court-bouillon* in which the COLD STRIPED BASS is poached; the clarified aspic made from the *court-bouillon,* which decorates the platter (chicken- or beef-stock aspics are made the same way); and the *mayonnaise collée* which contains a portion of the same aspic and which masks the fish. Lastly, there is the *mirepoix bordelaise,* a vegetable mixture traditionally reserved for flavoring shellfish, in the recipe for LOB-STER À L'AMÉRICAINE.

Note, finally, that the directions for broiling, sautéing, or poaching fish and shellfish in any of these recipes will serve as a guide to handling those procedures correctly whenever you encounter them elsewhere. And, if you are looking for a new sauce to serve with poached or broiled fish, see AVGOLEMONO SAUCE on page 210.

*

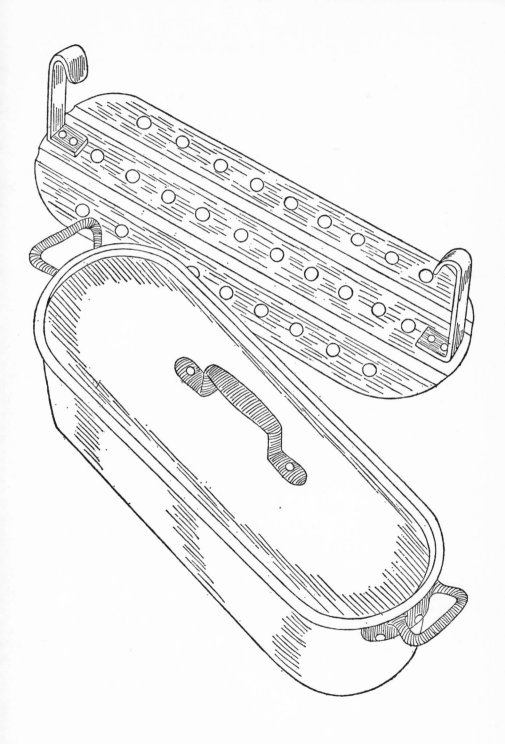

*

FILLETS OF MACKEREL EN ESCABECHE

THE SPANIARDS have devised a method of pickling fish so simple and effective that it must be ranked as a great culinary achievement. *Escabeche,* as it is called—and which means pickle, literally—consists of sautéing lightly floured fish in oil, and then immersing it for at least twenty-four hours in a highly acidulated vegetable marinade. Although an *escabeche* can be made successfully with almost any variety of fish—and meat and poultry, too—the boldly assertive flavor of mackerel lends itself particularly well to this treatment.

] To serve six or eight [

2 pounds mackerel fillets
¼ cup fresh lime or lemon juice

MARINADE:

½ cup olive oil
1 cup thinly sliced onions
½ cup thinly sliced carrots
½ cup thinly sliced celery
1 large green pepper, seeded and thinly sliced
6 cloves garlic, whole, or thinly sliced
2 bay leaves, crumbled
½ teaspoon thyme
10 whole black peppercorns
1 tablespoon salt
1 cup cold water
½ cup white-wine vinegar

Salt
Chili powder
½ cup flour, sifted
¼ cup olive oil

2 tablespoons finely chopped parsley
Black olives
2 whole limes or lemons

Ask your fish man to leave the skin on the mackerel after he fillets it, otherwise the fish will fall apart when you cook it. Wash the fillets under cold running water, pat them dry with paper towels, and slice them crosswise into the serving sizes of your choice: small for hors d'oeuvres, somewhat larger for a first-course or luncheon dish.

Lay the pieces in a large, shallow glass or porcelain dish, in one layer if possible, and sprinkle the fish with the ¼ cup of lime or lemon juice, making sure each piece is thoroughly moistened. Let them soak in the juice for about 20 minutes—no longer, or the acid will begin to "cook" them—then pat the pieces dry again, and refrigerate until you are ready to sauté them.

For the marinade, combine in a small saucepan the ½ cup of olive oil, the sliced onions, carrots, celery, green pepper, garlic, thyme, peppercorns, and salt. Heat slowly and, stirring almost constantly, cook until the onions begin to wilt—about 8 to 10 minutes. Don't let the vegetables brown. Now pour into the pan the 1 cup of water and ½ cup of vinegar and, still stirring, bring to a boil. Immediately lower the heat to the barest simmer, cover the pan, and let the marinade cook undisturbed for about 20 minutes, until the vegetables are tender but still firm.

While the marinade is simmering, start sautéing the fish. Ideally, the fish and the marinade should be ready simultaneously so that they can be combined while they are both hot. Rest assured, however, that a stop watch is not essential to the success of the *escabeche*; if need be, the marinade can always be reheated.

Prepare the fish as follows: Sprinkle each piece generously with salt, then with your fingers gently redden the fleshy sides of the fish with a few specks of chili powder. Sift ½ cup of flour on one end of a long strip of waxed paper. Dip the fish into the flour, vigorously shake the excess flour off each piece and, as you proceed, lay them side by side on the waxed paper.

Now, in a large, heavy frying pan, heat almost to smoking the ¼ cup of olive oil. Fry the fish in this a few pieces at a time, and regulate the heat so that they brown rather quickly but without burning. About two minutes on each side should be enough. Place the sautéed fish, skin side down, on a large glass or porcelain platter at least one half inch deep. For best results, arrange the fish in one layer; if you must, use two platters.

Pour the marinade over the fish while it is still hot and spread the vegetables over the top as evenly as possible. Cool to room temperature, then cover the platter loosely with waxed paper and refrigerate for at least 24 hours before serving.

The *escabeche* may be served directly from this platter or rearranged more impressively on a large silver platter. In either case, sprinkle the fish with the chopped parsley, scatter a handful of black olives over the top, and surround with quartered limes or lemons. Serve with crisp, hot French or Italian bread, as a first-course hors d'oeuvre.

AFTERTHOUGHTS:

✳ The Latin Americans and Mexicans sprinkle their *escabeche* with chopped *cilantro,* or Chinese parsley, as it is sometimes called. Try it if you can find it, but with caution; its pungent flavor is not to everyone's taste.

✳ Experiment with other varieties of fish until you discover the ones you like best. Red snapper and sole are prepared *en escabeche* almost as frequently as mackerel, but be careful not to overcook them. Fillet of sole, particularly, should not be cooked any longer than a minute or so on each side.

✳ If you have used whole cloves of garlic in the marinade instead of slicing them, remove them from the *escabeche* before you serve it.

✳ If you live anywhere near a Spanish or Mexican grocery store, buy dried chilis and make your own chili powder; it is far superior to the commercial variety. After removing the seeds and stems, merely pulverize the chili pods in the electric blender.

*

CLAMS ROCKEFELLER

THE WELL-KNOWN specialty, oysters Rockefeller, is presumed to have originated in New Orleans. Be that as it may (there are voices in Louisiana to the contrary), it is certainly to the Creoles that the dish owes its world-wide fame. However, for some of us the forth-right flavor of the hardshell clam lends itself better to this prep-aration than the more diffident oyster. The gratin topping of spinach, fresh herbs, Pernod (or Louisiana Herbsaint), Tabasco, butter, and bread crumbs somehow needs a more aggressive adver-sary. Clams Rockefeller make an impressive first course at an ele-gant dinner or a substantial main course at luncheon.

] To serve six [

3 dozen Little Neck or Cherrystone clams, about 2
    inches across
1 package frozen chopped spinach
½ cup small, stemmed sprigs parsley, well packed
½ cup water cress leaves, well packed
¼ cup coarsely chopped celery
½ cup coarsely chopped scallions, including some of
    the green tops
½ teaspoon finely chopped garlic
1 teaspoon lemon juice
⅜ pound butter (1½ sticks), melted and cooled
¼ cup Pernod
¼–½ teaspoon Tabasco
1 cup dry bread crumbs
½ cup heavy cream and ½ teaspoon salt,
    whipped together stiffly

The most practical way to manage 3 dozen clams on the half shell, unless you can open them easily yourself, is to have the fish man

73

open them, place the clams and their juice in a container, and wrap the shells separately. When you get them home, you can wash the shells and replace each drained clam on a shell.

For the vegetable topping, first defrost the spinach thoroughly and squeeze it absolutely dry. In the jar of an electric blender, combine the spinach, parsley, water cress, celery, scallions, garlic, lemon juice, melted butter, Pernod, Tabasco, and salt. Blend at high speed until the vegetables are reduced to a smooth purée. Should the machine clog at any point, turn off the motor and, with a rubber scraper, push the mixture down the sides of the jar before blending again.

Turn the purée into a mixing bowl, and stir into it 6 tablespoons of dry bread crumbs. If the mixture seems too fluid, add 1 or 2 more tablespoons of the crumbs. With a small knife, spread a thin layer of the purée over each clam, masking it completely and spreading the purée out to the edges of the shell. Then sprinkle each clam lightly with bread crumbs.

Preheat the oven to **500° F.** It is customary to bake and serve the clams in large or individual baking dishes filled with rock salt; the salt retains the heat and gives the clam shells a secure base. However, you can bake the clams without the salt but handle them gently, as the shells do tend to tilt and slide around.

Bake the clams in the hot oven for 8 to 10 minutes, or until the crumbs are ever so lightly browned. Then remove the pans from the oven and spread each clam with a scant teaspoon of the salted whipped cream. Now slide the clams under the broiler for a few seconds (watch them, for they burn easily) and, when the tops are a crusty brown, serve at once.

AFTERTHOUGHTS:

✶ If, after they are opened, the clams seem excessively sandy, wash them quickly under cold running water and dry them well in paper towels.

✶ Preparing the green purée without a blender is something of a chore, but it can be done. Chop all the vegetables as finely as possible, then pound them in a mortar, adding the butter a little at a time. Stir in the bread crumbs, Pernod, and seasonings, and, if you have the patience, rub the purée through a sieve.

✻ If you prefer, oysters may of course be used in place of clams. Whichever you use, make sure the half shells are thoroughly drained of all liquid before you spread on the purée.

✻ The clams may be prepared hours ahead, set up on rock salt in their baking dishes, and refrigerated until they are ready to be baked. Unfortunately they cannot be cooked ahead successfully and reheated; this makes them quite rubbery and tough.

BROILED SHRIMP WITH TARRAGON AND GARLIC

BROILED shrimp, as served in many Italian restaurants, are almost always listed on the menu as scampi; and, in truth, a dish of *scampi* broiled with olive oil, butter, herbs, and garlic is one of the glories of the Italian cuisine. But *scampi,* indigenous to the Adriatic, are not shrimp at all and are never available here. Large shrimp, however, do quite as well, though it is best to disregard the Italian practice of broiling the shellfish in their shells. What little flavor the shrimp might gain is more than offset by the difficulty you will have eating them. Compromise before broiling the shrimp by shelling them but leaving the tails on.

] To serve six [

2 pounds fresh shrimp
¼ pound butter
½ cup olive oil
2 teaspoons lemon juice
¼ cup finely chopped shallots
1 tablespoon finely chopped garlic
1 tablespoon finely chopped fresh tarragon
    or 1 teaspoon dried tarragon

75

Freshly ground black pepper
Coarse salt
2 tablespoons finely chopped parsley, mixed with 1
    tablespoon finely chopped fresh tarragon, if
    available

Fresh shrimp are, of course, to be preferred to frozen ones; but if you must use the frozen, defrost them thoroughly first. The size of the shrimp you buy will be determined by how many there are in a pound. For broiling, 16 to the pound is best but 18 or, in a pinch, even 20 will do, but no more; they would simply be too small.

Shell each shrimp carefully, breaking off the shell just above the point where it joins the tail. It is almost impossible to do this evenly so don't fuss with it. With a small sharp knife, make a shallow incision down the back of each shrimp and carefully lift out the black or white intestinal vein, whichever color it happens to be; frequently there won't be any at all. Wash the shrimp thoroughly under cold running water and pat them dry with paper towels.

Choose an ovenproof baking pan just large enough to hold the shrimp in one layer and attractive enough to bring to the table. On top of the stove, over the lowest possible heat, slowly melt the butter in the pan. Don't let it brown. Remove the pan from the heat, let it cool a bit, then stir into the butter the olive oil, lemon juice, shallots, garlic, tarragon, and a few grindings of black pepper. Lay the shrimp in the pan, and turn them over and over in it until they are thoroughly coated with the oil, garlic, and herbs.

Preheat the broiler to its highest point. Sprinkle the shrimp with a little coarse salt, and slide the pan onto the rack 3 inches or so below the heat. Broil for about 5 minutes, basting the shrimp with the pan juices at the end of 3 minutes with a large spoon or basting syringe. When they have browned lightly, turn the shrimp over, one by one, with a pair of kitchen tongs. Again sprinkle them with a little salt, and broil them anywhere from 5 to 10 minutes longer, depending upon their size. Baste them every 3 minutes and don't overcook them; you can be sure they are done when they are lightly browned, the tails are almost blackened, and the flesh is definitely resistant to the touch. If you have any doubts, simply taste one.

Sprinkle the finished shrimp with the combined parsley and tarragon, and serve them directly from the baking dish, accompanied by hot French or Italian bread.

AFTERTHOUGHTS:

✳ Broiled shrimp make a fine first course served in the baking dish or kept warm in a chafing dish. Or serve them as a main course, garnished with water cress, with a RICE PILAF (see p. 285) and, naturally, lots of hot French bread to dunk into the sauce.

✳ You may set up the uncooked shrimp in the butter-oil mixture hours before you broil them; if you refrigerate them, the oil and butter will congeal without, however, any ill effects to the shrimp.

✳ Omit the tarragon if you prefer, and merely sprinkle the finished shrimp with chopped parsley. If possible, use the flat-leaf parsley; it has far more flavor and pungency than the curly type.

BROILED SWORDFISH
WITH COLD CUCUMBER AND DILL SAUCE

MANY Americans are noticeably unenthusiastic about fish; but swordfish, if statistics are to be believed, appears to rate in a contrary category all its own. Regrettably, the immense popularity of swordfish must be attributed to its unfishlike characteristics: When really fresh, it is completely free of odor; it has no bones to speak of; and its flesh when cooked doesn't separate into flakes but remains quite dense, with a texture resembling that of very young veal. The flavor of swordfish is delicate and unique, so that it is quickly dissipated or masked if it is too elaborately prepared. Broiling it quickly with the simplest of seasonings is undoubtedly the best way to cook it. The cold cucumber sauce served with the hot fish is an unexpected surprise to the palate.

] To serve six or eight [

3 pounds fresh swordfish, cut 1 inch thick
6 tablespoons softened butter, in all
Salt
Freshly ground black pepper

SAUCE:

1 cup peeled, seeded, and diced cucumber
1 pint sour cream
3 teaspoons white-wine vinegar
1 teaspoon salt
⅛ teaspoon cayenne
2 teaspoons grated onion
3 tablespoons finely chopped fresh dill

More than most fish, swordfish can be savored at its best only if it is really fresh. Use frozen swordfish if you must, but be certain it is thoroughly defrosted and patted dry with paper towels before you broil it; rubbing the fish with a little lemon juice as soon as it is defrosted may restore a little of its vanished bloom.

Preheat the broiler for 15 minutes and remove the fish from the refrigerator; it will cook more evenly if it isn't chilled.

Meanwhile, prepare the sauce. With a vegetable scraper, peel the cucumbers and cut them in half lengthwise. Run the tip of a teaspoon down the seeded length of each cucumber half and scoop out and discard the seeds. Dice the halves into approximately one-quarter-inch cubes. If they seem overly moist, spread them out on a strip of paper toweling and pat them dry.

In a small glass, porcelain, or stainless-steel mixing bowl, combine the sour cream, vinegar, salt, cayenne, and grated onion. Mix thoroughly, then gently stir in the chopped dill and the diced cucumber. Taste the sauce for seasoning; it will probably need more salt.

Allow approximately 15 minutes to broil the fish. With a pastry brush, grease the hot broiler rack with 1 tablespoon of soft butter. Spread another tablespoon of butter on the fish, sprinkle lightly with salt and a few grindings of black pepper, and broil the swordfish about 3 inches from the heat for about 3 minutes. Brush it again with another tablespoon of butter, and broil it 2 or 3 minutes longer, or until the surface of the fish is lightly browned.

Carefully turn the fish over, using two spatulas if necessary. As before, brush it with a tablespoon of butter and season it with salt and pepper. Broil for 5 minutes, brush with butter again, and then broil 10 minutes longer. The surface of the swordfish should be quite brown and the flesh should be firm to the touch. Transfer it to a hot platter immediately, brush it with the remaining butter, and serve at once. Pass the cucumber sauce separately.

AFTERTHOUGHTS:

✳ Omit the cucumber sauce if you prefer, and simply serve the broiled swordfish with lemon quarters. In that event, sprinkle the broiled fish with a little chopped parsley or dill before serving.

✳ You may broil a 1-inch-thick halibut steak in exactly the same fashion and serve it with the cucumber sauce. Don't overcook the halibut; if it flakes easily when pierced with a fork, it is done.

✳ If you want to make the sauce ahead, put the diced cucumbers, sprinkled with a little salt, in a small bowl, and put the mixed sour cream and seasonings in another bowl. Store them both, covered with Saran wrap, in the refrigerator. Drain the cucumbers well before adding them to the sour cream and add the fresh dill at the last.

✳ This, and any other broiled fish, is delicious with hot AVGOLEMONO SAUCE, page 210, or BÉARNAISE SAUCE, pages 212 and 213.

*

SAUTÉED SEA SQUABS PROVENÇALE
WITH TOMATO FONDUE

THE SEA SQUAB, or blowfish, as it is more commonly known, is a singular little fish, able, when alarmed, to inflate its body to twice its size. Were this its only claim to distinction, it would be easy to understand why fishermen for years always tossed it aside as a nuisance when it strayed into their nets. It was not until an imaginative soul discovered the technique of stripping the fish and exposing the succulent flesh surrounding the spine that the sea squab came rightfully into its own. Not unlike frogs' legs in flavor and texture, the sea squab is considerably cheaper and has, moreover, the advantage of being a fish and not a frog, a biological fact of some importance to less venturesome American cooks.

The recipe which follows is an adaptation of the classical procedure used in Provence to cook frogs' legs. An added refinement is a brown, clarified garlic butter which is poured over the fish before it is served. Scallops, and, of course, frogs' legs, may be prepared with equal success in the same manner.

] To serve four [

12 sea squabs (about 1½ pounds)
Juice of a small lemon

CLARIFIED GARLIC BUTTER:

¼ pound sweet butter
1 teaspoon finely chopped garlic

TOMATO FONDUE:

4 firm ripe tomatoes (medium size)
1 teaspoon salt
½ teaspoon freshly ground pepper
¼ teaspoon sugar

80

1 tablespoon fresh minced basil
   or 1 teaspoon crumbled dry basil
2 tablespoons butter

Salt
Freshly ground pepper
½ cup sifted flour
4–6 tablespoons olive oil

2 tablespoons finely chopped parsley (flat-leafed
   variety, if possible)
Lemon quarters or slices

Wash the sea squabs quickly under cold running water and dry them with paper towels. With a pastry brush paint the fish thoroughly with the lemon juice and let them rest while you prepare the clarified garlic butter and tomato fondue.

❋ *To clarify the ¼ pound of butter, cut it first into 8 or 10 pieces. In a small saucepan let it melt over fairly low heat but don't let it brown; that will come later in this particular recipe. Remove the pan from the heat and carefully skim all the foam from the top. Now tilt the pan away from you and, with a large metal spoon, ladle off as much of the clear butter as you can, scrupulously avoiding the milky solids which have settled at the bottom of the pan. Throw these away, wash the pan, and pour the clarified butter back into it. This is the plain clarified butter required in several recipes in this book.*

Over fairly low heat, cook the clarified butter slowly again until it turns a light brown and gives off a delicate nutlike odor. Remove the pan from the heat at once and stir in the teaspoon of minced garlic; the heat of the butter and of the pan will be sufficient to cook the garlic while you proceed with the next step.

❋ *To make the tomato fondue, first drop the tomatoes into a saucepan of boiling water. If they seem thin skinned, count to ten slowly; if thick, make it fifteen. Remove them from the water at once, plunge them into cold water, then peel. Cut the tomatoes in quarters lengthwise, and run a sharp knife under the pulp of each piece, separating it from the solid tomato shell beneath; save the pulp for soups or stocks. Cut the tomato quarters into quarter-inch strips, pat them dry with a paper towel, and toss them in a small bowl with the salt, pepper, sugar, and basil.*

Now melt the 2 tablespoons of butter over moderate heat in a heavy, medium-sized frying pan. Stir in the tomatoes with a wooden spoon and cook them briskly for about 5 minutes, shaking the pan from time to time. When the tomatoes are soft but not yet disintegrating, turn up the heat and boil rapidly until almost all the liquid in the pan has evaporated. Don't carry this too far, however, or you may end up with a tomato purée which is not your intention at all. Remove the pan from the heat while the tomato strips still retain a semblance of their shape. Taste for seasoning (the fondue will probably need more salt), cover, and set aside to be reheated when the sea squabs are ready to be served.

Plan to start cooking the fish 20 minutes before dinner, so preheat the oven to **200–250° F.** accordingly. Sift about ½ cup of flour onto a strip of waxed paper. Sprinkle the sea squabs liberally with salt and discreetly with freshly ground pepper, and roll them in the flour; shake off any excess flour.

Heat the olive oil in a large heavy skillet. When it begins to smoke, arrange the sea squabs in the pan but don't crowd them. They are exceedingly delicate fish and tend to break as they cook; the more room you have when you turn them over the better. Sauté them about 5 minutes on one side and 3 minutes on the other, adjusting the heat so that they cook as quickly as possible without burning. Add a little more oil to the pan if you think it needs it.

As the fish are done, transfer them carefully to the ovenproof platter you intend to serve them on, laying them neatly in one line down the center, slightly overlapping. Keep them warm in the slow oven until all are cooked. If dinner is delayed, they can remain in the oven, door ajar, for 10 minutes or so, but certainly no longer.

———————————

Just before serving, heat the garlic butter and the tomato fondue. Pour the butter over the sea squabs, making sure each fish is thoroughly anointed before dusting them heavily with the chopped parsley. Spoon the hot tomato fondue around the fish and decorate the platter with lemon quarters or slices. Serve at once with hot French bread and a chilled dry white wine—a white Côtes du Rhône, a Pouilly-Fuissé, or a good Chablis.

HALIBUT MOUSSE WITH SHRIMP SAUCE

To PREPARE a fish mousse in the classical French style requires the most exacting technical skill, to say nothing of sheer physical brawn: Filleted fish is pounded to a pulp in a mortar, rubbed through a sieve, beaten and mixed with egg whites and heavy cream until it is a smooth paste; it is then chilled and finally poached to an unbelievable, airy lightness. Be assured immediately that almost the same result can be achieved with the electric blender, and with no effort at all. The accompanying sauce, like so many of the fine French fish sauces, is based on an easily prepared fish *velouté,* fish stock thickened with a *roux* of flour and butter.

] To serve six or eight [

MOUSSE:

1 pound ground halibut (about 2 cups)
1½ teaspoons salt
⅛ teaspoon cayenne
3 egg whites
1½ cups heavy cream

1 teaspoon grated onion
1 teaspoon lemon juice
1 tablespoon finely chopped fresh dill
   or 1 teaspoon dried dill weed
Soft butter for ring mold

SAUCE:

1 cup fish stock (see pp. 87-88)
   or ½ cup bottled clam juice mixed with ½ cup
   fresh or canned chicken stock
2 tablespoons butter
2 level tablespoons flour
3 egg yolks
½ cup heavy cream
Salt
Cayenne pepper
1 teaspoon lemon juice
1 tablespoon finely chopped fresh dill
   or 1 teaspoon dried dill weed
1 cup cooked shrimp, whole or diced
4 tablespoons soft butter

Beg, borrow, or buy an electric blender if you don't have one. Of course, you can put the fish three or four times through a meat grinder and then make the mousse by hand; but it won't be quite the same thing unless you also have the patience to force the ground fish through a sieve.

In the blender jar put the ground halibut, salt, cayenne, egg whites, and cream, and blend at high speed, turning the machine off after the first few seconds and scraping down the sides of the jar with a rubber scraper. Continue to blend until the fish is reduced to a smooth purée. Should the blender clog at any point, add more cream, up to ½ cup, if necessary. Transfer the purée from the blender to a mixing bowl, and stir in the grated onion, lemon juice, and dill. Cover, and refrigerate until you are ready to cook the mousse.

The sauce may be cooked at any time and simply reheated. Make the stock first, following the recipe for fish stock on page 88 and using the halibut trimmings and extra fish bones or heads. Strain it, and boil it down to 1 cup. Or, if you are pressed for time, combine ½ cup of clam juice and ½ cup of chicken stock from which you have removed every trace of fat.

In a small saucepan, melt the 2 tablespoons of butter without letting it brown. Remove the pan from the heat and stir in the 2 level tablespoons of flour, mixing it in thoroughly to a smooth paste. Return the pan to the heat and cook the *roux* for about 30 seconds before pouring over it the cup of stock. With a wire whisk, mix this together, and as it comes to a boil continue to stir until the sauce is smooth and thick. Turn down the heat at once and simmer another 5 minutes so that no taste of raw flour remains.

In the meantime, combine the 3 egg yolks, and ½ cup of cream in a small bowl. Stir into this 2 or 3 tablespoons of the hot *velouté* sauce, then reverse the process and pour the now heated cream mixture into the remaining sauce. Continuing to stir, bring the sauce almost to a boil, and cook it slowly until it is thick enough to coat a spoon lightly. It might reassure you to know that this sauce, with its *velouté* base containing flour, is not likely to curdle at this point. But do stir deep into the sides of the pan as the eggs thicken, for it is there that they will thicken the fastest.

Season the sauce now with salt (be careful if you have used clam juice) and a few specks of cayenne, then remove the pan from the heat and stir into it the lemon juice, dill, and cooked shrimp. So that the sauce doesn't continue to cook as it cools, set the pan in cold water for a minute or two, then cover it tightly with Saran wrap, and put it aside until you are ready to use it. If it is to remain waiting for any length of time, refrigerate it.

About 45 minutes before you plan to serve the mousse, preheat the oven to **350° F.** Brush the inside of a 1½-quart ring mold with about a tablespoon of soft butter. Stir the mousse thoroughly before spooning it into the ring, and bang the ring sharply on the table once or twice so that the mousse settles evenly.

Cover the mold with a sheet of buttered aluminum foil and place it in a baking pan on the lower-third shelf of the oven. Pour into the pan enough boiling water to come half way up the side of the ring, and cook the mousse, undisturbed, for about 25 minutes, or until it is firm to the touch. Then remove the ring from the oven and let the mousse rest for about 5 minutes so that it will unmold more easily.

Meanwhile reheat the sauce. Stir it constantly over moderate heat and, when it has almost reached the boiling point, beat into it, off the heat, the 4 tablespoons of soft butter.

To serve the mousse, have ready a heated round platter about 2 or 3 inches wider in diameter than the ring mold. Carefully pour off, or draw off with a baster, all the liquid (there will be lots of it) which has accumulated on top of the mousse. Then run a sharp knife around the two inside circumferences of the mold. To unmold the mousse, place the hot platter over it, upside down, then grip the ring and platter together and quickly reverse them. Still holding them together tightly, rap the platter sharply on the table, and the mousse should drop out of the ring without any difficulty. Clear the platter of liquid, and pour half the sauce over the mousse.

Serve at once, and pass the remaining sauce separately. Steamed new potatoes in parsley butter and a fresh SPINACH SALAD with fennel (page 297) would be fine accompaniments.

AFTERTHOUGHTS:

✳ If dinner must wait, the mousse may remain in its pan of water in a turned-off oven for 10 or 15 minutes before being unmolded.

✳ Substitute cooked crabmeat or lobster for the shrimp if you wish. And if you want to be really lavish, garnish the ring with extra poached shellfish.

✳ In place of halibut, you may use an equal amount of any firm white fish such as pike, sole, flounder, cod, and the like.

∗

BOURRIDE OF SOLE WITH AÏOLI SAUCE

THE *bourride* in Provençal cookery is generally a fish soup made with the small whole fish of the region and thickened with *aïoli*, a garlic-laden mayonnaise. In this unusual version, the *bourride* is no longer a soup. Instead, the fish is filleted and gently poached, rather than boiled, in a rich, highly flavored stock or *fumet*. The stock is then reduced to intensify it further and finally combined with the *aïoli* to produce a piquant and tantalizing sauce, a perfect counter to the bland and delicate flavor of the poached fish. Oddly enough, the formidable amount of garlic indicated—conservative by Provençal standards—is not at all as overpowering as one might think.

] To serve six [

2½ pounds fillet of sole

FISH STOCK:

½ cup dry white wine
1 cup water
Fish trimmings
Small bay leaf
10 whole peppercorns
1 stalk celery, with leaves, cut up coarsely
1 leek, white part only, thinly sliced
1 small onion, thinly sliced
1 small carrot, thinly sliced
¼ teaspoon thyme
½ teaspoon salt
3 sprigs parsley
1 teaspoon lemon juice

AÏOLI:

4 large cloves garlic, coarsely chopped

87

1 tablespoon dry bread crumbs
1 tablespoon wine vinegar
3 egg yolks
1½ cups olive oil
½ teaspoon salt
⅛ teaspoon cayenne
2 tablespoons lemon juice

2 tablespoons heavy cream
2 tablespoons finely chopped parsley (flat-leafed
    variety, if available)

Any type of filleted American sole—grey sole, lemon sole, or flounder—will do for a *bourride* provided it is at least a half inch thick.
Thin fillets cook too quickly and tend to fall apart. To be sure
your fillets are really fresh, have the fish filleted just before you
buy it. Reserve the trimmings for the stock, and ask your fish man
to add to them a couple of fish heads and whatever other trimmings
he can spare.

✳ *To make the fish stock or* fumet, *combine in a 2- or 3-quart
enamel or glass saucepan the wine, water, and washed fish
trimmings, and bring it slowly to a boil. As the scum and froth
rise to the top, skim carefully; when the liquid is fairly clear,
add all the remaining ingredients. Turn the heat down to the
barest simmer, half cover the pan, and cook for about 40 minutes, but not much longer or the stock may develop a slightly
bitter flavor. Strain it through a fine sieve, pressing down on
the trimmings and vegetables with the back of a spoon before
throwing them away.*

✳ *The* aïoli *is really no more than a standard mayonnaise in
which pounded garlic is incorporated in the egg-yolk base.*
    *Don't be tempted to crush the garlic in a garlic press, nor to
make the* aïoli *in an electric blender; the results simply will
not be the same. Proceed traditionally by soaking a tablespoon
of bread crumbs in a tablespoon of vinegar. Squeeze these dry*

*with your fingers and combine them with the chopped garlic
in a mortar or small wooden bowl. With a wooden pastle or
the bottom of a small beer bottle, mash the garlic vigorously
until it has merged with the crumbs to form a smooth paste.
Don't be too concerned if it is lumpy here and there; it will
be strained out later.*

*When the paste is as smooth as you can get it, mix in the
3 egg yolks one at a time, and with the third yolk add the salt
and cayenne. Pound and beat the paste a few seconds longer,
then, with a rubber scraper, transfer it to the bowl of an electric mixer, or, lacking that, to a large mixing bowl.*

*With the mixer set at medium speed, or with a rotary beater
or wire whisk, start beating in the olive olive oil about ⅛ teaspoon at a time. Beating constantly, continue to add the oil
at this rate until ½ cup has been used and the aïoli has begun
to thicken into a dense, smooth cream. Now you may add the
oil at a faster rate, increasing it to ½ teaspoon at a time for the
next ½ cup and then a teaspoon at a time for the rest.*

*When the sauce is finished, it will be a thick, heavy mass.
Thin it with 2 tablespoons of lemon juice, cover it tightly
with Saran wrap, and put it aside until you are ready to use it.*

With these basic preparations out of the way, the actual cooking
of the *bourride* is a simple matter. Preheat the oven to **350° F.** Butter heavily the bottom and sides of a 1½- to 2-inch-deep flameproof
baking dish; it should be large enough to hold the fillets in one
layer. For easier handling, it is a good idea to cut the fish into serving pieces before poaching them. If any of the pieces are considerably thinner than the others, fold them in half lengthwise. Don't
worry if the pieces are disparate in size and shape; they will be
masked with the sauce before serving.

Arrange the fish in the baking dish, salt it lightly, then pour in
enough fish stock so that it is about half as deep in the dish as the
fillets are thick. Dot each piece with a little butter, and heat the
dish on top of the stove until the stock begins to simmer. At once,
transfer the dish to the center shelf of the oven, and cover it loosely
with a piece of buttered waxed paper slightly larger than the dish

89

itself. This is not only to prevent the fish from browning but to generate enough moisture to poach the fish without boiling it.

Poach the fish for about 10 minutes, 12 if the pieces are really thick, but certainly no longer. Remove it from the oven immediately and turn the oven off.

With a kitchen baster, drain all the liquid from the dish and put it into a small enamel or glass saucepan. Bring this to a boil and continue to boil it over high heat until it has reduced to about ½ cup. In the meantime, return the fish, still covered with the waxed paper, to the oven; this will keep it warm without cooking it while you finish the sauce.

Put all the *aïoli* in the top of a double boiler. Little by little, pour the hot reduced stock into it, stirring constantly, until the sauce is fluid enough to coat the back of the spoon rather heavily. Add 2 tablespoons of heavy cream—more if the sauce is thick—and, directly over moderate heat, still stirring constantly, bring it almost but not quite to the boil; if you allow it to really boil, it *will* curdle. Taste the sauce for seasoning, and add a little more salt, cayenne, and lemon juice if you think it needs it. If, for any reason, dinner must wait, keep the sauce warm over tepid, not hot water, stirring it every now and then.

Don't sauce the fish until you are ready to serve it. Remove the pieces from the baking dish with a spatula and arrange them on a heated serving platter. Be sure to mop up any liquid that accumulates with a paper towel or it will spoil your sauce. Through a fine sieve, strain the sauce over the fish, coating each piece as thoroughly as you can. Sprinkle with the chopped parsley and serve surrounded with boiled and buttered new potatoes, the traditional and perfect accompaniment to *bourride*.

AFTERTHOUGHTS:

✱ If you plan to make the *bourride* early in the day and reheat it later, poach the fish for only 8 minutes, as it will continue to cook as it cools. let the poached fish remain in its baking dish after you have drained off the stock. Prepare the *aïoli* and combine it, as described in the recipe, with the reduced stock, but don't heat it; cover the pan tightly with Saran wrap and put it aside until you are ready to use it.

To reheat the fish, set the baking dish over a pan of boiling water. Have it still loosely covered with its buttered waxed paper, and let it steam until the fish is heated through. Don't overcook it. Heat the sauce, stirring it constantly over direct heat, but in no circumstances let it come to a boil. Serve as described earlier, but you may, if you like, serve the fish directly from the baking dish. Just be sure to drain off all the accumulated liquid in the dish with a basting syringe before straining the sauce over the fish.

✱ You may complete the *aïoli* sauce hours before poaching the fish. Simply make twice the amount of stock indicated. Reduce half of it to ½ cup, and combine it with the *aïoli*, to be reheated later. Poach the fish in the remaining stock.

COLD STRIPED BASS IN MAYONNAISE COLLÉE

WITH SAFFRON ASPIC

HOW OFTEN have you admired that crowning glory of the professional chef's buffet table—a splendidly decorated whole fish reposing on a bed of shimmering, golden aspic? If the thought of recreating this masterpiece in your kitchen has occurred to you at all, you have probably dismissed it as impractical, if not totally impossible. Actually, the three basic techniques involved are rather simple once you decide to learn them, and they have many applications in other dishes. Explored here in precise detail are: poaching a fish in the highly seasoned broth called a *court-bouillon;* transforming the bouillon into a clear aspic; and preparing the firm mayonnaise known in classical cooking as a *mayonnaise collée.*

91

] To serve eight [

4-pound striped bass

COURT-BOUILLON:

2 quarts cold water
1 bottle dry white wine (about 3½ cups)
¼ cup tarragon vinegar
2 tablespoons salt
2 carrots, sliced
3 medium onions, sliced
4 stalks celery, cut up coarsely
2 bay leaves
4 sprigs parsley
5 sprigs fresh dill
    or ½ teaspoon dried dill weed
1 teaspoon thyme
20 whole black peppercorns

ASPIC:

4 cups reduced *court-bouillon* (above)
½ teaspoon lemon juice
5 whole black peppercorns
Small pinch powdered saffron
2 envelopes unflavored gelatine
½ cup cold water
Whites of 2 eggs and the crushed shells

MAYONNAISE COLLÉE:

2 cups mayonnaise (see p. 300)
1 cup liquid aspic (above)
1 level tablespoon unflavored gelatine
3 tablespoons cold water

GARNISH:

Sliced black olive
10 small cooked shrimp
1 or 2 lemons, thinly sliced
Sprigs of fresh dill or parsley

A difficulty you may encounter when you decide to cook a whole fish is finding a pan large enough to hold it. The practical French use a special fish poacher called a *saumonière,* a long, narrow pan equipped with a removable rack. Available in a variety of sizes, it can be bought in restaurant-supply houses or stores specializing in French cooking ware. However, a large, shallow roasting pan with a cover will do almost as well.

Your first concern with the fish itself should be its freshness. The difference between a fish freshly caught and one refrigerated for any length of time is enormous. Patronize a fish dealer you can trust, of course, but trust him to a point only. Examine the fish closely before you buy it. A pronounced fishy odor, though not always conclusive, should alert you to other signs of possible deterioration: dull, instead of bright, bulging eyes; scales hanging loosely from the skin instead of clinging closely to it; gills a pale pink rather than a bright red; and the flesh flaccid instead of firm and resilient to the touch.

Have the striped bass you finally choose scaled and cleaned, but be sure the head and tail are left intact. Unlike most Europeans, we tend to take a dim view of fish heads, cooked or uncooked, so of course the head may be removed if you insist. But it does add considerable flavor to the broth and lends a professional touch to the finished dish besides.

Plan to poach the fish and make the aspic the day before you serve them; the *mayonnaise collée* can wait.

❋ *First prepare the* court-bouillon, *a simple procedure: In a large pot, combine all the listed ingredients except the pepper-*

corns. Bring the pot to a boil, then simmer, partially covered, for 45 minutes; add the peppercorns and cook 20 minutes longer. Strain the bouillon through a fine sieve into the fish poacher or roasting pan and let it cool until lukewarm.

Wash the striped bass under cold running water. Without drying it, wrap it securely in a large piece of cheesecloth, leaving at least 6 extra inches of cloth at each end. Twist the ends tightly and tie them with string. The fish is now enclosed in a hammock, as it were, ready to be placed on the rack of the fish poacher and immersed in the *court-bouillon.*

If you are using a roasting pan, prepare the fish the same way, but tie the ends of the cheesecloth to the handles outside the pan. This helps, later, to remove the fish from the broth without having to grapple with it unnecessarily. Be sure in either case that the fish is well covered with liquid; if there isn't enough *court-bouillon,* add water.

To heat the broth quickly, cover the pan tightly and place it over two burners of the stove at once. When the *court-bouillon* just begins to boil, lower the heat at once, low enough so that the liquid makes only the slightest surface movement. Poach the fish in this fashion for 15 minutes, timing it from the moment the liquid be-began to boil. Then let the *court-bouillon* cool until it is lukewarm before removing the fish to a large chopping board or platter.

Unwrap the fish, but leave it on the cheesecloth. With a small knife make a small slit at the base of the tail and peel off the skin from tail to gill. Again using the cheesecloth as a hammock, lift up the fish and cautiously flip it over onto the most elegant platter you own. As before, peel off all the skin on the second side. Cover the fish with waxed paper or Saran wrap, and refrigerate it until it is thoroughly chilled.

✳ *To make the aspic, first transfer the* court-bouillon *from the poaching pan to a smaller pan. Reduce it by boiling it furiously until there are 4 cups left; this may take an hour, possibly longer. Then add to the reduced bouillon the lemon juice,*

94

peppercorns, and saffron. Be careful with the saffron, for a speck too much will give an unpleasant medicinal taste to the aspic instead of flavoring and coloring it delicately.

Sprinkle 2 packages of gelatine into ½ cup of cold water. While it is softening, beat the 2 egg whites to a froth. Crush the egg shells into the bouillon, and add the egg whites and softened gelatine at the same time. Over high heat, stir this disparate mixture constantly with a wire whisk, and don't stop stirring until it boils and threatens to overflow the pot. Then turn off the heat and let the aspic rest for about 10 minutes.

Now strain it through a fine sieve lined with a moist kitchen towel. Don't at any point disturb the liquid as it drips through the towel or you will cloud the aspic by dislodging the sediment now clinging to the cooked egg whites.

Put aside 1 cup of the clarified aspic for the *mayonnaise collée.* Pour the rest into a shallow dish or pan and chill it until firm.

✻ *Make the* mayonnaise collée *the next day, at least 3 or 4 hours before you plan to serve the fish. Ideally, the only mayonnaise worth eating is one you make yourself; commercial mayonnaise, whatever its dubious virtues, is generally too sweet and blend. There is a recipe for mayonnaise on page 300; start it with the 2 egg yolks left over from clarifying the aspic. If, for any reason you must use commercial mayonnaise, heighten its flavor with extra salt, cayenne, and lemon juice.*

Heat the reserved cup of aspic in a small pan; when it boils, stir into it the level tablespoon of gelatin first softened in 3 tablespoons of cold water. Cook the aspic a minute or two, cool it, then, with a fork, beat it bit by bit into the mayonnaise until it is all absorbed.

Remove the fish from the refrigerator and cover the platter with strips of waxed paper, sliding them slightly under the fish on all sides.

Pour the *mayonnaise collée* into a small china bowl, and set it in a larger bowl filled with ice. Stir it constantly with a large metal spoon until the mayonnaise thickens to the "point of setting"; in other words, when the mixture has almost but not quite congealed and still runs off the spoon. At this point, spoon the mayonnaise in even streams along the surface of the fish until the body and head are thoroughly coated. Traditionally, the tail is left exposed.

Garnish the fish immediately, and be sure to anchor each decorative piece into place as you proceed by pressing it gently into the still soft mayonnaise: Lay a round of black olive over the eye; then arrange the split shrimp in a row, to simulate scales, along one side of the fish, slightly overlapping one over the next. Arrange thin half circles of unpeeled lemon along the other side in the same fashion, and fix a few sprays of fresh dill or parsley on the mayonnaise for additional color.

Carefully remove the splattered strips of waxed paper from the platter, and refrigerate the fish until the mayonnaise and decorations are set.

When the mayonnaise is firm to the touch, a matter of an hour or so, turn out the aspic onto a double thickness of waxed paper; either dip the pan into hot water until the aspic is loosened and comes out easily, or you may scoop it out with a spoon. With a large knife, chop the aspic fine, and arrange it evenly on the platter, piling it up around the sides of the fish so that it appears to be floating in a sea of golden foam. Return the platter to the refrigerator for the last time to await the moment you proudly present it.

AFTERTHOUGHTS:

✳ To serve individual portions of the bass with very little bone, cut the top layer of the fish into sections without cutting through the spine. Gently remove each piece with a spatula. Lift out the backbone in one piece, and divide the bottom layer of the fish.

✳ Striped bass cooked in the same fashion may be served hot. Add 10 minutes to the cooking time and remove the fish from the hot *court-bouillon* as soon as it is done. Lemon butter or hollandaise sauce would be fitting accompaniments. Cut the fish as described for the cold version. If you have no immediate use for the *court-bouillon,* freeze it, to be used later in any fish recipe calling for fish stock.

96

✳ If, by some mischance, the fish has been overcooked, it will probably break when you first unwrap it. In that event, don't attempt to remove it from the cheesecloth; put the fish, as is, in the refrigerator. It will become firm as it cools and you will be able to handle it easily from then on. If the cheesecloth sticks when you try to remove it, moisten it lightly with cold water.

✳ Any left-over fish may be used to advantage in a fish salad. Flake it into small pieces and combine it, after removing all the small bones, with a little mayonnaise, minced chives, dill, or parsley, salt, lemon juice, and cayenne. Sprinkle a few washed and dried capers over the top, and serve the salad on a bed of shredded Boston or romaine lettuce.

LOBSTER À L'AMÉRICAINE

THIS, the best-known of the more elaborate French lobster recipes, is a far cry from the boiled or broiled lobster typical of American cooking. Lobster *à l'américaine* comes by its name not through any connection with America but through a series of migrations within France itself that culinary historians have delighted in arguing about since the nineteenth century.

The original dish, flavored as it is with olive oil, tomatoes, and garlic, can hardly have come from any region but the south of France, and a simpler version continues to be well-known there as lobster *à la provençale*. The transformation of this antecedent into a classic of *haute cuisine* must have been effected by very fine chefs, presumably in Paris, where, as one story goes, a now vanished restaurant called the *Américain* made a specialty of it. However, the plot continues to thicken, for Brittany, the source of the finest lobsters of France, also came to specialize in the dish and another name evolved, *à l'armoricaine,* after the ancient coastal region of *Armorique.* This produced the theory that *à l'américaine* was a mere corruption of an authentic Breton name.*

Finally, the intricacies of the recipe multiplied and the flavoring

* Waverly Root, *The Food of France.* Knopf. N.Y., 1958.

of simmered vegetables called *mirepoix bordelaise* was added to the dish, causing some to say that the original must have been from Bordeaux (where crayfish, or *langoustes,* are indeed prepared with this *mirepoix*). This is the least likely claim of all, however, and some cooks positively object to the addition of a *mirepoix* to lobster *à l'américaine.* The recipe that follows nevertheless includes it, as it adds a final refinement to the sauce that is more than justified, whether the purists approve or not. This is a superb creation, worth every bit of the effort it takes to prepare—and worthy, as well, of all the learned argument about it.

] To serve four or six [

2 live lobsters, 2–2½ pounds each
      or 3 live lobsters, 1½ pounds each

MIREPOIX BORDELAISE:

4 tablespoons butter
2 small onions, finely chopped
1 medium carrot, finely chopped
1 tablespoon finely chopped parsley
1 teaspoon thyme
1 small bay leaf

6 tablespoons olive oil
1/3 cup brandy
5 shallots, finely chopped
5 large tomatoes, peeled, seeded, and chopped

4 tablespoons butter, creamed with:
      Tomalley and coral of the lobsters
      1 level tablespoon flour
      2 cloves garlic, finely minced
      ½ teaspoon lemon juice
      1 tablespoon chopped fresh tarragon
            or 1 teaspoon dried tarragon
      1 tablespoon finely chopped chervil or parsley

1 tablespoon tomato paste
1 teaspoon commercial meat essence (BV)
1 cup dry white wine
1 cup chicken stock, fresh or canned

Confronted for the first time with a couple of live lobsters squirming on a kitchen table, the adventurous cook embarking upon this recipe can scarcely be blamed for feeling a qualm or two. It is a simple matter, however, to have the fish dealer cut up the lobsters to your specifications. Be sure to have him save the tomalley and coral for you. But it is also useful to know how to cut up a lobster yourself; the instructions are in the AFTERTHOUGHTS to this recipe.

For this particular dish, two fairly large lobsters are better than three small ones; since they are not to be served whole, large ones are easier to manage and the proportion of meat to shell is greater. Unless you must, don't buy the lobsters from a tank. The lobsters will have retained two or three ounces of water, thus adding needlessly to their cost, high enough to begin with. Above all, the lobsters should not only be alive but lively when they are cut up. If you are going to cut them up yourself, be sure their claws are securely pegged.

✳ *To begin, prepare the* mirepoix bordelaise, *the name of the bed of vegetables upon which the lobsters will repose: In a large casserole, melt the 4 tablespoons of butter, and in it slowly cook the chopped onions and carrot until they are lightly colored—about 10 minutes; then add to them the parsley, thyme, and bay leaf.*

Meanwhile, sprinkle the cut-up lobster with 1 tablespoon of salt. Heat the 6 tablespoons of olive oil almost to the smoking point in a heavy frying pan large enough, if possible, to hold all the pieces in one layer. Toss in the lobster and sauté it over high heat until the shells turn red and the meat stiffens slightly; turn the pieces frequently with kitchen tongs. Then turn off the heat and, with a basting syringe, draw off most of the oil from the pan and throw it away.

99

The flaming procedure that follows can be done either with a ladle as described on page 115 or by simply heating the brandy in a very small pan and setting it alight with a match. However you do it, pour the burning brandy over the lobsters a little at a time, and shake the frying pan back and forth constantly until the flame dies out. Now, one by one, put the lobster pieces on the *mirepoix* in the casserole, and add the chopped shallots and tomatoes.

Ignore the casserole for a moment and return to the frying pan: In it blend together the tomato paste and the meat glaze. To this add the white wine and chicken stock, stir well, and bring the mixture to a boil. Let this cook a moment or two, then into the casserole it goes, to be combined with the lobster and *mirepoix*. Stir everything together around and around with a large spoon until the pieces of lobster are thoroughly coated.

Now turn on the heat under the casserole and, when the liquid begins to boil again, turn the heat down, cover the pot securely, and simmer the lobsters slowly for about half an hour. With a spoon or the basting syringe, baste the lobster pieces every now and then with the sauce to keep them moist.

While the lobsters are cooking, with a spoon cream 4 tablespoons of butter in a bowl; when it is soft and smooth, mash and beat into it the tomalley and coral, the flour, minced garlic, lemon juice, tarragon, chervil or parsley, and a little salt and cayenne.

Remove the lobster when it is done to the large heated platter you intend to present it on. You can serve the bodies or not, as you wish; except for the infinitesimal amount of meat in the small claws—a nuisance to get at—there is practically no meat in them. Keep the platter warm, covered loosely with foil, in a slow (**250° F.**) oven while you finish the sauce.

Strain the juices in the casserole through a fine sieve into a small saucepan; press hard against the vegetables with a spoon but don't force them through. Boil this sauce rapidly to reduce it to about half its original quantity; this will take 10 minutes or less, depending upon how much you start with. Then lower the heat and stir in the creamed butter mixture bit by bit. Cook the sauce slowly without boiling it for about 5 minutes; taste for seasoning, then pour it over the lobster.

———————

Serve lobster *à l'américaine* with plain boiled rice or RICE PILAF (see p. 285); a salad of Boston lettuce, simply dressed with olive oil, lemon juice, salt and freshly ground pepper; hot French bread; and a bottle of white Bordeaux Graves if you can still afford it.

AFTERTHOUGHTS:

✳ There are many ways to present lobster *à l'américaine*. Most correctly, it is served in a timbale—a drum-shaped mold or dish—, the bodies of the lobster (with the little claws removed) standing upright against the sides of the dish, the tail sections and claws in the center, and the sauce over all. Frequently the tail and claw meat is removed from the shells. Another alternative is to serve only the shelled meat, covered with the sauce, in a chafing dish.

✳ The chicken stock in this recipe is not traditional; the sauce is usually made with fish stock. If you have some around, or want to go to the trouble to make it (see p. 87), by all means use it. Otherwise, chicken stock is quite satisfactory; some cooks even prefer it.

✳ Lobster *à l'américaine* may be prepared a few hours ahead, if you must, and reheated in a double boiler.

✳ Any left-over sauce can be used to advantage to cook other shellfish. This is particularly successful with shrimp. Sauté them lightly first, raw and shelled, in a little butter or oil, cover with the sauce, and simmer them with a lid on for 10 or 15 minutes. Serve the shrimp sprinkled with chopped parsley as a first course or, with rice, as a main course.

✳ *Lastly, to cut up a live lobster, this is how you proceed:*
Wash it first, and lay it on its back on a chopping board. Put a kitchen towel over the head and claws and grasp towel and lobster together firmly with one hand. With a large, very sharp and rigid knife, cut off the tail section, crosswise, at the point where it joins the body. This will dispatch the lobster quickly and mercifully by severing the spinal cord, although the claws will continue to wave around in reflex for a while.

101

Slice the tail crosswise into 4 or 5 pieces. Now cut the claws from the body. If you find them too resistant, place the sharp edge of the knife on the claw joint and hit the back of the knife sharply with a mallet. Similarly, make a gash on the flat side of each of the large claws so that the meat may be extracted easily when the lobster is served. Finally, cut through the body section lengthwise, between the two rows of small claws, using the mallet if necessary.

Spread the split body shell flat. Remove and discard the gelatinous sack near the head, but save the greenish-brown substance called the tomalley, or liver; scoop it out with a spoon and put it in a small bowl to be used later. If the lobster is a female, you may also find a black, caviarlike deposit which will turn red when it is cooked. Unattractive as it may seem in its uncooked state, it is a great delicacy; collect every bit of it and reserve it with the tomalley.

Poultry

POULTRY may be sautéed, fried, or deep-fat fried, braised, broiled, or roasted, and stuffed or sauced as well. Each of these processes is represented in this chapter, each requiring a particular type and size of bird, which may also be whole, halved, quartered, or cut up. Chicken, of course, is the most adaptable poultry of all, and it may also be boiled (simmered, really; see CHICKEN STOCK on page 34). In short, there is practically no end to the number of ways you can cook a bird.

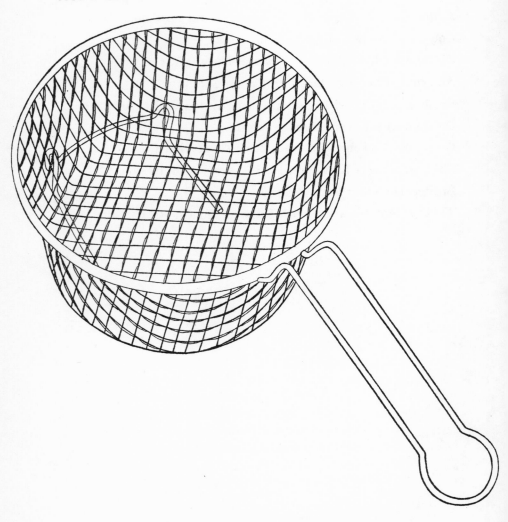

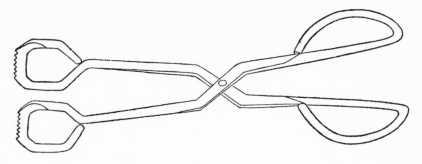

There are several basic techniques here that you can refer to when you are cooking many other recipes. Learn, for one thing, what to tell your butcher when you want him to disjoint a chicken for you properly; see SAUTÉED CHICKEN. How to truss a bird is described for CHICKEN IN A COCOTTE; a turkey is trussed in almost the same way. The TRUFFLED TURKEY recipe further tells how to stuff a bird and the simple though mysterious-appearing way in which truffles can be inserted under its unbroken skin; this can be done with a roasting chicken as well. Boning a chicken breast is a most useful technique to know, used in a show-piece recipe, CHICKEN CUTLETS KIEV, and for the CHICKEN CURRY. In CHICKEN CUTLETS KIEV, the standard method of deep frying is described; their coating *à l'anglaise* is no more than the conventional egg and bread crumb coating used for many deep-fried foods, including the ordinary croquette. The expert method for flaming brandy is described in CHICKEN VALLÉE D'AUGE.

These poultry recipes also demonstrate some of the various ways sauces are arrived at in cooking. COQ AU VIN is essentially cooked in its own sauce, while CHICKEN VALLÉE D'AUGE has a sauce made afterwards with the cooking liquid. The cooking liquid *is* the sauce in a braised dish such as CHICKEN IN A COCOTTE. For sautéed, broiled, and roasted birds, the extended pan juices become unthickened gravies, or pan sauces, the most developed one here being the orange sauce for BROILED DUCKLING. Cream gravy for AMERICAN FRIED CHICKEN is a thickened pan sauce. The sauce for CHICKEN CURRY is quite different from any of the others—an almost finished sauce being made for the chicken then to be cooked in.

*

SAUTÉED CHICKEN
WITH WHOLE SHALLOTS AND ARTICHOKE HEARTS

A SIMPLE provincial dish. The number of shallots required may appear formidable at first glance but, oddly enough, they don't overpower the flavor of the chicken. Instead, they give it a subtle, indefinable distinction. But they must be shallots; no other member of the onion family will do.

] To serve four [

2½- to 3-pound frying chicken, disjointed
Salt
Freshly ground black pepper
4 tablespoons butter
2 tablespoons vegetable oil

16 large shallots, uniform in size if possible
1 bay leaf
2 tablespoons butter
1 teaspoon lemon juice
1 package frozen artichoke hearts
½ cup chicken stock, fresh or canned
2 tablespoons finely chopped parsley

* *Ask the butcher to disjoint the chicken with care; that is, to separate the joints cleanly with a knife instead of hacking through them with a cleaver. The average butcher tends to be much too casual about this dissection, with the result that the pieces are frequently unattractive and, moreover, difficult to eat because of protruding bone splinters. If he does a really good job, the backbone will have been cut away from the rest of the bird, as will the wing tips; all these and the gizzard, heart, and neck should go into your freezer, first well washed,* *to be used for stock (see p. 34). All disjointed chickens should be handled in the same way.*

Wash the pieces of chicken quickly under cold running water and pat them dry with paper towels; and they must be thoroughly dry, or they won't brown well. Salt the pieces generously but sprinkle them ever so lightly with the black pepper.

Choose a large, heavy frying pan, or a true sauté pan, that has a closely fitting lid, and in it heat the butter and oil until they fairly sizzle. Over high heat, brown the chicken a few pieces at a time, starting them skin side down and turning them with kitchen tongs. Add more oil to the pan if necessary to prevent the chicken from sticking or burning. As each piece reaches a deep golden brown on all sides, remove it to a platter and add a fresh piece to the pan until all the chicken is done.

In the same pan and over fairly high heat, brown the whole peeled shallots, shaking the pan back and forth occasionally so that they color evenly without burning. This should take no more than 2 or 3 minutes.

Push the shallots to the side of the pan and, with a large spoon or basting syringe, remove all but 2 tablespoons of the fat in the pan. However, if the fat should seem badly burnt, pour it all off and in its place add 2 tablespoons of butter.

Return the chicken to the pan (with whatever liquid has collected on the platter), arranging the pieces in one layer if possible. Scatter the shallots at random on top of the chicken. Add the bay leaf, cover the pan, and cook over high heat until you hear the fat begin to sizzle. At once, turn the heat down to the barest simmer, and cook the chicken slowly for 30 to 40 minutes. Baste it well every 10 minutes or so; as in all sautés, enough liquid will collect in the pan after a while so that the chicken can be continually moistened with its own shallot-flavored pan juices.

Meanwhile, prepare the artichokes: For the best results, they should be thoroughly defrosted, or at least to the point where they can be separated from one another. Heat the 2 tablespoons of but-

107

ter in a small enamel or Pyrex casserole (don't use aluminum or cast iron; they will turn the artichokes a slate grey) and, when it is melted but not brown, stir in the lemon juice. Toss the arti-chokes in the lemon butter until they are well coated, sprinkle them lightly with salt, and cook them, covered, over low heat, for 10 or 15 minutes. Shake the casserole every now and then to keep the artichokes from sticking. Don't overcook them; turn off the heat when they are tender but still slightly resistant to the touch.

When the chicken is done (one way to tell is to test the leg for tenderness with a two-pronged fork), arrange the pieces down the center of a large heated platter. If the shallots were small, they will probably have lost their shape; if so, remove them from the pan with a slotted spoon and scatter them over the chicken. If they are presentably whole (large ones will be), alternate shallots and arti-choke hearts in a neat ring around the chicken.

Working quickly, add ½ cup of chicken stock to the juices left in the frying pan and bring it to a boil. Scrape up all the brown sediment on the bottom and sides of the pan and stir it into the boiling stock. Boil this rapidly for a couple of minutes or until the sauce is reduced again to about ½ cup. Taste it for seasoning, then pour it over the chicken. Sprinkle with the chopped parsley and serve at once, accompanied by buttered rice and hot French or Italian bread.

AFTERTHOUGHTS:

✳ This sautéed chicken is at its best served the moment it is done. But if it must be made ahead, brown the chicken and shallots and put them aside without cooking them further. Half an hour before dinner, re-turn them to the frying pan, with their accumulated juices, and finish the cooking, basting the chicken frequently. It should be tender in 15 to 20 minutes, as it will have continued to cook earlier as it cooled. The artichokes may be cooked at any time and simply reheated, pref-erably over hot water.

✳

COQ AU VIN À LA BOURGUIGNONNE

Coq au vin is simply a chicken or, literally, a rooster stewed in wine, whether it is called *coq au vin alsacienne, Pouilly, jurassienne, bourguignonne,* or anything else. Each wine-producing region of France has its own version of this classic dish but the Burgundian *coq au vin* is the best known here. Ideally, it should be made with the best Burgundy you can buy and the American types, though lacking a certain robustness, should certainly be considered. However, your *coq au vin* will only be as good as the wine it is cooked in. Never, then, attempt to make it with a so-called "cooking" wine, a misnomer, if ever there was one.

In earlier times, when farmers' wives dressed their own poultry, the blood of the rooster was used to thicken the sauce of a *coq au vin.* This ingredient, you may be relieved to know, is not essential to the success of the dish and is not used in the following recipe.

] To serve four [

½ pound salt pork, cut into ¼-inch dice
1 tablespoon butter
12–16 little white onions, all approximately 1 inch in
     diameter, peeled and left whole

3-pound frying chicken, disjointed (see p. 106)
Salad oil, if needed
¼ cup brandy

2 cups Burgundy

2 tablespoons flour
½ cup chicken or beef stock (or brown chicken
     stock; see p. 35)
A bouquet consisting of 3 sprigs parsley, a bay leaf,
     2 celery tops, all tied together
½ teaspoon thyme
1 teaspoon salt

4 tablespoons butter
½ pound mushrooms
2 tablespoons finely chopped shallots
½ teaspoon finely chopped garlic

2 tablespoons finely chopped parsley

Wash the pieces of chicken quickly under cold running water and dry them thoroughly with paper towels; they won't brown well if they are the slightest bit damp. Sprinkle the pieces liberally with salt and sparingly with pepper, and put them aside while you prepare the salt pork and the little white onions.

Here begins the traditional garnish of onions browned in rendered salt pork that is described in detail for BEEF BOURGUIGNON; if you have not made this before, be sure to refer to page 159. Preheat the oven to **350° F.**

Blanch the diced salt pork in a little boiling water, and drain and pat it dry. In a large frying pan, sauté the pieces in the tablespoon of butter until they are crisp and brown, then drain them on paper toweling.

In the rendered fat left in the pan, brown the little white onions over moderate heat, shaking the pan often to brown them as evenly as they can be. Then transfer them to a shallow baking dish, add 3 tablespoons of the fat to the dish, and bake them in the preheated oven for about 30 minutes, turning them occasionally. Don't overcook them. Remove them from the dish, and put them aside in a bowl lined with a paper towel.

While the onions are baking (or, if you prefer, after they are done), heat the fat remaining in the frying pan, adding a couple of tablespoons of vegetable oil if there isn't enough fat left to cover the bottom of the pan. Over fairly high heat, brown the chicken in this, starting the pieces skin side down and turning them with kitchen tongs to brown each side. Each piece should be a deep golden brown when you finish.

While the chicken is browning, reduce the 2 cups of Burgundy to 1½ cups by boiling it hard in an enamel or stainless-steel pan. If you think the double operation too fraught with potential disaster, finish browning the chicken first and reduce the wine afterwards. It might be interesting to note here, that heat not only volatilizes the alcohol in wine but changes the wine's character as well. Any unfortified wine, no matter how fine its quality, will taste sharp and raw if it is not cooked long enough. Reducing it insures you a rich, smooth-tasting sauce without any acrid aftertaste.

When the chicken is brown, turn off the heat and, with a basting syringe, remove all but a thin film of fat from the pan. Warm ¼ cup of brandy and set it alight, stepping back as you do so (see page 115). Pour the burning brandy over the chicken a little at a time, shaking the frying pan back and forth until the flame dies out. Transfer the chicken to a heavy 3- or 4-quart casserole with a closely fitting lid.

Into the dark-brown glaze remaining in the frying pan, stir the 2 tablespoons of flour, mixing it to a paste with all the fat and sediment you can scrape up from the bottom and sides of the pan. Add to this *roux* the reduced wine and ½ cup of chicken or beef stock. Bring the mixture to a boil, stirring constantly with a wire whisk, and let it cook for a moment or two until it is smooth and thick. Strain the sauce through a fine sieve over the chicken in the casserole, and add the bouquet, the thyme, and a teaspoon of salt.

Now prepare the mushrooms. If they are large, slice or quarter them; if small, use them whole. Don't wash or peel them, but wipe them lightly with a moist towel and dry them thoroughly. Over moderate heat, melt 4 tablespoons of butter in a large frying pan. When the foam subsides, add the chopped shallots and garlic; stirring all the while, cook these together for about 30 seconds before adding the mushrooms. Now raise the heat and, turning the mushrooms constantly with a wooden spoon, cook them for no more than 2 or 3 minutes. Then, using a rubber scraper, add them and all the pan juices to the chicken in the casserole.

Give the *coq au vin* a gentle turn or two with a large spoon so that the mushrooms, chicken, and herbs are all well moistened with the sauce. Then cover the casserole and bring it to a boil. At once, slide it onto the center shelf of the oven, which should still be at **350° F.,** and cook the chicken, barely simmering, for 30 to 40 minutes, until it is tender. Add the baked onions to the casserole about 10 minutes before the chicken is done.

The *coq au vin* may be served directly from the casserole, or more impressively, on a platter, the pieces of chicken arranged down the center, surrounded by the mushrooms and onions. However you serve it, remove the bouquet from the sauce, and dust the surface of either casserole or platter with chopped parsley. Scatter the reserved salt pork scraps over the dish now, unless you prefer not to use them at all.

Steamed whole potatoes, boiled rice, or POTATOES ANNA (see page 278) go well with this. Certainly the chicken deserves to be served with a bottle of the same Burgundy it was cooked in. Above all, have plenty of hot French or Italian bread with which to sop up the sauce.

AFTERTHOUGHTS:

✻ More often than not, the sauce, when the chicken is done, will be of exactly the right density. However, should it be too thick, thin it with a little chicken stock. If it is too thin, boil it down to the desired consistency after first removing the chicken, onions, and mushrooms. Or, stir into it ½ teaspoon of arrowroot powder dissolved in a tablespoon of cold water; boil for a minute or two until the sauce thickens.

✻ *Coq au vin,* like all stews, may be prepared hours ahead and reheated; whether this improves it, as some cooks maintain, is open to some dispute. But if you do cook *coq au vin* in advance, undercook it a bit; it will continue to cook as it cools and will in all likelihood be properly done by the time you are ready to reheat it. The braised onions, of course, may be made at any time prior to the cooking of the chicken.

✻ You may, if you like, cook *coq au vin* wholly on top of the stove instead of in the oven. In that event, for the best results, your casserole *must* be a heavy one equipped with a tightly fitting cover.

✳ If you object to the dark-purple color of a Burgundian *coq au vin* as, unaccountably, some people do, combine 1 cup of red Burgundy with 1 cup of white Burgundy—a Pouilly or an American Pinot Chardonnay—and reduce this to 1½ cups as indicated in the recipe. This will lighten the color of the sauce without impairing its flavor.

✳ The dish may be made with white wine only, with excellent results, though it can then no longer be called *à la bourguignonne*.

CHICKEN VALLÉE D'AUGE
WITH SAUTÉED APPLE RINGS

Eggs, cream, apples, Calvados, products for which Normandy is famous, are used in this regional dish. Calvados, a brandy distilled from apples, is as indigenous to Normandy as is maple syrup to Vermont. A truly aged Calvados, however, is quite rare in the United States. If you are fortunate enough to find some, by all means use it; it has a unique flavor that will give your *poulet Vallée d'Auge* the proper note of authenticity. Otherwise, the American applejack will do. In fact, good applejack is likely to be superior to immature Calvados, and it is certainly less expensive.

] To serve four [

3-pound chicken, disjointed (see p. 106)
Salt
Freshly ground black pepper
4 tablespoons butter
2 tablespoons vegetable oil

¼ cup Calvados or applejack
½ cup chicken stock, fresh or canned

2 tablespoons butter
2 tablespoons finely chopped shallots
¼ cup finely chopped celery

2 small tart apples, peeled, cored, and coarsely
 chopped
½ teaspoon thyme

2 egg yolks
 or 3 if the yolks are small
½ cup heavy cream
½ teaspoon lemon juice
Cayenne

2 tablespoons finely chopped parsley
Water cress

APPLE RINGS:

3 firm large apples, cored, *un*peeled, and sliced
 ½ inch thick
4–6 tablespoons butter
1–2 tablespoons granulated sugar

Wash the chicken pieces quickly under cold running water and pat
them dry with paper towels; and they must be thoroughly dry or
they won't brown well. Salt the pieces generously, but sprinkle
them ever so lightly with freshly ground pepper.

Choose a large, heavy frying pan, preferably enamel, which can
be covered securely later, and in it heat the 4 tablespoons of butter
and 2 tablespoons of oil until they fairly sizzle. Over high heat
brown the chicken pieces, a few at a time, starting them skin side
down and turning them with kitchen tongs. Add more oil if necessary to prevent the chicken from sticking or burning. As each piece
reaches a deep golden brown, remove it to a platter and add a fresh
piece to the pan until all the chicken is done.

Turn off the heat. Pour off all but a tablespoon of the sautéeing
fat and replace all the chicken in the pan to be flamed.

✱ *Flaming, or blazing, with brandy may be done in any number of ways. The most expert method is first to warm the*

114

brandy in a soup ladle held directly over the burner, tipping the ladle then towards the flame to ignite it. But, if you have an electric stove, or if the ladle procedure strikes you as too hazardous (it does take practice), do it less spectacularly by heating the brandy in a small saucepan and setting it alight with a match. However you do it, be careful to step back as it catches fire. Pour the flaming brandy, a little at a time, into the frying pan with one hand while you shake the frying pan gently back and forth with the other; shake it until the flame has burnt itself out.

Pour the ½ cup of stock over the chicken, and scrape into the liquid all the brown bits you can find under and around the chicken.

Over moderate heat, melt the 2 tablespoons of butter in a small saucepan; then add the chopped shallots, celery, and apples, and the thyme. Stirring occasionally, cook these together very slowly for about 10 minutes, until they are soft but not brown. Scrape the mixture out over the chicken in the frying pan, cover the pan tightly, and bring to a boil. Then lower the heat at once, and cook the chicken until it is tender—30 to 40 minutes. Baste thoroughly every 10 minutes or so.

Meanwhile, prepare the apple rings: Heat 4 tablespoons of butter in a large frying pan and, when the foam subsides, add the apple slices first sprinkled with a little sugar on each side. A few slices at a time, sauté the apples rapidly until they are lightly browned and glazed on each side. When they are done they should be on the firm side so that they will retain their shape and texture. With a spatula, carefully place them on a cooky sheet, and keep them warm in a **250° F.** oven until you are ready to serve them.

When the chicken is tender, remove the pieces from the frying pan with kitchen tongs and arrange them neatly in the center of a large ovenproof platter. While you prepare the sauce, keep the chicken warm in the slow oven with the apples.

115

Pour and scrape the remaining contents of the frying pan into a fine sieve set over a small saucepan. Press down on the vegetables with the back of a spoon, and when the pulp is dry, throw it away. Let the juices rest a moment, then skim off most but not all of the surface fat. There should be about a cup of liquid in the pan. Bring it to a boil and cook it rapidly until it is reduced to exactly ½ cup, measuring it to be sure.

Meanwhile, in a small bowl, combine the egg yolks with the ½ cup of heavy cream, beating them together briefly with a wire whisk or with a rotary beater. Add to this, a tablespoon at a time, mixing all the while, the reduced hot sauce. Then pour the sauce all back into the saucepan. Cook over low heat, stirring constantly and deeply with a spoon around the bottom and sides of the pan. In no circumstances allow the sauce to come to a boil, or it will most assuredly curdle. When it begins to thicken, raise the pan off the heat and stir deeply and vigorously for about 10 seconds, at which point return the pan to the heat once more and continue to cook the sauce until it clings tenaciously to the spoon. Raise the pan from the heat again from time to time to keep it from reaching the boiling point.

When the sauce is done, turn off the heat and, still stirring, season it with the ½ teaspoon of lemon juice, a few grains of cayenne, and as much salt as you think it needs. If you are a perfectionist, strain it.

Spoon the sauce carefully over each piece of chicken on the platter so that they are all thoroughly coated. Sprinkle the sauced chicken with parsley, and surround it with a circle of alternating glazed apple rings and sprays of crisp water cress. Serve at once, with boiled and buttered rice.

AFTERTHOUGHTS:

✳ If you are fearful, after the egg yolks are added, of thickening the sauce over direct heat as most professional chefs do, cook it instead in a double boiler. This will take considerably longer; you might use an extra yolk beaten into the cold cream to hasten the process.

116

✳ Like most sautéed chicken dishes, *poulet Vallée d'Auge* is at its best served the moment it is done. But if you must prepare it ahead, undercook the chicken somewhat; it will continue to cook as it cools, and reheating it will cook it even further. Put the cooked chicken and finished sauce aside separately, and cover them each tightly with Saran wrap.

Twenty minutes or so before dinner, reheat the chicken in a covered casserole with a couple of tablespoons of chicken stock. Reheat the sauce in a double boiler; if it seems too thick after it has warmed through, thin it with a little stock or cream.

✳ For a spectacular effect, you might flame the apple slices with a little warm applejack or Calvados before serving.

✳ If you can get it, add a teaspoon of chopped fresh tarragon to the sauce before pouring it over the chicken.

✳ If you plan to increase the recipe, it is useful to know that the consistency of the final sauce depends upon the proportion of egg yolks to liquid. In this case, 2 large or 3 small yolks to 1 cup of liquid (half reduced pan juices and half cream) is a fairly reliable formula for a sauce which will cling to the chicken when it is poured on. Multiply accordingly.

AMERICAN FRIED CHICKEN
WITH CREAM GRAVY

FRIED chicken, that mainstay of the church supper, Sunday family dinner, and country picnic, is, at its best, one of the fine achievements of American cooking. Not for fried chicken the elaborate marinades, fancy sauces, and off-beat seasonings; its virtue lies in simplicity.

Different sections of the country have their own firm notions of how best to fry a chicken, and woe to anyone, away from home ground at least, who dares question them. There is a batter-cum-deep-fat school; an egg-cum-cracker-crumb school. For some, to fry a chicken without first soaking it in milk or buttermilk is rank heresy; for others, the frying fat, whether it be butter, bacon fat, lard, vegetable shortening, or oil, is what really matters.

The following version is one of the simplest and for many cooks one of the most effective. It results, when the procedures are carefully followed, in crisp, thinly crusted pieces of fried chicken, moist and tender inside.

] To serve three or four [

2- to 2½-pound frying chicken, disjointed (see p. 106)
Salt
Juice of small lemon
1 cup flour
1 teaspoon salt
¼ teaspoon dry mustard
¼ teaspoon white pepper

½ cup vegetable shortening, approximately
½ cup lard, approximately

1 tablespoon flour
½ cup chicken stock, fresh or canned
½ cup cream, light or heavy, or a mixture of both
¼ teaspoon lemon juice
Salt
Pepper

For really successful fried chicken, choose a bird no larger than 2½ pounds, though smaller ones, 1¾ to 2 pounds, are preferable. If they are very small, buy two chickens to serve four. Since the chicken will be cooked with only the simplest of seasonings, its quality and freshness are of the utmost importance. Avoid any dubious bargains, go to the best store you know, and ask the butcher to disjoint the chicken with care.

Although the actual frying of the chicken is an easy matter, it should be a continuous operation once you start. To make it as smooth as possible, to say nothing of avoiding burnt fingers, a flour-strewn floor, and a frayed temper, have all your materials organized carefully ahead of time.

Begin by washing the chicken pieces quickly in cold water and patting them dry with paper towels. Sprinkle each piece first with lemon juice, then lightly with salt.

Coat them with flour in the following fashion: Sift into a sturdy, medium-sized paper bag, the flour, 1 teaspoon of salt, and the dry mustard and white pepper; drop the chicken into the bag a few pieces at a time, and shake the bag vigorously until each piece is thoroughly coated. Remove the chicken from the bag, shake the pieces free of all excess flour (there will be a lot of it), then lay them side by side on a long strip of waxed paper. Put them near the stove where you can get at them easily when you start to fry them.

Ideally, the pan in which you fry the chicken should be 10 inches in diameter, one you can cover, and as heavy as possible, preferably made of iron or copper. Of course, a light aluminum pan will do if it must, but it won't retain heat well and the chicken is likely to burn over a high flame unless it is carefully watched.

In the frying pan, melt over moderate heat ½ cup each of vegetable shortening and lard. A larger pan will require more fat; a smaller one, less. In any case, the fat when it is melted should be about one quarter inch deep. While it is heating, turn on the oven to 250° F. and on the middle shelf place a large shallow baking dish, this to receive the finished chicken as each piece is fried.

When the fat is hot but not smoking, put into it the legs and thighs (second joints), and cover the pan at once. Let the chicken fry over moderate heat, lifting the cover every now and then to check its progress. When the pieces are a deep brown on one side, turn them over with tongs and cover the pan again. As each piece of chicken is done, transfer it to the baking dish in the oven, and put an uncooked piece in the frying pan in its place.

Fry all the remaining chicken in the same way, remembering that the wings and breast will need less time than the dark meat to brown and cook through. It should take a little over half an hour

119

to cook all the pieces and, if the chicken was the proper size to begin with, you need have no fear that it will be underdone. Leave it in the oven with the door closed while you make the gravy.

Pour off all the fat in the frying pan and replace it with 2 tablespoons of butter. Melt this over low heat, meanwhile scraping up all the brown crust clinging to the bottom and sides of the pan. Remove the pan from the heat, add 1 tablespoon of flour, and mix it to a smooth paste with the butter. Cook very slowly for a minute or two, being careful the mixture doesn't burn. Now pour in ½ cup of chicken broth and, stirring all the time, bring it to a boil. Reduce the heat, and let the thickened gravy simmer for a couple of minutes before adding the cream and lemon juice. If the gravy at this point seems too thick, as it may well be, thin it with a little more cream or stock. Make sure it has enough salt and pepper before pouring it into a gravy boat.

Remove the chicken from the oven, arrange it attractively on a heated platter, and decorate it with a wreath of crisp water cress or parsley. Serve it with the hot gravy and, if you like being traditional, with mashed potatoes and corn on the cob.

AFTERTHOUGHTS:

❋ The gravy for the chicken can be varied in any number of ways; one of the best is giblet gravy. Cook the giblets in enough water to cover, with a small onion, a couple of sprigs of parsley, a small piece of bay leaf, salt and pepper, and any stray bits of uncooked chicken that are not worth frying, such as the neck, back, and wing tips. When the giblets are tender, mince them and add them to the finished gravy. Use the stock as the gravy base.

❋ For those who prefer their gravy without flour, follow almost the same directions for the gravy but, instead of making the paste of flour and butter, leave out the flour and add the chicken stock directly to the melted butter. Then, in a small bowl, beat 2 egg yolks into the ½ cup of cream. Pour the hot stock into this a little at a time, stirring constantly. When the two mixtures are thoroughly combined, pour them back into the pan, and, still stirring, bring the sauce just to the boiling point but not beyond it. Add the lemon juice, taste for seasoning, and serve.

✳ If you plan to have the chicken cold, remove it from the refrigerator at least an hour before you serve it. Cold fried chicken should always be served at room temperature.

✳ You can fry two, three, or four times the amount of chicken in this recipe, but don't try to do it all in one pan; it will take forever. With a little practice, you can learn to manipulate two or three pans at the same time.

BROILED CHICKEN WITH LEMON-GARLIC BUTTER
AND COARSE SALT

OF THE innumerable ways to broil a chicken, this is one of the most successful. The lemon-garlic butter is fresh and intriguing and the coarse salt gives the skin an unusual texture. Although broiling a chicken requires no great technical skill, it does demand constant attention. Because it has little interior fat, a young chicken must be basted persistently and thoroughly if you would have a superbly broiled bird, moist and succulent inside and crisply brown on the outside.

] To serve four or six [

Two 2½-pound broiling chickens, halved or
    quartered
¼ pound sweet butter, softened
1 teaspoon lemon juice
2 teaspoons soya sauce
½ teaspoon finely chopped garlic
Freshly ground black pepper
2 tablespoons coarse salt
4 tablespoons finely chopped parsley
Water cress

121

Preheat the broiler for at least 15 minutes—it must really be hot—and allow 25 minutes to half an hour to broil the chickens. Be fairly precise about this, for the broiled chickens will be at their best only if they are served immediately.

Wash the chickens quickly under cold running water and dry them well with paper towels. If the butcher has not already done so, cut out the backbones with a small sharp knife, remove the wing tips, and twist the wing joints in their sockets so that the chickens will lie flat.

Cream the softened butter by beating it in an electric mixer or mashing it against the sides of a bowl with a large spoon. When it is perfectly smooth, beat in the lemon juice a couple of drops at a time, then gradually beat in the soya sauce, and stir in the finely minced garlic. With a pastry brush, spread both sides of the chickens with as much butter as they will hold and reserve the rest, if any, for basting. Lay the chickens, skin side down, on the broiler rack, grind a few specks of black pepper over them and sprinkle evenly with about a tablespoon of coarse salt.

Start broiling the chickens with the rack about 4 inches below the heating unit. Although you should broil them quickly—that is, about 15 minutes on the first side and about 10 on the other—in no circumstances do you want the outsides to char before the insides have begun to cook. If it appears that the birds are browning too slowly or too quickly, adjust the distance of the rack from the heat accordingly.

Baste the chicken every 5 minutes while it is under the broiler; and do this quickly and thoroughly, using first the remaining lemon-garlic butter, then the drippings in the pan. A basting syringe is almost indispensible for this, but a long-handled spoon will do if it must. At the end of 15 minutes, carefully turn the chickens over, using kitchen tongs or two wooden spoons to avoid breaking the skin. Baste thoroughly, sprinkle with a little pepper and the remaining tablespoon of salt, and broil the chickens skin side up for 10 minutes. Baste once or twice so that the skin remains constantly moistened.

122

The chickens will be a glistening, golden brown when they are finished, charred slightly here and there. But to make sure they are done, pierce the fleshy part of one of the legs or thighs with the point of a sharp knife. The juice that spurts out should be a clear yellow. If it is tinged with pink, return the chickens to the broiler for a few minutes longer, basting once again. Be careful, at this point, that they don't burn and lower the heat somewhat if necessary.

When the chickens are done, remove the broiler pan from the stove and, with the tongs or spoons, transfer them to a hot platter. Scrape up the brown crust clinging to the bottom and sides of the broiling pan and mix them into the drippings. Pour these over the chicken, making sure each piece is moistened. Scatter the chopped parsley over all and garnish the platter with the water cress.

AFTERTHOUGHTS:

✳ If there seem to be very little drippings in the pan after the chicken is broiled, stir into them ½ cup of strong chicken broth. Bring this to a boil directly in the pan, on top of the stove, and boil until the liquid is reduced by half. Pour over the chicken.

✳ Coarse salt is available in many forms. The kosher variety is most easily purchased, but you will have to search for Malden or sea salt which really has more flavor.

✳ Naturally, if no coarse salt is available, regular salt will do, but use somewhat less of it.

✳ To avoid overcooking the chicken, some chefs like to remove it from the broiler while the juices still show a tinge of pink. They maintain that the chicken will be fully cooked by the time it completes its journey from the kitchen to the dining room.

*

CHICKEN IN A COCOTTE BONNE FEMME

A TENDER young chicken braised with bits of browned salt pork, small white onions, carrots, and potatoes is one of those straightforward, honest dishes representative of French bourgeois cooking at its best. Because the chicken is cooked in nothing but its own juices, it has a moist succulence and a unique flavor quite impossible to achieve by any other method.

] To serve four [

Whole 3-pound chicken
4 tablespoons softened butter
½ teaspoon finely minced garlic
½ teaspoon thyme
½ teaspoon lemon juice
Salt

1 tablespoon butter
½ pound salt pork, cut in ¼-inch dice

2 tablespoons butter
16 small white onions, all approximately the same
   size—1½ inches in diameter
Twelve 2-inch pieces carrot
16 potato balls, or potatoes cut into small ovals or
   1½-inch dice

Salt
Freshly ground pepper
A bouquet consisting of 2 celery tops and 4 sprigs
   parsley, tied together
Small bay leaf

2 tablespoons finely chopped parsley

124

The success of this dish will depend first of all upon the quality and freshness of your chicken for, when it is cooked, it will emerge innocent of any disguising wines or sauces. Be certain, therefore, that the bird you buy is a superior one. Wash the chicken quickly under cold running water, and dry it thoroughly inside and out; it won't brown well if it is damp.

Cream 2 tablespoons of the softened butter by beating it vigorously in a bowl with a wooden spoon. Mix into it the ½ teaspoon each of minced garlic, thyme, and lemon juice; if the butter is sweet, add ½ teaspoon of salt. With a pastry brush or with your fingers, spread the seasoned butter inside the chicken.

✳ *Now truss the chicken. For the average cook this can be something of a trial and, more often than not, the chicken can hardly be seen for the strings around it. Here is the wonderfully simple way to truss a bird with a single string that anyone can master with a little practice:*

For a small bird, cut off a 3-foot length of white kitchen cord. Place the chicken on its back with its legs pointing away from you. Grasp a drumstick firmly in each hand and force them down and against the breast as far as they will go; this will raise the point of the breastbone above the legs. Now slide the middle of the string under the ends of the drumsticks, and cross the two ends of the strings over them. Then pull the strings tightly around the drumsticks and under the breastbone that is directly above. Pull the strings toward you like a pair of reins, and slide them, on each side, between the legs and the body of the bird. Now turn the bird over; its tail should now be facing you, and the strings should come up on each side between the legs and the body.

With the strings again as tight as you can get them, slide each one now under the wings, and bring them up in the large V's of the wings and over the chicken's back. Close the neck opening by bringing the loose neck skin up and towards you. Now tie the string firmly in place over the back and the end of the neck skin. Twist each protruding wing tip up over the back. Firmly tuck the tail into the opening that is above it. Now turn the chicken over again. It will sit on its haunches in a nice compact bundle.

A great advantage of this method of trussing a bird is that, when the time comes to remove the string, all you need to do is to cut it at the point where it hold the ends of the drumsticks together; you can then pull the whole string away from the bird in one piece.

Rub the chicken all over with the remaining 2 tablespoons of softened butter, and it is ready for the *cocotte* or casserole. Preheat the oven to **350° F.**

A small, oval, enameled-iron *cocotte*—heavy, with a tightly fitting cover and just about large enough to hold the chicken and the vegetables—is the ideal utensil for the browning and braising procedures that follow. Your casserole need not be the traditional oval *cocotte*, but it must not be too large; if it is, there will be too rapid a condensation of moisture and the dish will be dry.

Blanch the salt pork to rid it of excess salt: Cover it with cold water in a small pan, bring it to a boil, and let it simmer for a couple of minutes; drain and pat it dry. Melt a tablespoon of butter in the casserole and, over fairly high heat, cook the pork bits in this, turning them constantly with a wooden spoon as they render their fat. When they are brown and crisp, scoop them out with a slotted spoon, and put them in a small dish lined with a paper towel.

Turn the heat under the casserole down to moderate, and place the chicken, breast side down, in the remaining hot fat. After about 5 or 6 minutes, turn the bird on its side, holding it with a kitchen towel or with two large wooden spoons to avoid breaking the skin. Turn it in a few minutes to the other side. Then, when the legs and thighs have browned to your satisfaction, place the chicken on its back for about 5 minutes. All in all, it should take about 20 to 25 minutes to brown the bird properly. Don't, in any circumstances, try to rush this.

126

With a basting syringe, remove all but about a tablespoon of fat from the casserole, and in its place put back the reserved browned pork bits.

If you feel up to managing two operations at the same time, sauté the vegetables while the chicken is browning in the *cocotte*; otherwise, do it either before or after. In any case: Heat 2 tablespoons of butter in a large heavy frying pan and, when the foam subsides, add the onions, carrots, and potatoes. Cook them over moderate heat for about 5 minutes, or just long enough to glaze them with butter and give them a light gold patina. Shake the pan from time to time to insure even coloring.

When they are done, remove the vegetables from the frying pan with a slotted spoon, and scatter them around the browned chicken in the casserole. Sprinkle both chicken and vegetables rather generously with salt and with a few grindings of black pepper. Toss in the celery and parsley bouquet and the bay leaf, and cover the casserole. Place a sheet of aluminum foil under the cover if it is light or doesn't fit snugly.

Heat the casserole on top of the stove until you hear the fat bubbling, then place the casserole at once on the center shelf of the preheated oven. Cook for about an hour, basting both the chicken and the vegetables every 20 minutes with the liquid which will accumulate in the pot; after a while, there will be a surprising amount of it.

The best way to tell whether the chicken is done is to lift it out of the pot with a wooden spoon inserted in the tail opening and all the way into the body. Hold it almost upright and allow the liquid to drain out of the body back into the casserole. If the juice is a light yellow, the chicken is assuredly done; if it is slightly pink, return the chicken to the oven for another 10 minutes or so.

How you will serve the chicken depends on how skillful a carver you are. Brought to the table in its *cocotte,* the chicken is a most attractive sight and should be carved on a carving board right then and there. If you are diffident of your ability to handle this publicly, cut up the chicken in the privacy of your kitchen and put it back in the casserole. Arrange the top layer of chicken neatly, moisten it with the cooking juices, surround it with some of the vegetables, and sprinkle these with finely chopped parsley. Or, make a similar arrangement on a hot platter. Serve with hot French bread.

AFTERTHOUGHTS:

✳ The chicken may be cooked on top of the stove instead of in the oven. It will require more basting—every 15 minutes or so—and will probably take a little longer to cook. And in this case, the casserole you use *must* be a heavy one.

✳ If, by some mischance, the chicken is done before the vegetables are, merely remove it to a warm platter, and cook the vegetables alone in the casserole, over moderately high heat, on top of the stove. Add a little chicken stock if the liquid shows any sign of cooking away. The chicken itself will only benefit by its short wait outside the pot before being carved.

✳ Other vegetables may be cooked with the chicken or substituted for the ones suggested. Although you can then no longer call it a chicken *bonne femme,* you may add frozen (but defrosted) artichoke hearts to the casserole 10 minutes before the chicken is done, basting them well with the casserole juices. Or, whole, quartered, or sliced mushrooms, first sprinkled with lemon juice and sautéed briskly in a little hot butter, may be added to the casserole 5 or 10 minutes before it is done.

✳ And, if you're worried about whether the potatoes will be done or not, leave them out of the casserole and sauté them separately until they are brown and tender. Add them to the casserole just before serving, or present them in a separate serving dish.

BREAST OF CHICKEN CURRY
WITH NINE CONDIMENTS

EITHER you love curry or you hate it; there never seems to be a middle ground. And frankly, when it is prepared, as it too frequently is, with leftovers in a curry-flavored white sauce, it isn't a dish to excite much admiration. But the real thing is something else again and may well make your confirmed curry hater change his mind.

Lengthy as this recipe may appear, it is in reality rather simple. Most of the condiments are available commercially and require little or no preparation. Moreover, the curry and rice can be prepared hours ahead and reheated quite successfully. This is a fine and practical dish for a large buffet dinner.

] To serve eight [

3 pairs of chicken breasts (about 3 pounds in all)
Juice of small lemon
Salt
¼ cup flour
4 tablespoons butter
2 tablespoons vegetable oil

SAUCE:

2 tablespoons butter
2 medium onions, finely chopped (about 1 cup)
½ teaspoon finely chopped garlic
1 small tart apple, peeled, cored, and coarsely chopped
2 tablespoons flour
3 tablespoons curry powder
2 cups strong chicken stock, fresh or canned
½ cup heavy cream
1 teaspoon lemon juice
1 tablespoon grated lemon rind

CONDIMENTS:

½ cup dried currants, soaked in ¼ cup Port
½ cup yellow seedless raisins, soaked in ¼ cup brandy
1 cup shredded coconut

8 to 10 scallions, very thinly sliced
½ pound bacon, cooked crisp and crumbled
Small jar chutney
2 ripe avocados, sliced and sprinkled with lime juice
1 small can chopped toasted almonds
16 poppadums

Ask the average person what curry powder is, and the uncertain response will usually be, "Some sort of powdered spice, isn't it?" Actually, curry is a combination of five to twenty-five herbs, seeds, and spices, their relative proportions giving each curry its particular distinction. The commercial varieties differ enormously in flavor, color, and intensity. Unless you intend to make your own (curry enthusiasts do), experiment until you find a brand you like.

Buy chicken breasts minus the wings, and ask your butcher to skin and bone them. If he won't, can't, or wants an exorbitant price, do it yourself. It's not difficult if you follow the precise directions in the AFTERTHOUGHTS to the recipe for CHICKEN CUTLETS KIEV, on page 137. When the breasts are boned and trimmed of all fat, tendons, and gristle, cut them into fairly uniform 2-inch pieces, and moisten each piece with a little lemon juice.

Sift ¼ cup of flour onto one end of a long strip of waxed paper. Salt the chicken pieces liberally, then dip them one at a time into the flour, and shake them vigorously as you proceed so that they are only barely coated. Lay them side by side on the waxed paper.

Heat together in a large, heavy frying pan the 4 tablespoons of butter and 2 tablespoons of vegetable oil. Cook over moderate heat until the foam subsides. Add the chicken, a few pieces at a time, and brown them rather briskly for about 3 or 4 minutes on each side, turning them with tongs. Transfer them to a shallow 2-quart casserole that you can cover later.

The fat in the frying pan will have become quite brown by now. Pour off and throw away most of it, and replace it with 2 tablespoons of fresh butter. Stir in the cupful of chopped onions and cook them very, very slowly, turning them with a wooden spoon until they are delicately colored but not brown. Then mix in the cut-up apple and ½ teaspoon of minced garlic. Still over low heat, cook until the apple is soft enough to be mashed with the back of the spoon. Now remove the pan from the heat.

In a small bowl combine the 2 tablespoons of flour and 3 tablespoons of curry powder. Dump this over the apple-onion mixture and, with a large spoon, mash everything together into as smooth a paste as you can. Stir into this, a little at a time, the 2 cups of chicken stock, then the ½ cup of heavy cream. Set the pan over moderate heat and, stirring continuously with a wire whisk, bring the sauce to a boil. It will have thickened considerably and must be watched lest it burn. Lower the heat and cook it as slowly as possible for about 15 minutes, partially covered. Stir every now and then, reaching down to the bottom of the pan with a spoon to make sure the sauce doesn't stick.

You may now strain the sauce or not, depending on how smooth you want it to be. If you strain it, use a fine sieve and press down hard on the vegetables to extract all their juice before throwing them away. Strained or unstrained, the sauce should be thick enough to cling lightly to the back of your spoon; if it too thick, thin it with a little more stock or cream.

Mix in the lemon juice and rind, and taste the sauce for seasoning. For those who like their curry hot, add some ground chili powder, but with discretion. Remember that the aftertaste of curry is delayed, so give your palate a chance before deciding to add more of anything.

———————————

Now pour the sauce into the casserole and baste all the pieces of chicken with it. Then, over moderate heat, bring it almost to the boil. Cover the casserole, lower the heat, and simmer the curry for about 20 to 30 minutes, or until the chicken has cooked through and absorbed the flavor of the sauce. Check every now and then; if the sauce seems to be getting too thick, stir in a spoonful of hot stock.

Serve directly from the casserole with plain boiled rice and the condiments. Cold beer is really the only drink to serve with curry;

131

a white wine, no matter how full-bodied, cannot cope with the insistence of even the mildest curry.

AFTERTHOUGHTS:

✳ About the preparation of the condiments: Soak the currants in the Port and the raisins in the brandy for at least 3 hours or overnight, if possible; they need time to absorb the liquor and to plump up.

Solve the coconut problem by simply buying a box of shredded, *un*sweetened coconut; however, better still, grate your own if you have the time. Follow the directions for shelling them on page 324.

Peel and slice the avocado just before serving; the lime juice sprinkled over it gives it a piquant flavor and will prevent it from discoloring, but not for too long.

Scallions are scallions, and need only be trimmed, washed, patted dry, and cut into thin rounds, green tops, and all. As for the bacon, make sure it is crisp and well drained of all fat before you crumble it.

Bottled chutney and canned chopped toasted almonds may be purchased anywhere. Your only real problem is the poppadums which can be ordered from fine food shops or department stores carrying imported foods. The poppadum is a crisp, highly seasoned wafer served in place of bread. Directions for preparing them are in the package. They are in every way worth making a determined effort to find.

✳ For a large party, serving curry buffet style is the easiest way to manage what might otherwise become an exercise in logistics. Keep the curry warm in two chafing dishes if you have them—the chicken and sauce in one and the rice in the other. Arrange the condiments in small separate dishes. Suggest to your guests that they help themselves in the following fashion: a mound of rice first, the chicken and sauce over that, then a spoonful of each condiment on top of the chicken or around it.

✳ The curry may be made hours ahead and reheated. Simmer it only until it is heated through; the chicken must not overcook or it will be dry and tasteless.

✳ Many other condiments may be served with curry and they may be substituted for the ones suggested above: peanuts, pignolia nuts, shredded fresh pineapple, caramelized or fresh sliced bananas, sieved hard-cooked eggs, pickled onions, deep-fried onion rings, and Bombay duck, a dried salted fish imported from India.

✳ Curry fanciers insist that curry powder should be warmed in a slow oven for 10 minutes or so before being cooked. The dry heat presumably releases flavors which would otherwise be lost.

✳ Though the dish will lose some of its refinement, you may use for it the skinned and boned meat of a poached hen (see CHICKEN STOCK on page 34). Simmer the completed curry sauce for an extra 20 minutes, then add the cut-up chicken meat and continue to simmer until it is heated through.

CHICKEN CUTLETS KIEV
WITH HERBED LEMON BUTTER

THE REPERTOIRE of every serious cook should include at least one great virtuosic dish like cutlets Kiev. Admittedly, this is not a venture to embark upon lightly: Boned chicken breasts are pounded thin, rolled around nuggets of chilled, fragrantly seasoned butter, sealed with a coating of flour, egg yolks, and bread crumbs, and finally deep fried. Formidable as this may sound, the cooked cutlets look disarmingly innocent when they appear and give no indication of the dramatic effect they are about to create. When pierced with a fork, the cutlets will release a stream of hot, aromatic butter—which will rise in the air like a miniature geyser, drenching the unwary guest unless he has been forewarned.

] To serve six [

6 pairs of chicken breasts, ½ to ¾ pound each, skinned, boned, and pounded

12 tablespoons unsalted butter (1½ sticks)
1 teaspoon lemon juice
½ teaspoon finely minced garlic
½ teaspoon salt

133

1 teaspoon dried tarragon
    or 1 tablespoon finely minced fresh tarragon
1 tablespoon finely chopped parsley

1½ teaspoons salt
4 egg yolks
2 tablespoons vegetable oil
½ cup flour
1 cup finely grated and sieved bread crumbs

1½ quarts oil for deep frying
    or one 3-pound can vegetable shortening

A competent butcher will bone the chicken breasts for you, but usually at a price. Although it does take time, the boning process is not very difficult. If you would like to try it, detailed instructions are included in the AFTERTHOUGHTS to this recipe.

––––––––––

To prepare the herbed butter, first let it soften a bit, then cream it by beating it in an electric mixer, or by mashing it against the sides of a mixing bowl with a large wooden spoon. When the butter is perfectly smooth, beat 1 teaspoon of lemon juice into it drop by drop, then add the minced garlic, parsley, tarragon, and salt. But, if the butter is salted to begin with, don't add any salt at all. With a rubber scraper, gather up the seasoned butter and shape it into a ball. Wrap it loosely in waxed paper and refrigerate until it is firm. If you are in a hurry, a half hour in the freezer will do as well.

––––––––––

One of the most important steps in making successful cutlets Kiev is the pounding of the chicken breasts. You can have your butcher do this, too, if you can rely upon him to follow your directions exactly, but it is far less hazardous to pound them yourself.

Lay the chicken breast, smooth side down, between two sheets of waxed paper about 4 inches wider all around than the breast. Ideally, the best implement with which to pound it is the flat of a butcher's cleaver. Lacking that, a wooden meat mallet, even a croquet mallet, or the bottom of a quart-size beer bottle will do the job almost as well. However you pound the meat, do *not* pound it paper thin. Flatten each breast to a thickness of about an eighth of an inch, and don't be overly concerned at their disparate shapes and sizes; they can be trimmed later if you wish.

More important are the torn holes which may appear in the meat after it is pounded. Slightly overlap the edges of the tear, cover this patch with waxed paper again, and pound it gently until the meat comes together. Chicken is a gelatinous meat and easily mended when ragged or torn.

When you are ready to assemble the cutlets, carefully peel the top layer of waxed paper from the first chicken breast. Sprinkle the breast with ⅛ teaspoon of salt. Then turn it so that the wide end is toward you. On this end, place about a tablespoon of the chilled butter. With the help of a small knife, lift the same wide end of the meat over the butter, and roll up the breast around the butter, tucking in the sides as you go and eventually freeing the meat entirely from the bottom sheet of waxed paper. It doesn't really matter what the cutlet looks like at this point, provided it is cylindrical and the butter is snugly enclosed in the chicken.

Give the remaining breasts the same treatment, and line them up on a baking sheet or dish covered with waxed paper. If the cutlets seem soft, it is wise to refrigerate them for 15 minutes or so, or to put them in the freezer, until they are fairly firm again.

At least an hour, or two, before you intend to cook and serve them, shape the cutlets and give them their coating, *à l'anglaise* as it is called, of egg and bread crumbs.

In a small bowl, break up the 4 egg yolks with a fork and slowly mix into them the 2 tablespoons of oil. Arrange separate mounds of flour and fine sieved bread crumbs on a long strip of waxed paper, and proceed as follows: Dip a cutlet into the flour, and shake it gently free of excess flour. Holding the cutlet carefully cupped in one hand, with the other hand pat and shape it into a long cylinder slightly pointed at the ends. Firmly press together any fissures that may appear in the meat, sealing them with a little more flour if necessary. Now dip a soft pastry brush into the egg-yolk mixture,

135

and paint the cutlets thickly with the egg, carefully filling in every crack, particularly at the ends. Finally, roll the cutlet in the bread crumbs, and make sure there are no exposed surfaces left when you finish; for good measure, dip each end of the roll lightly in the crumbs again.

As they are done, line up the breaded cutlets on fresh waxed paper on a baking sheet, and cover them lightly with more waxed paper. Refrigerate. If you carry out all these procedures thoroughly, the butter inside will not burst through when the cutlets are cooked.

✳ *The actual cooking of the cutlets is not difficult, particularly if you own an electric deep fryer. The principle is the same as for all deep frying. A deep-frying basket and a 2- or 3-quart saucepan, containing the hot fat, in which the basket can be immersed will do almost as well as an electric fryer. But, in this case, a deep-frying or candy thermometer is imperative; fortunately, these are quite inexpensive and, moreover, have a multitude of uses besides the present one.*

A half hour or so before you plan to serve dinner, preheat the oven to **250° F.,** *and on the center shelf place an ovenproof platter lined with a double thickness of paper towelling. At the same time, slowly heat the frying fat to a temperature of* **370° F.** *Fry no more than three or four cutlets at the same time, otherwise the temperature of the fat will drop. Cook the cutlets about 4 minutes, or until they turn a deep golden brown. Remove them from the basket with kitchen tongs as they are done, and lay them gently on the paper-lined platter.*

When all the cutlets are done, they may remain in the oven for 10 minutes or so, but not much longer; leave the oven door slightly ajar after the first 5 minutes.

Serve the cutlets Kiev on a hot platter, surrounded with crisp fresh water cress. Baked buckwheat groats (KASHA; see page 291), combined perhaps with sautéed mushrooms, would lend the proper Russian note, and a chilled Pouilly-Fumé would be the perfect wine.

AFTERTHOUGHTS:

✳ Don't make the mistake of preparing cutlets Kiev with large chicken breasts, as is often suggested. They will be ungainly, difficult to manage, and really too large for an average serving.

✳ Although the cutlets cannot be cooked ahead of time and reheated, the initial preparations can be staggered so that the going becomes a little easier: Trim and pound the breasts, after you yourself or your butcher has boned them, and refrigerate them, waxed paper and all, until you are ready to roll them (but for no longer than a day). The butter filling may be made at any time, even a day ahead. When you roll up, shape, and flour the cutlets, you can then freeze them for future use; or wrap them in waxed paper and put them in the refrigerator to be breaded as much as a day later, whenever you have time. If you freeze them, defrost them before putting on the coating à l'anglaise. Finally, once they are breaded, they may remain in the refrigerator all day if necessary, but not much longer.

✳ The amount of filling may vary from breast to breast, depending on their size and shape. If there is any butter left over, it may be used to advantage on a broiled or pan-fried steak, or on poached, broiled, or baked fish. If you have no immediate use for it, freeze it.

✳ Commercial frozen chicken breasts won't do for cutlets Kiev; they are too pulpy and will fall apart.

✳ *Finally, if you bone the chicken breasts yourself, this is how you proceed:*

Begin by skinning a pair. Starting at the pointed end, insert your thumb under the skin and peel it off like a glove. Next, hold the breast firmly with both hands, flesh side down, and bend it back in two until the shovel-like breastbone pops up, as it inevitably will. Pull the bone out and, with a heavy sharp knife, cut the breasts apart into two neat halves.

For the actual boning operation, it is imperative that you have a pointed, 4- to 6-inch knife sharpened to the finest possible edge; if you don't, give up the whole idea. Lay one breast bone side up on a chopping board, with the pointed end away from you. Slip the point of the knife under the base of the single small rib bone you will discover radiating away from the rib cage proper. Press the flat of the knife up against the small bone and pull the cutting edge of the knife away from you, freeing the bone from the flesh.

Now hold the freed bone in your left hand like a rudder and, while you cautiously pull it up and towards you, cut through the flesh adhering to the other ribs next to it; use short, sawing, and scraping motions, always holding the flat of the knife against the ribs. The ribs are your guide; follow them wherever they take you and shortly, if all goes well, you will have freed the entire rib cage in one piece from the breast meat. Now cut and scrape the flesh away from the larger bones still attached to it at the base of the ribs.

The breast will probably look a bit mangled when you finish, but the meat is gelatinous and will come together again quite easily. Pat the boned breast into its original oval shape and trim it neatly of all fat and pieces of cartilege.

BROILED DUCKLING WITH ORANGES

The Long Island duckling, a bird of incomparable flavor, is unfortunately difficult to cook properly because of the thick layer of fat beneath its skin. Some suggest roasting the bird slowly to dissolve the fat; but even then, if the meat is kept slightly rare as it should be, a goodly part of the fat remains. Short of roasting the bird to death (which most people do), the best way out of the dilemma is not to roast the duck at all but to broil it. Although this method is exacting, you will be rewarded with crisply browned quarters of duck, moist and delicately flavored, yet almost entirely free of fat.

] To serve four [

4- to 5-pound duckling, quartered

½ cup orange juice
¼ cup lemon juice

138

1 teaspoon salt
1 teaspoon powdered ginger
    or ½ teaspoon grated fresh ginger root
3 bay leaves, coarsely crumbled
1 medium onion, thinly sliced
2 cloves garlic, thinly sliced

SAUCE:

2 small navel oranges
2 tablespoons granulated sugar
1 tablespoon red-wine vinegar
1 cup chicken stock, fresh or canned
1 teaspoon arrowroot powder
2 tablespoons cold water
2 tablespoons Grand Marnier

4 tablespoons softened butter
1 tablespoon vegetable oil

Water cress

The younger the duck, the more tender it will be; so don't buy a bird over 5 pounds, drawn weight, if you can help it. Four-pounders are even better for broiling but are usually difficult to find. Ask the butcher to split the duck, remove the backbone and wing tips, then cut, not chop, the duck into neat quarters. Trim the pieces yourself of all extraneous skin and fat.

Prepare the marinade in a glass, porcelain, or stainless-steel mixing bowl just about large enough to hold the duck comfortably. Combine the orange and lemon juices, the salt, ginger and crumbled bay leaves, stir them together thoroughly, and add the sliced onion and garlic. Wash the duck quarters quickly under cold running water and dry then with paper towels. Immerse the quarters in the marinade, baste well, and marinate them 1 to 3 hours, turning the pieces over occasionally.

Sometime before you broil the duck, make the sauce: Peel off the rind of the 2 oranges with a vegetable scraper and cut it into small julienne strips about an eighth of an inch wide and half an inch long. Drop them into a small saucepan, cover them with cold water, and bring to a boil. Reduce the heat and simmer slowly, uncovered, for about 10 minutes. In the meantime, with a small sharp knife, remove all the white underpeel on the oranges, and slice them as thinly and as evenly as you can. They will be used later as a garnish.

When the simmering orange peels are soft to the touch, drain them through a fine sieve, run cold water over them to stop their cooking, and pat them dry on a paper towel. Now mix together in a pan the 2 tablespoons of sugar and 1 tablespoon of red-wine vinegar. Without stirring, cook this over moderate heat for about 3 minutes, or until the sugar dissolves, begins to boil, and caramelizes into a thick, dark syrup. Watch carefully that it doesn't burn for it will taste bitter if it does. Immediately pour over the syrup a cup of chicken stock; the sugar will harden instantly. Bring the stock to a boil, then simmer it slowly until the caramel dissolves, stirring occasionally to help it along.

Meanwhile, remove the duck from the marinade. Strain the marinade through a fine sieve directly into the simmering sauce. Add the teaspoon of arrowroot powder or cornstarch, first mixed to a paste with 2 tablespoons of cold water. Stir constantly until the sauce comes to a boil, then reduce the heat, and simmer it slowly for about 10 minutes. The sauce should now be fairly thick and clear; add a little more stock if it seems excessively thick. Stir in the simmered orange peel and the 2 tablespoons of Grand Marnier. You may use a little more liqueur if you like, but be careful the sauce doesn't become too sweet; it should have a pleasantly tart flavor. Put it aside to be reheated later.

✳ *Allow about 40 or 50 minutes to broil the duck and before that 15 minutes to preheat the broiler to* **350° F.** *With a large spoon, beat together the 4 tablespoons of softened butter and 1 tablespoon of vegetable oil. Pat the duck quarters dry, and* *spread them on each side with as much of the butter as they will hold. Lay the pieces skin side down on the broiler rack, and slide in the rack about 4 inches below the heat.*

*Broil the duck for 15 minutes, basting it after 10 minutes with the drippings in the pan. Then raise the heat to **400° F.**, and, still basting periodically, broil for another 15 minutes. Now, with kitchen tongs, turn the duck quarters over, and broil them skin side up for 10 minutes, still at **400° F.** Finally, raise the heat to **450° F.**, and broil 10 minutes longer.*

At this point, the duck should be crisply brown and just the slightest bit underdone. If you prefer it well done, broil the duck five minutes longer, lowering the heat if the skin shows signs of burning.

During the last 5 minutes of broiling, heat an ovenproof platter in the oven, and bring the orange sauce to a simmer on top of the stove. When the duck is done, remove the quarters to the hot platter. Pour off all the accumulated fat in the broiling pan, but be careful not to lose a drop of the brown glaze and sediment in the bottom of the pan. Scrape up as much of it as you can with a spatula, and stir it into the orange sauce. Taste the sauce for salt, then spoon it over the duck. Garnish the platter with the thin slices of orange and sprays of crisp water cress. Serve at once.

AFTERTHOUGHTS:

✳ The orange sauce will improve immeasurably if you use a duck-flavored stock in place of the straight chicken stock. You can make this easily by bringing a couple of cups of fresh or canned chicken broth to a boil with the cut up giblets, backbone and wing tips of the duck. Skim the stock, then add a small onion, a few slices of carrot and celery, and a sprig of parsley. Simmer slowly for at least half an hour or longer if you can. Strain and use as directed.

✳ Broilers without temperature controls will have to be played more or less by ear. Broil the duck rather slowly at first, then raise the heat gradually as you proceed. If you allow the duck to brown too quickly at the start, you will have trouble cooking it through without burning it.

*

TRUFFLED ROAST TURKEY
WITH SAUSAGE AND CHESTNUT STUFFING

THE FRENCH, with morbid whimsicality, describe a poached truffled turkey as a *dindonneau en demi-deuil*, or "young turkey in
half mourning." And a bird, poached or roasted, with slices of black
truffle showing through the skin of the breast and legs does have a
mournful appearance if you choose to view it that way. But if the
truth be known, here is more cause for rejoicing than sorrow, for
the truffles flavor the bird so distinctively that without them a turkey, thereafter, never tastes quite the same.

] To serve eight or ten [

9-pound turkey
2-ounce can black truffles
¼ cup Madeira

STUFFING:

2 tablespoons butter
½ cup finely chopped onions
¼ cup finely chopped shallots
½ pound sausage meat

2 tablespoons butter
Turkey liver and 2 chicken livers, coarsely chopped

2 cups coarsely grated dry white bread crumbs
½ teaspoon thyme
2 tablespoons finely chopped celery leaves
3 tablespoons finely chopped parsley
1 tablespoon salt
½ teaspoon freshly ground pepper
1 teaspoon lemon juice

142

20 peeled, partially cooked chestnuts
   or 1 can whole chestnuts packed in water
4 tablespoons heavy cream

3 tablespoons softened butter
Salt
1 thin slice salt pork, large enough to cover turkey
   breast
2 medium onions, thickly sliced
2 medium carrots, cut in 3-inch pieces
2 stalks celery, cut in 3-inch pieces

2 cups chicken stock, fresh or canned

Before the turkey appears on the scene, open the can of truffles and, with a very sharp knife, slice each truffle into rounds an eighth of an inch thick. Lay the slices in a shallow glass or porcelain dish, pour over them the ¼ cup of Madeira and the canned truffle liquid and let them marinate, covered, for an hour at least.

As for the turkey, there is little reason to buy a frozen bird unless you must; fresh-killed birds are now available all year round and in every way are superior to the frozen ones. Whatever turkey you buy, make certain all the leg tendons and the wing tips have been removed. And have the neck cut off as close to the body as possible so that you can stuff the breast if you wish.

Wash the turkey quickly under cold running water, and clear the cavity of all its extraneous tissues. Dry it thoroughly with paper towels, inside and out.

You will find it easy enough to insert the truffles under the turkey's skin if you loosen it first. Start at the breast, and separate the skin from the meat by forcing your fingers between them. Slide your hand under as far as you can go and gently free the skin on both sides of the breast. Although you can continue around the legs in the same way, a rubber spatula will do a neater job. Insert it at the breast opening and, holding it flat against the flesh, move it sideways and loosen the skin around the upper part of each leg. Stop about half way down the leg. If necessary, push the leg in on itself to give you more traction.

Remove the truffles from their marinade (save it) and, without drying them, one by one insert them under the skin, arranging them as symmetrically as you can, first on the legs, then on either side of the breastbone. Reshape the loosened skin on the bird by patting it gently back in place; it will sag here and there, but don't let that worry you for it will come together again as the bird is cooked. Wrap the turkey loosely in waxed paper and let it rest in the refrigerator for at least 3 hours, preferably overnight.

The stuffing may be made at any time, but be sure it has time to cool before it is put in the turkey. Furthermore, it is well to remember that stuffed, uncooked poultry of any kind tends to spoil quickly, even when refrigerated. So stuff the turkey no earlier than 2 or 3 hours before you roast it.

To make the stuffing: Melt 2 tablespoons of butter in a large heavy frying pan. In this, slowly cook the ½ cup of onions until they begin to color lightly, then add the shallots. Cook a few minutes longer until both are a light even brown. Now add to the pan the ½ pound of sausage meat and break it up with a fork as it cooks. When the meat has become granular and lightly browned, transfer the entire contents of the pan to a fine sieve set over a small bowl. Allow the fat to drain through.

Meanwhile, in the same frying pan, melt another 2 tablespoons of butter. Quickly brown in it the chopped turkey and chicken livers, turning them constantly with a spatula; they will be done in 2 or 3 minutes. Pour over them the Madeira-truffle marinade, and boil it down rapidly until it all but disappears.

With a rubber spatula, scrape the sautéed livers and every bit of the pan's drippings into a large mixing bowl. Stir into it the drained sausage-onion mixture. Dump in the 2 cups of bread crumbs, and add the thyme, celery leaves, parsley, salt, pepper, and lemon juice. With a large wooden spoon and a light hand, mix everything together gently.

144

If you are using fresh chestnuts and have any doubt as to how to prepare them, look at the first AFTERTHOUGHT at the end of this recipe. Purée 10 of the chestnuts in an electric blender or a food mill; lacking either of these, rub the chestnuts through a not-too-fine sieve with the back of a spoon. Stir the purée into the stuffing, and crumble in the remaining chestnuts.

The stuffing will be rather dry at this point. Moisten it with the heavy cream, mixing it in a tablespoon at a time.

Salt and pepper the inside of the turkey before stuffing it, then fill the cavity loosely. Sternly fight the impulse to pack the stuffing in; it will expand as it cooks and if too tightly packed will most assuredly break through. If you have any stuffing left over, and you probably will, stuff the breast and bring the long neck flap over to hold it in. Sew up all the openings carefully with a large needle and strong white kitchen thread so that no stuffing can escape. Or you can, if you like, use small metal skewers and lace them up with cord.

Truss the turkey securely, as described for the CHICKEN BONNE FEMME on page 125. Unlike a small chicken, however, the turkey will have had its wing tips removed, so the wings will have to be tied closely to the body.

Now rub the truffled, stuffed, and trussed turkey all over with 3 tablespoons of soft butter, sprinkle it generously with salt, and lay the slice of salt pork over the breast, tying it in place if it is too small to stay on by itself.

Preheat the oven to **350° F.** Scatter the sliced onions, carrots, and celery on the bottom of a shallow roasting pan, and set the turkey on a rack directly over the vegetables. Place the pan on the center shelf of the oven, and roast it for approximately 2 hours, basting it every 20 minutes or so with the drippings in the pan.

If, after the first hour, the vegetables seem to be dry and show signs of blackening, *after* each basting add a couple of tablespoons of hot stock or water to the pan.

The turkey should be thoroughly cooked at the end of 2 hours, but make sure by inserting the point of a sharp knife in the fleshiest part of the thigh. If the juice spurts out yellow, remove the turkey from the oven at once; if the yellow is tinged with pink, cook it 5 or 10 minutes longer.

When the turkey is done, lift it carefully onto a heated platter or a carving board, and remove the trussing strings and the salt pork. Let it remain on the platter for at least 15 minutes before serving it; contrary to your possible fears, the turkey will *not* get cold but will be juicier and easier to carve.

Meanwhile, pour into the roasting pan the 2 cups of chicken stock and bring it to a boil on top of the stove. With a metal spatula, scrape up all the brown particles and sediment encrusting the bottom and sides of the pan, and stir them into the boiling stock. Continue to cook rather rapidly for about 3 minutes, or longer if the sauce doesn't have enough flavor to suit you. Then pour the entire contents of the pan into a sieve set over a small saucepan. With the back of a large spoon, press down hard on the vegetables to extract their juice before throwing them away. Allow the sauce to settle for a few minutes so that the fat can rise to the surface, then skim off most but not all of it. Before serving, bring the sauce again to the boil, taste for seasoning, and pour into a heated gravy boat.

AFTERTHOUGHTS:

✳ To prepare fresh chestnuts, with a small, very sharp knife, first cut a long gash in the flat, softer side of each chestnut. Put the chestnuts in a saucepan, cover them with cold water, and bring them to a boil. Cook briskly for a couple of minutes, then remove the pan from the heat. Working quickly, with a slotted spoon remove a few nuts at a time from the water and peel off their shells and inner skins. This takes no effort at all while the chestnuts are hot but, if they cool too much, you may have to heat them again in order to proceed.

When you have finished, put the peeled nuts in a saucepan, cover them with cold salted water or, better still, with a highly seasoned chicken or beef stock if you have it. Bring this to a boil, half cover the pan, and simmer the chestnuts for about half an hour, or until they are tender but not falling apart. Drain.

✳ After slicing the truffles, mince finely any scraps you may have left over and add them to the stuffing.

146

CHAPTER V

Beef

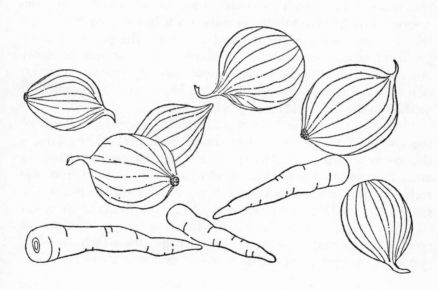

*

THE TWO famous provincial beef stews given here each begin with rudimentary processes without which one could not start the most ordinary brown beef stew: the correct searing of pieces of beef in fat and then the making of a *roux* in the same fat to start the sauce. The easier stew, the CARBONNADE, is completely assembled once sauce and beef are together in the pot. In principle, if not in ingredients, a classic BEEF BOURGUIGNON is the same, but there are several special refinements, starting with the blanching and rendering of salt pork and the cooking *à brun* (or brown cooking) of onions for the garnish. These little onions may accompany almost any brown stew you wish (see VEAL MARENGO on page 184). Together with sautéed mushrooms and salt-pork scraps, the onions constitute the classic *garniture à la bourguignonne*. (The same elements are prepared in almost the same way for Burgundian COQ AU VIN on page 109.)

The recipe for BEEF À LA MODE is a continual sequence of classic operations, all of which you will encounter again and again elsewhere: larding; marinating; braising on a bed of browned vegetables (with less liquid than is used in a stew); the *garniture bourgeoise* of onions and carrots, standard accompaniment to many other dishes; and the clarifying of aspic, done here for the cold version of beef *à la mode*, very different in ingredients but parallel in method to the fish aspic on page 94.

The BORDELAISE SAUCE for steak provides a perfect example of the system of theme and variations in French classic cooking— this being a reduced red-wine sauce which changes its name to *sauce marchand de vins* if the beef marrow is removed from the recipe, or which becomes a *sauce Bercy* if a dry white instead of a red wine is used. This sauce is cooked independently of the meat on which it is served—making it technically a completely different type of sauce from those described on page 105, which are components of recipes rather than "named" sauces in themselves.

*

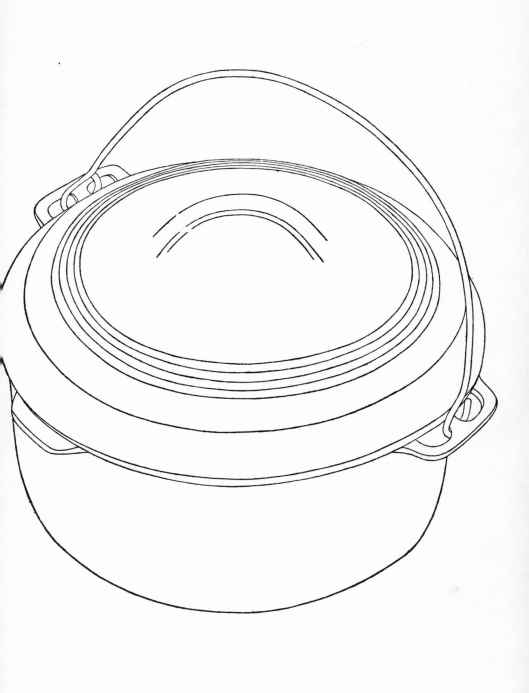

*

PAN-FRIED SIRLOIN STEAK
WITH BORDELAISE SAUCE

THE QUICKEST, neatest and, really, the best way to cook a small or medium-sized steak is to pan-fry it as the French do. After it is seared quickly on both sides, the steak is cooked *à point*, or medium rare, in a matter of 10 minutes or so without the fuss of a messy broiler or a hot, smoke-filled kitchen. Moreover, the steak is always in full view and therefore easier to control and test for the degree of doneness you prefer.

As for the classic Bordelaise sauce, a sublime distillation of shallots, red wine, herbs, poached marrow, and butter, it may be prepared hours earlier and given its final touches just before the steak is served.

] To serve six [

BORDELAISE SAUCE:

2 tablespoons butter
½ cup finely chopped shallots
1½ cups dry red wine
1 bay leaf
10 whole black peppercorns
2 cloves garlic, unpeeled
2 level teaspoons commercial meat essence (BV)

¼ cup beef marrow

10 tablespoons butter (1¼ sticks)
1 tablespoon fresh lemon juice, strained
2 tablespoons finely chopped parsley

3 tablespoons rendered beef fat
    or 2 tablespoons vegetable oil combined with 1
    tablespoon melted butter

150

3½-pound sirloin steak, cut 1 inch thick
Salt
Freshly ground black pepper

It is a truism but still worth repeating: The best way to get a good steak is to buy it from a butcher you can trust. And all talk of prime and choice grades, marbleizing, color, and the rest are useful facts to learn about meat if you have time, but they will avail you nothing if you can't tell whether the meat has been aged or not. Only a good butcher will do this, and it is probably the most important point in determining whether the steak will be tender or tough. Since the aging of meat results in its shrinking perceptibly, thus automatically raising its price, it is unlikely that you will find a good steak at supermarket prices. So be prepared to spend a goodly sum.

A competent butcher will usually make small incisions along the fatty outside edge of the steak. If he hasn't, do it yourself, spacing the cuts at half-inch intervals; this will prevent the steak from curling as it cooks. Have the butcher give you some of the trimmings of fat to render later before you cook the steak.

Start the sauce before you cook the steak, or, if you prefer, hours earlier: In a small saucepan, slowly melt the 2 tablespoons of butter, stir in the ½ cup of minced shallots, and cook them over moderate heat for about 3 minutes without letting them brown. Then add the wine, bay leaf, peppercorns, and garlic cloves, and mix together thoroughly. Bring the wine to a boil, then reduce the heat to moderate, and simmer it, uncovered, until it has reduced, or cooked down, to half its original volume.

At this point strain the sauce through a fine sieve into a small mixing bowl and, with the back of a spoon, press down hard on the shallots and garlic to squeeze them dry before throwing them away. Return the strained wine to the saucepan, and stir into it the 2 level teaspoons of meat essence which you have dissolved first in a couple of tablespoons of hot water. Let the wine remain in its pan and put it aside until later.

If you were able to get the marrow (a matter of cajoling the butcher into splitting a marrow bone lengthwise for you and removing the marrow in one piece), bring a couple of cups of water to a boil in a small pan. Meanwhile, with a sharp knife dipped in hot water, slice the marrow into quarter-inch rounds. After the water comes to a full boil, remove the pan from the heat, and gently drop in the pieces of marrow. Give them about 4 minutes to heat through, off the stove, then remove them with a slotted spoon to a small dish.

Now cream the 1¼ sticks of butter by beating it either by hand with a large wooden spoon or in an electric mixer. When the butter is soft and creamy, beat into it, a few drops at a time, the tablespoon of lemon juice. Stir in the chopped parsley.

When you are ready to fry the steak, start the wine simmering on the lowest possible heat, and make sure the butter, marrow and, particularly, the steak are all at room temperature.

In a heavy frying pan, preferably one just large enough to hold the steak comfortably, heat several pieces of beef fat trimmings until they have rendered about 3 tablespoons of melted fat. Throw the solid scraps away, and heat the remaining fat until it literally begins to smoke. (You may use combined butter and oil instead.) Lay the steak in this, and let it sizzle over high heat for about a minute. Turn it quickly with kitchen tongs and sear it for about a minute on the other side.

Now adjust the heat so that the steak may cook rapidly, but without burning. Fry for about 5 minutes on each side, lifting it and looking under it from time to time. If it is cooking too fast, regulate the heat accordingly. After a little experience, you should be able to tell the degree of doneness the steak has reached by pressing it lightly with your finger: Raw meat is soft and pulpy; medium-rare is slightly resistant; and well-done is quite firm. If you don't trust either your judgment or your sense of timing with this, make a small incision near the bone with a small knife. If the meat still seems bloody, fry it a few minutes longer.

However you determine when the steak is done to your taste, remove it at once to a heated platter, sprinkle it lightly with salt and freshly ground pepper, and let it stand while you rapidly finish the sauce.

Remove the simmering wine from the heat and, with a wire whisk or wooden spoon, quickly beat into it the creamed butter, about a tablespoon at a time. Gently stir in the poached marrow, and pour the completed sauce into a hot sauceboat. Pass it separately and serve the steak sliced. POTATOES ANNA and TOMATOES NIÇOISE (see page 278 and page 271) or plain broiled tomatoes would be correct and colorful accompaniments.

AFTERTHOUGHTS:

✳ If you don't own a pan large enough to hold the steak, cut out the bone and skewer the separated pieces of meat together with small wooden or metal skewers. Naturally, the butcher can do this for you easily.

✳ See the variations on *sauce bordelaise* described on page 148, which are equally good, and try, for a change, the SAUCE BÉARNAISE on page 213.

✳ Another and more expert way to handle the steak is to sear it for 1 minute on each side first, and then to turn it every 2 minutes for a total cooking time of 10 minutes. This will usually produce a more evenly browned steak.

CARBONNADE OF BEEF FLAMANDE

BELGIUM has created a number of national dishes of the first order, but much of her cuisine is frankly indebted to the French and the Dutch. The *carbonnade*, of French origin, was adapted by the Belgians so successfully that by now it is almost always described, even by the French themselves, as a *carbonnade de boeuf à la flamande*, or Flemish beef stew.

At first glance, the *carbonnade* seems an unlikely concoction, composed of beef and a rather staggering quantity of onions cooked together in beer. Contrary to what you might expect, however, the stew, when it is properly prepared, is both distinctive and delicate in flavor. Although an authentic *carbonnade flamande* is usually made with one of the strong, dark Belgian beers, not easily come by here, any good American brand will do quite as well.

] To serve six or eight [

3 pounds boneless chuck, middle or bottom, in one
    piece
Salt
Freshly ground pepper

¼ pound salt pork, cut into ¼-inch dice
1 tablespoon butter

5 large onions
4 tablespoons butter

3 level tablespoons flour

1 pint beer, approximately, preferably dark
1 cup brown beef stock or canned bouillon
1 teaspoon granulated sugar
1 tablespoon vinegar
1 teaspoon finely chopped garlic
1 teaspoon thyme
A bouquet consisting of 4 sprigs parsley, 2 celery tops,
    1 bay leaf, all tied together

2 tablespoons finely chopped parsley

Almost any cut of beef may be used for a *carbonnade,* but most chefs prefer bottom or middle chuck. It has a pronounced flavor and can be cooked for a considerable length of time (indispensable for a good stew) without falling apart. Have the butcher leave the meat in one piece, but ask him to trim off all fat and gristle.

When you get the meat home, wipe it with a damp cloth, and cut it into approximately 2-inch chunks, keeping them as uniform as possible. Of course, the butcher can do this for you, but it is easier to control the size of the pieces if you do it yourself. Salt and pepper the meat liberally, and set it aside while you render the salt pork and start the onions.

Blanch the ¼ pound of diced salt pork in a little boiling water, and drain and pat it dry. In a large heavy frying pan, fry the blanched dice in the tablespoon of butter until they are brown and crisp, and remove them to a double layer of paper towelling to drain. (If you have never done this before, see page 159.) Pour the rendered pork fat into a small bowl, leaving a thin film of fat in the pan in which to brown the meat later.

In another large frying pan, heat the 4 tablespoons of butter. When it foams, add the sliced onions, and cook them over moderate heat, turning them frequently with a spatula or a large spoon. They will take at least 20 minutes to color lightly, during which time you can brown the meat and start the sauce. Don't try to cook the onions any faster; they will merely char on the outside and give the *carbonnade* a rough and bitter taste.

Now that the onions are started, heat the first frying pan to the point where the pork fat almost smokes. Don't make the common mistake of trying to brown the meat in this all at once. If you do, the heat of the pan will drop sharply; the surface of the meat, instead of contracting upon contact with the intense heat as it should, will expand instead and release the moisture within. You will then probably find yourself with a pan full of a greyish-brown broth that makes it impossible to brown the beef at all.

So, put 4 or 5 pieces of meat in the pan at a time and, over moderate heat, brown them carefully on all sides. As they are done, remove them with kitchen tongs to a Dutch oven or a heavy casserole with a tightly fitting cover. As you continue to brown the meat, add to the frying pan some of the pork fat you saved earlier. But, though it may seem paradoxical, remember that the less fat you use, the more quickly the meat will brown. And, while you are doing this, preheat the oven to **325°F.**

When you have deposited the last piece of browned meat in the casserole, mix into the pork fat remaining in the frying pan the 3 level tablespoons of flour. Remove the pan from the heat when you do this, or the flour will burn. Stir the fat and flour together until they form a thick paste, or *roux* as it is called. If there isn't enough fat in the pan to absorb the flour, add a bit more.

Now cook the *roux* very, very slowly, stirring it constantly until it turns a deep brown. This will take longer than you might suppose; in no circumstances must the *roux* burn, so don't rush it. When it gives off a characteristically nutty odor and is the color of dark chocolate, it is ready to have the liquid for your sauce added.

Pour into the *roux*, all at once, the pint of beer and the cup of beef stock. Bring this to a boil, stirring vigorously with a wire whisk until the *roux* and liquid have combined and the sauce is quite thick and smooth. Mix into this the sugar, vinegar, garlic, and thyme, simmer a few minutes, then pour the sauce over the meat in the casserole. By now the onions should be done. Add them to the casserole also. The sauce should just about cover the meat and onions; if it doesn't, pour in a little more beer.

With a large spoon, give everything a gentle turn or two, toss in the herb bouquet, and cover the casserole. Bring it to a boil on top of the stove, then put it in the preheated oven to simmer until the meat is tender but not falling apart. Variations in cuts of meat being what they are, it is impossible to say with accuracy how long this should take. Allow certainly a minimum of an hour and 15 minutes to a maximum of 2 hours, possibly a bit more. In any case, at the end of the first 20 minutes, taste the sauce for salt; it will undoubtedly need some.

When the *carbonnade* is done, sprinkle it with the crisp pork bits and the chopped parsley, and serve it directly from the casserole. Unadorned boiled potatoes usually accompany this dish, but there is no reason why you can't have buttered noodles, white or green, if you wish. It would seem illogical, however, to serve with the *carbonnade* anything but ice-cold beer to drink.

AFTERTHOUGHTS:

✳ Like most beef stews, the *carbonnade* may be made hours ahead and reheated quite successfully. It is generally wise, if you plan to do this, to undercook the meat somewhat for it will continue to cook as it cools, particularly if the pot is heavy, as it should be, and retains its heat. In all likelihood, the meat will be tender when you are ready to reheat it. If it isn't, simply simmer it a while longer.

✳ The use of salt pork, a characteristic of French regional cooking, is not traditional with the Belgians. If you prefer, substitute as they do, lard, rendered beef fat, or butter.

✳ The meat may be cooked like a pot roast in one piece and sliced at the table. A solid piece of bottom round, top round, or brisket will be a more attractive cut than chuck for this purpose. Be sure to have it tied securely so that it keeps its shape while cooking.

✳ The *carbonnade* may be cooked on the top of the stove. In this case, the pot *must* be a heavy one and the lid close fitting. Keep the heat down to the lowest possible simmer. The two methods produce almost identical results, but in the oven there is less danger of the stew sticking to the pot or burning.

✳ If you happen to have any left-over beer around, use it. It is just as effective in this dish as freshly opened beer.

✳ Beer, like wine, will taste raw if it is undercooked. Taste the sauce when the meat is done; if it seems to be the least bit acrid, remove the meat and reduce the sauce by boiling it vigorously for a few minutes.

✳ For a smoother sauce, chop the onions fine instead of slicing them. For an even smoother sauce, use sliced onions, but strain them out of the sauce before serving the *carbonnade*.

*

BEEF BOURGUIGNON

THIS is a stew that Americans have taken to their hearts. The red wine in which the beef is cooked and the typical Burgundian garnish of salt pork, small browned onions, and mushrooms give this famous dish its special character. Vigorous and full-bodied, like the good Burgundy it should be made with, beef *bourguignon* is appropriate on the simplest family table, yet it can hold its own with assurance on an elaborate buffet. Its flavor is incomparable and, moreover, it can be made well ahead of time and reheated successfully even on the second or third day. But remember, this is not a dish to be thrown together carelessly; the cut of beef, the quality of the wine and stock, the careful browning and slow simmering of the meat, all these elements and more will determine how good your beef *bourguignon* will be.

] To serve six to eight [

½ pound fat salt pork
1 tablespoon butter
16–18 small white onions, all approximately the same
    size—1 to 1½ inches in diameter

3 pounds boneless chuck, middle or bottom, in one
    piece

6 shallots, finely minced
1 medium carrot, finely minced
3 level tablespoons flour

2 cups imported French red Burgundy
    or an American Pinot Noir
1 cup brown beef stock or canned bouillon
A bouquet consisting of 6 sprigs parsley, 2 celery tops,
    1 large bay leaf, all tied together
1 teaspoon finely chopped garlic

1 teaspoon thyme
Salt
Freshly ground black pepper

3 tablespoons butter
¾ pound mushrooms

2 tablespoons finely chopped parsley

The cut of beef you choose for your beef *bourguignon* is of great importance to the success of the dish. The long slow cooking necessary to produce a richly flavored stew would reduce to shreds a tender piece of meat from the sirloin, or even the top of the round, long before the stew was done. The cut which seems to stand up best, both in texture and flavor, is the middle of the chuck, sometimes called bottom chuck.

Have the butcher leave the meat in one piece, but ask him to trim it of all fat and gristle. Cut it yourself into approximately 2-inch chunks—no smaller. Few butchers will go to the trouble to do this properly, with the result that the pieces are either too large or too small. Pat each piece of meat dry with a paper towel; any dampness will prevent it from browning well. Season with salt and pepper.

❋ *Cut the salt pork into quarter-inch dice. To make sure the salt in the pork doesn't oversalt the stew, blanch it. That is, cover the pork bits with cold water in a small pan, bring it to a boil, and simmer for about 5 minutes. Drain the pork and pat it dry with paper towels.*

In a large heavy frying pan, melt 1 tablespoon of butter. Add the blanched salt pork, and cook it over high heat, stirring constantly with a wooden spoon, until it has rendered all its fat and the bits have crisped and turned a golden brown. Be careful not to let them burn. With a slotted spoon, remove them to a small bowl lined with a double layer paper toweling to absorb their excess fat.

159

❋ *Preheat the oven to* **350°F.** *Have the little white onions ready peeled and left whole. To cook them* à brun, *reheat now the rendered pork fat left in the frying until it begins to smoke, and add the onions. Let them cook over moderate heat, and shake the pan from time to time so that they roll around in the fat and brown on all sides. They never brown evenly, so don't work too hard at this.*

With a slotted spoon, transfer the onions to a shallow baking dish large enough just to hold them in one layer. Spoon 3 tablespoons of the pork fat into the dish, and sprinkle the onions with a little salt and pepper. Bake them on the center shelf of the oven for about 30 minutes, or until they can be pierced easily with a pointed knife. Turn them from time to time. Don't overcook them—they should retain their shapes when they are done. Then put them aside; you won't need them until the stew is almost done.

The size of the casserole in which you are going to cook and serve the beef *bourguignon* is important. A 4-quart ovenproof casserole is just about right for the amounts specified in this recipe; if it is much larger, you will need too much liquid to immerse the meat adequately. Have the casserole ready.

While the onions are baking, start browning the meat in the same pork fat the onions were browned in. Begin by pouring most of the fat out of the frying pan into a small bowl, and keep this handy so you can dip into it as you need it. Leave only a thin film of fat in the frying pan. Heat this almost to the smoking point, and in it brown 4 or 5 pieces of meat at a time; if you try to do much more than this at once, the heat of the pan will drop too much and the meat may not brown at all.

As each piece becomes a dark crusty brown all over, transfer it with tongs to the casserole. Add more pork fat to the pan as you proceed, but use as little as possible for the best results.

When the last piece of meat has been deposited in the casserole, add the chopped shallots and carrot to the fat remaining in the

160

pan. Cook them slowly over low heat until they are lightly colored. Then remove the pan from the heat, and stir the 3 tablespoons of flour into the browned vegetables. Mix this thoroughly until it forms a paste; if the mixture is too dry or crumbly, stir in a little more pork fat.

Now return the pan to the heat and slowly cook this *roux* until the flour begins to turn brown. It is worth taking extra precautions here: Stir the *roux* constantly, and don't try to cook it too fast or it will burn and give the sauce a bitter taste; but get it as brown as you can without burning it.

Then, pour into the pan the 2 cups of Burgundy and the cup of brown stock in which you have dissolved the tablespoon of tomato paste. Bring this to a boil, stirring constantly with a wire whisk. The sauce will be lumpy at first but will thicken and smooth out as it heats through. Continue to cook it slowly until it is quite smooth, then pour it over the meat in the casserole.

The sauce should come almost to the top of the meat but not above it. If there isn't enough, add a little more stock or wine. Push the herb bouquet below the surface of the liquid, and stir in the minced garlic, thyme, and crisp pork bits you saved earlier. Add a scant tablespoon of salt and a few grindings of black pepper to start with; you can tell how much more to add later, after the stew has simmered a while.

Cover the casserole tightly and bring it to a boil. Then put it in the hot oven, lower the heat to **325° F.**, and cook the beef anywhere from 2 to 3 hours, depending on the quality of the meat.

While the beef is cooking, prepare the mushrooms. If they are large, slice or quarter them; if small, use them whole. Don't wash them, but wipe them lightly with a moist towel and dry them carefully. Heat the 3 tablespoons of butter in a large heavy frying pan and, when it begins to splutter, add the mushrooms. Cook over high heat no more than 3 or 4 minutes, turning them over constantly with a wooden spoon, until they are lightly browned. Remove them from the pan and set them aside in a small bowl; after they have cooled a bit, cover them with Saran wrap.

When the beef is tender but not pulpy or falling apart, add to the casserole the browned onions and mushrooms and whatever juices have accumulated with them during their wait. Mix everything together carefully with a large wooden spoon, cover the casserole again, and simmer slowly for about 15 minutes, or until the onions and mushrooms have heated through.

Skim off any fat that has accumulated on the surface, taste for salt, and sprinkle the finished beef *bourguignon* with the chopped parsley. Serve directly from the casserole, accompanied by either boiled potatoes, or buttered noodles, or steamed rice. Hot French or Italian bread to sop up the sauce is a must with this, as is a bottle of the same wine the meat was cooked in.

AFTERTHOUGHTS:

✳ If the sauce lacks character or suavity when the meat is done, reduce it. Pour the beef *bourguigon* into a large strainer set over a saucepan. When all the liquid has gone through, remove the strainer. Skim off most, but not all of the fat from the sauce, and bring the sauce to a boil. Continue to boil, tasting frequently. When the sauce reaches the intensity of flavor you want, combine it again with the meat and vegetables in the casserole; reheat, and serve.

✳ To thicken the sauce if it is too thin, mix ½ teaspoon of arrowroot powder or cornstarch to a paste with 2 tablespoons of water. Stir this into the sauce, bring it to a boil, and cook until it thickens. To thin a sauce that is too thick, add more stock; never add uncooked wine.

✳ For a change of texture, try sprinkling the crisp pork bits over the stew just before serving it, instead of cooking them earlier in the sauce.

✳ You can substitute diced bacon for the salt pork if you prefer, but make certain to blanch it for about 10 minutes. Bacon is smoked and unless it is well blanched tends to blot out the flavor of everything it is cooked with.

✳ If you want to double this recipe, don't double the amount of wine and stock or you will turn the stew into a soup. Half again as much liquid as in the original recipe generally works pretty well; the best gauge is still to have the liquid come almost to the top of the meat.

✳ Try cooking the meat in one piece and slicing it at the table when it is done. In that case, tie it securely before you brown it, so that the piece will hold its shape while cooking. You might omit the chopped garlic from the sauce, and insert slivers of garlic into the meat instead. Or lard the meat as described for BEEF À LA MODE on page 165.

✳ Stews in general may, of course, be cooked on top of the stove. The two methods—oven or burner—produce almost identical results. On top of the stove, keep the heat very low and be sure to use a heavy pot with a closely fitting lid so that the stew will not stick or burn; there is less risk of this in the oven.

BEEF À LA MODE

MARCEL PROUST in *The Remembrance of Things Past,* writes rhapsodically of a cold *boeuf à la mode* served "upon enormous crystals of jelly, like transparent blocks of quartz," and goes on to describe its preparation as a task of great complexity. Literary license being what it is, cooking beef à la mode is in reality far less difficult than he implied. In fact, it is not difficult at all. Although the various steps in its preparation do take time, the techniques involved are well within the capabilities of any enterprising cook, and they display the logic with which a classic recipe is constructed that can be admired for its own sake.

] To serve ten [

4½ to 5 pounds boneless chuck or bottom round of
    beef, in one piece
6–8 strips larding pork, cut ⅛ inch wide and 2 inches
    longer than length of the meat
1 tablespoon salt mixed with 1 teaspoon freshly
    ground black pepper

MARINADE:

3 cups dry red wine, preferably Burgundy
1 cup thinly sliced onions
¾ cup thinly sliced carrots
1 teaspoon finely chopped garlic
2 bay leaves, roughly crumbled
2 tablespoons finely chopped parsley
1 teaspoon crumbled leaf thyme

GARNITURE BOURGEOISE:

½ pound fresh pork fat, cut in small dice
20 little white onions, 1 to 1½ inches in diameter
20 pieces of carrot, cut into 2-inch olive shapes or
     cylinders
Salt
Pepper

4 tablespoons butter
1/3 cup brandy

2 calves' feet, cut up
     and/or 1 large veal knuckle, cut up
2 large tomatoes, peeled, seeded, and coarsely
     chopped
3–5 cups brown beef stock or canned bouillon
A bouquet consisting of 1 large leek (white part
     only), 3 celery tops, 6 sprigs parsley, and 1 small
     bay leaf, all tied together
Salt

½ cup finely chopped parsley

To serve cold, in Aspic:

3 envelopes unflavored gelatine
¾ cup brown beef stock or canned bouillon

164

3 cups brown beef stock or canned bouillon, ap-
    proximately
3 egg whites, beaten to a froth
½ bay leaf, 10 black peppercorns, ½ teaspoon thyme,
    ½ teaspoon lemon juice

½ cup dry Madeira

If you plan to serve the beef à la mode hot, begin its preparation a day ahead; for the cold version, allow at least two days.

Choose a solid piece of beef not less than 5 inches wide and completely trimmed of all outside fat; have the meat tied in three or four places so that it will hold its shape while cooking. Ask the butcher to lard the meat with 6 to 8 strips of larding pork, but if he won't, or can't, do it yourself. Although it is not absolutely necessary for the success of the dish, larding the meat adds immeasurably to its flavor and tenderness.

Larding needles come in a variety of types and sizes. The best for your present purpose is a 13- or 14-inch grooved steel shaft attached to a round wooden handle. Comparatively inexpensive, these are available in restaurant-supply houses or shops carrying imported kitchen ware.

✳ *Chill the pork strips—lardoons—in the freezer for about 10 minutes, or until they have stiffened almost, but not quite to the point of rigidity. Insert the point of the larding needle 2 inches into the meat, heading into it lengthwise; then retract the needle about an inch, and lay the lardoon in the groove. Slowly force the needle through the meat until the lardoon emerges about an inch out at the other end.*

If, at first, or any time during this maneuver, the lardoon begins to buckle, slide your left hand down the length of the needle to the meat and, with your thumb, press the lardoon flat in the needle and push it simultaneously toward the meat to help guide it through.

To retract the needle, with your thumb, again press against

*the lardoon at the point where it went into the meat to keep
it in place, and slowly and cautiously pull out the needle.*

*Repeat the entire procedure with the other pork strips,
spacing them as evenly as possible throughout the meat, so
that later each cross-cut slice will be neatly patterned with
small pieces of the pork.*

Pat the combined salt and pepper into the surface of the beef
with your fingers. In a glass, porcelain, or stainless-steel bowl just
about large enough to hold the beef comfortably, combine the
marinade ingredients. Add the meat, and turn it about in the
marinade until it is moistened all over. Let the beef marinate for
at least 6 hours, preferably longer—even 24 hours is not too much—
and change its position every few hours so that a different area
rests in the seasoned wine each time.

Marinades are more effective if they aren't refrigerated, but,
if your kitchen is warm, let the beef marinate part of the time in
the refrigerator.

✳ *Before you braise the beef, render the diced fresh pork fat
and prepare the onion-and-carrot garniture bourgeoise: Fry
the pork fat over moderate heat in a large heavy frying pan,
stirring it constantly, until the scraps are brown and crisp.
Lift them out of the melted fat with a slotted spoon and throw
them away.*

*Preheat the oven to 350° F. Simultaneously, heat the ren-
dered fat in the frying pan almost to the smoking point. Add
the little white onions and the carrots and, shaking the pan
continuously, cook them for a few minutes until they are lightly browned. Then transfer the vegetables to a shallow baking
dish large enough to hold them in one layer. Pour over them
3 or 4 tablespoons of the hot pork fat, or enough to lightly
cover the bottom of the dish, and sprinkle them lightly with
salt and pepper. Leave the rest of the fat in the frying pan.*

*Bake the onions and carrots, uncovered, on the center shelf
of the oven for half an hour or so, turning and basting them*

every now and then, until they are tender but still firm to the
touch. Remove them from the baking dish and put them aside.

While the vegetables are baking, or after they are done, prepare
the meat for braising. Remove it from the marinade and pat it
thoroughly dry with paper towels; don't be careless about this,
for the meat won't brown well if it is damp. Strain the marinade
into a small bowl, and spread the marinated vegetables out on a
double thickness of paper towels to rid them of excess moisture;
it isn't necessary to dry them thoroughly.

Heat the pork fat that still remains in the frying pan until it
literally begins to smoke, then add the meat. Now regulate the
heat so that the meat browns evenly and thoroughly without burning. Turn it every few minutes so that each side colors gradually,
rather than allowing any part to brown completely at one time.
Done properly, this process takes from 20 to 25 minutes.

Meanwhile, in a heavy 6-quart casserole or Dutch oven, melt
the 4 tablespoons of butter. In it, over fairly low heat, cook the
marinated vegetables, turning them from time to time with a
wooden spoon, until all their moisture has evaporated and they
begin to color. Browning the meat and vegetables in their respective pans should take approximately the same time.

When the beef is a deep mahogany brown all over, turn off the
heat. With a basting syringe, draw off all but 2 tablespoons of the
fat in the pan. Heat 1/3 cup of brandy to lukewarm and set it
alight, stepping back as you do so (see page 115). Pour the brandy
over the meat a little at a time, shaking the frying pan until the
flame dies out.

Then transfer the beef to the casserole, placing it on top of the
browned vegetables. Surround it with the cut-up calves' feet and/
or the veal knuckle, and the chopped, drained tomatoes.

Now, to the dark-brown drippings remaining in the frying pan,
add the strained marinade and 3 cups of beef stock or canned
bouillon. Bring this to a boil over high heat, and scrape into it
every bit of brown sediment you can find on the bottom and sides

of the pan. Boil briskly for a minute or two, then pour the stock into the casserole. It should come a little more than half way up the sides of the meat; add more stock if it doesn't. Submerge the herb bouquet in the stock.

Bring the casserole rapidly to a boil on top of the stove. Cover it tightly then, and place it on the center shelf of the **350°F.** oven. If, after 10 minutes or so, the stock seems to be boiling too briskly, reduce the heat to **325°,** or even **300°** if necessary; the beef should braise at the barest simmer. Turn it every hour or so to insure its cooking evenly.

When the beef is tender, remove it from the casserole; it is impossible to be precise about how long this will take, but estimate at least 2½ to 3 hours, possibly longer. Pour the braising liquid, bones, vegetables, and all, into a large sieve set over a mixing bowl. Remove the bones. With a large spoon, press down hard on the vegetables to extract all their juices before throwing them away.

To serve hot:

Let the braising liquid rest for a minute or two, then skim off most but not all of the fat. Return the liquid and the meat to the washed casserole, and add the garniture of white onions and carrots you prepared earlier. Cover the casserole and, just before servingtime, simmer it slowly on top of the stove until the beef and vegetables are heated through.

Remove the strings and carve the meat in thin slices, against the grain. Arrange them, slightly overlapping, down the center of a large heated platter. Group the onions and carrots decoratively on both sides. Now keep the platter warm in a slow **(250°)** oven while you reduce the casserole juices.

Boil the juices vigorously on top of the stove for 5 or 10 minutes, until they are reduced by about half. When this sauce is as intense in flavor as you would like it to be (boil it down even more than half if you wish), spoon some of it over the meat and vegetables, and pour the rest into a sauceboat to be passed separately at the table.

168

Sprinkle the chopped parsley over the meat, and serve with buttered noodles or small boiled and buttered potatoes.

To serve cold, in Aspic:

Allow the beef to come to room temperature, then wrap it in waxed paper or Saran wrap and chill it for as long as you like. Wrap and chill the vegetable garniture separately. Don't reduce the braising liquid; after it has cooled, refrigerate it and later remove all the fat which will solidify on its surface.

When you are ready to make the aspic, soften the 3 envelopes of gelatine in ¾ cup of cold stock or canned bouillon. Meanwhile, measure the braising liquid (melt it first over lower heat if it has jellied). You should have 3 cups, more or less: whatever the amount, add to it enough cold, grease-free brown stock or canned bouillon to make, in all, 6 cups of liquid. Pour this into a 2- or 3-quart saucepan, stir in the softened gelatine, and, after beating the 3 egg whites to a froth, stir them into the liquid also. To augment the flavor of the aspic (most aspics, no matter how fine their color, are usually bland and tasteless), add to the pot the half bay leaf and the peppercorns, thyme, salt, and lemon juice.

Stirring constantly with a wire whisk, bring this mixture to a boil over moderate heat. Cook and stir it until the liquid begins to rise in the pot and threatens to boil over; whisk once or twice more, then turn off the heat and let the froth subside. Don't disturb the pot for at least 5 minutes.

Meanwhile, place a large fine-meshed sieve over a deep mixing bowl—deep enough so that the bottom of the sieve will not touch the surface of the 6 cups of liquid after it has drained through. Line the sieve with a kitchen towel moistened with cold water and wrung dry. Carefully pour the hot aspic, egg whites and all, into it, and in no circumstances disturb the mixture until the last drop of translucent amber aspic has dripped through. Remove the sieve, and stir ½ cup of Madeira into the finished aspic.

A quick way to assemble the chilled beef and aspic: Carve the

meat into thin, even slices and arrange them neatly in a large 2-
or 3-inch-deep baking dish; scatter a few of the braised vegetables
over the first layer of meat, and continue to build up the layers,
ending with one of the meat. Carefully pour enough aspic into
the dish to cover everything completely. Refrigerate for at least
5 hours, or until the aspic is firmly set.

If you prefer to present the beef more dramatically: Pour into
the baking dish a quarter-inch-deep layer of aspic, and chill (in
the refrigerator, *not* the freezer) until set. Upon this, arrange any
decorative garnish you like (sliced hard-cooked eggs, thin slices of
truffles, and the like), and place over it a few slices of beef. Spoon
enough aspic over the meat to cover it, and again chill until set.
Do the same with a layer of the vegetable garniture; then again
with slices of beef. Continue with the rest of the vegetables; then
the remaining beef, with aspic to cover each time. Chill until
set. The point of this careful procedure is to have the beef à la
mode "floating" between thin layers of its own aspic when you
finally see it unmolded.

However you have constructed your beef à la mode, the unmolding process is the same: Run a sharp knife around the inside rim
of the baking dish. Then dip the bottom of the dish in a shallow
pan of hot water and hold it there for 5 or 6 seconds. Dry the dish
with a towel, and place a chilled serving platter on top of it. Grasp
the platter and baking dish firmly together, quickly turn them over,
and rap the platter sharply on the table. The aspic should come out
easily. If it doesn't, either repeat the whole process, or rub a towel
wrung out in hot water over the upturned bottom of the dish.

Surround the jellied meat with chopped left-over aspic; if any;
if not, with a ring of crisp water cress. Serve with hot French bread
and a bowl of FRENCH POTATO SALAD (see page 299).

AFTERTHOUGHTS:

✳ You may, if you like, use vegetable oil in place of the fresh pork fat to brown the beef; but the pork fat is in every way preferable.

✳ Although it is not customary, the reduced braising juices may be thickened by adding to them 1 tablespoon of arrowroot powder mixed to a paste with 2 tablespoons of Madeira, stock, or water. Bring the sauce to a boil and cook until it thickens. Of course, do this only if the beef is to be served hot.

✳ The lardoons may be marinated in brandy for half an hour, and then coated with a paste of minced shallots, garlic, parsley, and salt and pepper before being chilled. Lard the meat as before.

✳ Cold VEGETABLES À LA GRECQUE (see page 26) may be used to augment the platter of jellied beef. In this case, omit the *garniture bourgeoise* entirely.

✳ For less formal occasions, or when using left-over beef cold, you need not clarify the liquid; in fact, the jelly will have more flavor if you don't, though it may not be firm enough to be unmolded. Arrange the meat and liquid in the same way, but serve directly from the baking dish.

CHAPTER VI

Veal

Veal Scaloppine Marsala with Prosciutto
Blanquette de Veau à l'Ancienne
Veal Marengo
Osso Buco
Roast Larded Rack of Veal
Galantine of Veal
Vitello Tonnato

You WILL find in cookbooks of all sorts recipes for sautéed veal *scaloppine* with quick and easy pan sauces. The crucial point, no matter what sauce is added, is to pound and sauté the veal correctly; detailed instructions are given in the recipe for VEAL SCALOPPINE MARSALA.

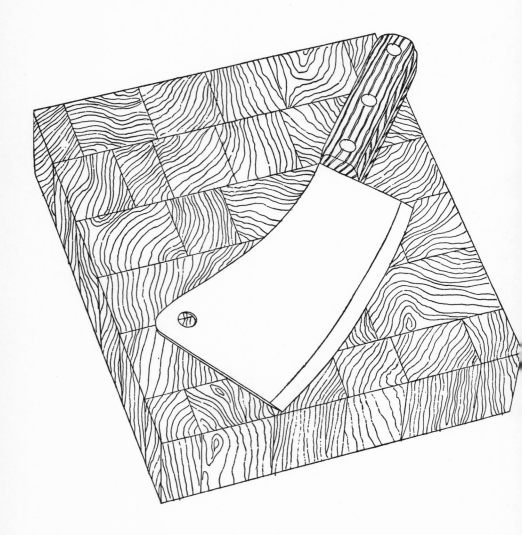

BLANQUETTE DE VEAU and VEAL MARENGO demonstrate at their best two principal types of stew. A *blanquette* is a white stew or fricassee for which any white meat—young veal or lamb, or a stewing hen (see page 35)—may be used. The meat is not browned at the beginning and the seasoning is restrained. As with many French stews, the garnish of little onions (and here, also, mushrooms) is cooked separately; the onions are stewed *à blanc,* not browned, in butter. In contrast, the veal is browned for a Marengo. The sauce, in this particular case, is highly seasoned in the Provençal manner. And onions, browned and braised in pork fat, are the garnish *à brun* identical to the braised onions that accompany the classic brown stews, COQ AU VIN and BEEF BOURGUIGNON (see Index).

OSSO BUCO is a typical braised dish, and also typically Italian. It offers an interesting contrast to the elaborate prototype of French braised meats, BEEF À LA MODE (see page 163). The Italian *osso buco* makes much of little, using veal rather than the (in Italy) scarcer beef and a lowly cut at that, the shank or shinbone. Also braised is the stuffed GALANTINE OF VEAL, a showpiece, but a simple one as galantines go. The masking of *chaud-froid* sauce is set with gelatine—a process comparable to the simpler *mayonnaise collée* on page 95.

The ROAST LARDED RACK OF VEAL explains itself—roasting is the simplest method of cooking meat, but to do it right you must be a perfectionist. Finally, VITELLO TONNATO is an Italian classic with no counterparts anywhere. It does, however, produce a veal stock which is different only in its Mediterranean seasoning from a French *fonds blanc*—which means in a general way a rich, light-colored stock made either with veal and veal bones, or chicken and veal bones, or all three. The stock can be made into an aspic for garnishing if you wish.

*

VEAL SCALOPPINE MARSALA WITH PROSCIUTTO

MOST national cuisines have their own way with slices of sautéed veal but, whether you call them scallops in English, *escalopes* in French, *Schnitzel* in German, or *scaloppine* in Italian, they are essentially the same—squares, rectangles, or circles of veal pounded to varying degrees of thinness and quickly sautéed. How they are sauced and what they are served with determines, finally, their particular category and distinction.

The Italians have developed through the centuries an almost endless variety of ways to cook *scaloppine—scaloppine Marsala* being one of the best known here. Thin pieces of veal are browned in butter and oil, then cooked ever so briefly in Marsala and stock which then become the sauce. The mildly salted *prosciutto* contributes a contrasting texture and heightens the flavor of the sauce.

] To serve four [

1½ pounds boneless leg or rump of veal, cut into
    slices ⅜-inch thick and pounded ¼ inch thick
½ pound prosciutto, in one piece
    or ½ pound Canadian bacon
Salt
Freshly ground black pepper
½ cup flour
3 tablespoons olive oil
2 tablespoons butter

½ cup dry Marsala
½ cup chicken or beef stock, fresh or canned
2 tablespoons soft butter
1 tablespoon finely chopped parsley

The quality of the veal is of the greatest importance to the success of this dish, and your safest bet is to buy it from an Italian or

176

French butcher if you can find one. If you can't, simply remember that the shade of pink in the veal determines its age; the younger it is, the paler and more tender it will be.

Ask your butcher to cut the veal into slices about three-eighths of an inch thick, and have him remove every bit of the surrounding skin and fat before pounding the slices one quarter inch thick. Slices thinner than this will cook too rapidly and will be dry and tasteless, so, if you don't trust the butcher, pound the veal yourself. Lay a slice on a chopping board between two sheets of strong waxed paper, and pound it, not too violently, with the flat of a cleaver, or a flat wooden mallet, the bottom of a large beer bottle, a rolling pin, or even a croquet mallet, if you must. The pieces of veal, when you finish, will probably be quite disparate in size and shape. Trim them as uniformly as you care to.

Cut the *prosciutto* (or Canadian bacon) into small sticks about 1 inch long and one quarter inch wide. Taste one. If it seems too salty, blanch the ham by covering it with cold water in a small pan and bringing it to a boil. Reduce the heat to a simmer and cook the ham for about 6 minutes. Taste it again; if it still seems salty, cook it a bit longer. Then drain it at once through a sieve, plunge it into a bowl of cold water to stop its cooking, and dry it on a paper towel. Canadian bacon is so mildly cured that it may be used as it is.

Salt each piece of veal generously on both sides, and grind black pepper over them more discreetly. Spread ½ cup of flour on a sheet of waxed paper, dip each slice of veal into it, then shake the meat vigorously like a flag to remove all but the faintest coating of the flour. This will help brown the veal without making it gummy, as too much flour usually does.

In a large sauté pan or frying pan you can cover, heat the 3 tablespoons of olive oil and 2 tablespoons of butter. When the fat begins to sputter, put in the pieces of veal, without letting them overlap. They will begin to shrink almost at once, so you will probably be able to fit all the pieces in the pan after a minute or two. If you can't or the pan is too small, remove each piece as it is done and

177

put a fresh one in its place. In any event, cook the *scaloppine* over fairly high heat for 3 or 4 minutes on each side, or until they are well but not too darkly browned.

Remove the pieces of veal to a shallow baking dish. Lower the heat under the frying pan and, in the same fat, brown the *prosciutto* for no longer than 2 minutes, turning it constantly with a large spoon. Remove the ham with a slotted spoon and add it to the veal in the baking dish.

Pour off all but a couple of tablespoons of fat from the frying pan, and in its place add the ½ cup of Marsala and ¼ cup of the stock. Cook this over high heat until it comes to a boil, meanwhile scraping into it all the brown crust on the bottom of the pan. Continue to boil for about a minute, then lower the heat to the barest simmer, return the veal and ham to the pan, and include any drippings that may have accumulated in the baking dish. Baste the meat carefully, cover the pan tightly, and simmer it for 10 or 15 minutes, or until the veal is tender. Test, if you must, by cutting off a small sliver and tasting it.

To serve, have ready a hot serving platter. Remove the *scaloppine* from the pan and arrange them down the center of the platter, slightly overlapping, and scatter the ham over the veal.

Pour the remaining ¼ cup of stock into the frying pan, repeat the earlier scraping process, and boil the sauce furiously for a minute or two, until it has reduced to about half the original amount. It should be somewhat dense and syrupy. Remove the pan from the heat, stir into the sauce the 2 tablespoons of soft butter, then quickly pour it over the veal.

Sprinkle with chopped parsley and serve at once. If you like, surround the *scaloppine* with TOMATOES NIÇOISE (page 271).

AFTERTHOUGHTS:

✱ The veal may, if it must, be prepared ahead, left in its sauce in the frying pan, and reheated slowly, just before serving. Don't, in that event, reduce the sauce until the veal is hot. Then proceed to complete the sauce as described before.

178

✻ For those of you unfamiliar with it, *prosciutto* is a distinctively cured Italian ham. Although it is now produced domestically, the imported variety is in every way superior. Food sections in large department stores and Italian grocers and butchers usually carry it. It is decidedly worth looking for. Sliced paper thin, it makes a delectable first course served with slices of chilled melon or with ripe figs. Certain brands are frequently oversalted as a preservative measure during the summer months; it is wise, before you buy the ham, to cajole a slice from the dealer and taste it.

✻ Be certain to use a dry Marsala and preferably an imported one. Sweet Marsala is too cloying and will spoil the dish.

BLANQUETTE DE VEAU À L'ANCIENNE

Despite the length of its name, *blanquette de veau à l'ancienne* spells "home" to the average Frenchman as surely as old-fashioned beef stew does to an American. And a *blanquette* of veal, unmasked, is really an old-fashioned stew, albeit in a creamy white *velouté* sauce embellished with heavy cream and egg yolks. Garnished with little white onions and mushrooms, it needs no more than the accompaniment of steamed rice and hot French bread to make a memorable meal. Moreover, a *blanquette* can be prepared well in advance and reheated with no loss of its original flavor.

] To serve six or eight [

3 pounds boneless leg or rump of veal, in one piece

6 cups chicken stock, fresh or canned
2 medium carrots, cut into chunks
1 large onion
1 teaspoon thyme
2 cloves garlic, unpeeled

A bouquet consisting of 4 sprigs parsley, 2 large
celery tops, 1 leek (white part only), 1 bay leaf,
all tied together
1 teaspoon salt

18 small white onions, about 1 inch in diameter,
peeled and left whole
2 tablespoons butter
2/3 cup chicken stock
1 teaspoon lemon juice
1 pound mushrooms, whole if small, quartered or
sliced if large

3 tablespoons butter
3 tablespoons flour
2 large egg yolks, 3 if small
1 cup heavy cream
Cayenne
Salt

2 tablespoons finely chopped parsley

In the place of the boneless leg or rump of veal, less expensive cuts
may be used for a *blanquette*. In fact, the cut-up breast, shoulder,
neck, and shank, used separately or together, are traditional for it
in France. But cartilege and gristle are not to the American taste,
so you are safer using the boned leg or rump.

However, whatever cut you use, any veal worthy of the name
should be the lightest pink in color, with the flesh firm and finely
grained and the outside fat white, smooth-textured, and pliable.
You may have to ferret around a bit to find such veal, but don't
settle for anything else. Veal in which the pink is more than a
delicate blush is more likely to be tough and flavorless very young
beef.

Buy the meat in one piece and cut it yourself into 2-inch chunks.
This is not much of a chore and much safer than entrusting the
job to a busy or careless butcher.

Because veal, when it is cooked in liquid, produces more scum than any other meat, it must be blanched first. In other words, in a 3- or 4-quart casserole, cover the veal with cold water, bring it quickly to a boil, and let it simmer for a minute before draining it in a large sieve.

Wash the accumulated scum off the pieces of meat under cold running water, scrub the casserole, and replace the veal in it. From a practical point of view, blanching the veal detracts nothing from its flavor and eliminates the nuisance of later having to skim it almost incessantly.

Pour over the blanched veal in the casserole the 6 cups of chicken stock, and supplement the stock with water (or more stock) if the meat isn't completely covered. Add the carrots, onion, thyme, garlic cloves, the bouquet, and the salt. Slowly bring the stock to a boil, and skim the surface of any residual scum that may appear. Then reduce the heat to the barest simmer—the liquid should barely move—and cook the veal, partially covered, for 1 to 1½ hours, or until it is tender. And the best way to tell is simply to taste it.

✳ *While the veal is simmering, prepare the little white onions and the mushrooms à blanc. (Note that these are the logical garnish for any white stew or fricassee.)*

In a large enamel frying pan or saucepan you can cover tightly, heat together the 2 tablespoons of butter and 2/3 cup of chicken stock. Slowly bring this to a boil and, when the butter has melted, add the onions. Cover the pan, reduce the heat, and simmer them for about 30 minutes. Shake the pan gently or turn the onions with a spoon every now and then to keep them well moistened; if the stock in the pan cooks away, add a little more from the veal in the casserole. The onions are done when they can be pierced easily with a pointed knife but are still slightly resistant to the touch. Remove them from the pan with a slotted spoon and put them aside in a small bowl.

Now stir a teaspoon of lemon juice into the stock remaining in the pan, bring it to a boil, and add the mushrooms. Cook them briskly for about 5 minutes, then remove them also from the pan with a slotted spoon and put them aside with the onions. Pour the remaining liquid into the simmering casserole.

When the veal is tender but still slightly firm, remove the pieces from the casserole with tongs and leave them in a bowl while you prepare the sauce.

Begin by straining the veal stock in the casserole through a fine sieve into a 2- or 3-quart saucepan; press down on the vegetables with the back of a spoon to extract every bit of their juice before throwing them away. Bring the stock to a boil, and boil it rapidly until it is reduced to exactly 2 cupfuls. (If you haven't the time, you may, of course, skip this step and use 2 cups of the stock as it is. But then the *velouté* sauce you are about to make will not be be the ideal.)

✱ *Melt the 3 tablespoons of butter in a small saucepan and, when it is melted but not brown, remove the pan from the heat and stir into it the 3 tablespoons of flour. Stirring constantly, cook this* roux *over low heat for about a minute without browning it, then pour over it the 2 cups of reduced veal stock. Raise the heat and bring the sauce to a boil, beating it all the while with a wire whisk until it is smooth and thick. Then lower the heat, and let the* velouté *simmer for about 15 minutes, skimming it every now and then of any scum which films the surface.*

Meanwhile, mix together in a small bowl the 2 or 3 egg yolks and the cup of cream. Stir into this a couple of tablespoons of the hot velouté *sauce; then reverse the process, and pour the egg mixture all into the pan of simmering sauce. Stirring constantly, cook over moderate heat until the sauce almost, but not quite reaches the boil. Remove it at once from the heat, and add to it the teaspoon of lemon juice, a touch of cayenne, and as much salt as you think it needs.*

182

Carefully drain the veal and the onions and mushrooms of any juices which may have collected in their respective bowls. Place meat and vegetables back in the original casserole, which you have first washed and dried. Pour the sauce over them and gently but thoroughly mix them together.

Heat once more, stirring occasionally, but don't let the sauce come to a boil. Make sure, however, that the meat is thoroughly heated through before you bring it to the table. Sprinkle the *blanquette* with the chopped parsley and serve it directly from the casserole, accompanied by hot boiled rice and crusty French or Italian bread.

AFTERTHOUGHTS:

✳ Should you make the *blanquette* in advance and wish to reheat it, allow a good 15 or 20 minutes of very slow, covered cooking for the meat and onions to heat through thoroughly. For reasons of flavor, it is not advisable to let the sauce boil, but no great tragedy takes place if it does; the flour in the *velouté* will be a safeguard against the egg yolks curdling. If the sauce is too thick after reheating, thin it with a little chicken stock or cream.

✳ *Blanquette de veau* is a most effective dish for a large buffet dinner. Serve it from two chafing dishes, one for the *blanquette* and the other for rice.

✳ For an unusual summer luncheon dish, try serving left-over *blanquette* chilled, sprinkled with minced chives or fresh dill, or a combination of both. A cold rice salad mixed with string beans or carrots and moistened with a tart *vinaigrette* dressing would be a fine way to use any left over rice. Garnish the *blanquette* with quarters of lemon.

✳ If you like the flavor of curry, you can transform your *blanquette de veau* into a *blanquette de veau à l'indienne* by adding 1 tablespoon, more or less, of good curry powder to the *velouté* sauce before you add the egg yolks and cream. The French meaning of *à l'indienne* is curry used as a seasoning, not as a hot spice.

✳

VEAL MARENGO

AT THIS point in history, the north Italian town of Marengo appears to be celebrated more for the chicken and veal dishes named after it than as the scene, so long ago, of Napoleon's victory over the Austrians. The famous story of Napoleon's chef, Dunand, inventing chicken Marengo on the spot for his famished master is surely more entertaining than accurate, for, truth to tell, the dish was well known before that as chicken *à la provençale*. And, like the chicken, veal Marengo is really a Provençal stew, composed of pieces of browned veal simmered in a sauce of wine, stock, tomatoes, and herbs and garnished with sautéed mushrooms.

] To serve six or eight [

3 pounds boneless leg or rump of veal, in one piece
4 tablespoons olive oil

2 tablespoons butter
¾ cup finely chopped onions
¼ cup finely chopped shallots
½ teaspoon finely chopped garlic

2 level tablespoons flour
1 teaspoon salt
½ teaspoon freshly ground black pepper
1 teaspoon thyme
½ cup dry white wine
1½ cups brown beef stock, fresh or canned
Two 2-inch strips lemon peel
1 cup canned drained tomatoes, coarsely chopped
A bouquet consisting of 4 sprigs parsley, 1 celery top,
     1 large bay leaf, all tied together
3 tablespoons butter
¾ pound fresh mushrooms

2 tablespoons finely chopped parsley

184

In place of the boneless leg or rump of veal, less expensive cuts may be used for veal Marengo. The characteristics of fine veal and how to select it are discussed at the beginning of the recipe for BLAN-QUETTE DE VEAU on page 180. Buy the meat in one piece, and cut it yourself into approximately 2-inch chunks.

Preheat the oven to **500°F.** In a large heavy frying pan, heat the 4 tablespoons of olive oil until it begins to smoke. Over fairly high heat, sauté the veal in this, a few pieces at a time, transferring them as they become dark brown on all sides to a 4- or 5-quart casserole. As you proceed, add more oil to the pan, if necessary.

When all the veal is browned, pour off and throw away all the oil in the frying pan, and in its place melt the 2 tablespoons of butter. Add the chopped onions, shallots, and garlic, and scrape into the mixture all the brown crust on the bottom and sides of the pan. Over low heat cook these slowly for about 10 minutes, until the onions are soft and quite brown; watch them, for they burn easily.

In the meantime, if you can do two things at once (if you can't, finish cooking the onions first and put them aside), add the 2 level tablespoons of flour to the veal waiting in the casserole. Sprinkle it also with the salt, pepper, and crumbled thyme and, with a large spoon, toss the pieces of meat around in the casserole until they are well coated with the flour and seasonings.

Place the casserole, uncovered, on the upper-third shelf of the hot oven for about 10 minutes, turning the meat over every few minutes until the pieces are slightly crusted and all trace of the gummy flour has disappeared. Remove the casserole from the oven and turn the heat down to **325°F.**

Now back to the frying pan: Pour into the browned onions the ½ cup of dry white wine and 1½ cups of stock. Again, scrape into this any brown crust in the pan, and bring the stock and onions to a boil over high heat. Let this bubble a couple of minutes, then pour it all into the casserole, using a rubber spatula to scrape the frying pan absolutely clean.

Mix the meat, onions, and stock together gently but thoroughly, then stir in the chopped, drained tomatoes, the lemon peel and the bouquet. Heat the casserole slowly on top of the stove and, when it comes to a boil, cover it and place it on the center shelf of the **325°F.** oven. In about an hour (possibly a little longer), the veal will have become quite tender. Look at it every now and then, and turn the meat in the sauce to make sure it isn't sticking to the bottom of the pot.

At some point during this period, melt the 3 tablespoons of butter in the frying pan and stir in the mushrooms—whole, if small; quartered, if medium; or sliced, if large. Cook them briskly in the butter for about 3 minutes, turning them almost constantly with a large spoon. After the veal has cooked about 50 minutes, add the mushrooms to the casserole along with whatever liquid they have collected in the frying pan. Continue to cook the veal until it is tender but not falling apart. And the best way to test is to taste it.

Now for the final refinement: Set a large fine sieve over a saucepan, and pour or ladle into it the entire contents of the casserole. Let all the sauce drain through, then replace the veal and mushrooms in the casserole, which you will first have washed and dried. Discard the lemon peel and the bouquet.

Tip the saucepan slightly to one side and, with a large spoon, skim the surface of the sauce of as much fat as you can. Bring the sauce to a rapid boil over high heat, and let it cook down to about half its original amount, or until it is lightly thickened and intense in flavor. Taste to see if further seasoning is needed before pouring the sauce over the meat. There should be just enough to moisten the meat without drowning it.

On top of the stove, reheat the meat in the sauce and, just before serving, sprinkle the surface copiously with chopped parsley. Small pasta shells, with butter and cheese, and hot French or Italian bread are all you really need to go with this. For wine, serve a chilled bottle of a superior rosé.

186

AFTERTHOUGHTS:

❋ Veal Marengo reheats perfectly. If you plan to make it early in the day, undercook the veal slightly, it will continue to cook as it cools and, when you reheat it, will cook again.

❋ Braised little white onions, as they are prepared in the recipe for BEEF BOURGUIGNON on page 159, may be added to veal Marengo when you add the mushrooms. They make for a more substantial dish and are quite traditional.

OSSO BUCO

AT FIRST sight, *osso buco* hardly seems to justify its reputation as one of Italy's culinary masterpieces. But, properly prepared, these unprepossessing stubby pieces of veal shank braised in wine, vegetables, and tomatoes have a vigorous uncompromising appeal. The traditional garnish is *gremolata,* a colorful mixture of grated lemon rind, chopped garlic, and parsley.

It has been long suspected that the Italians invented *osso buco* as an elaborate excuse to consume the marrow hidden in the veal shinbone; hence its name, "hollow bone." The Milanese, who claim the dish as theirs, go to such lengths to extract the precious marrow that they have a needle-like instrument especially designed for the purpose which they call *stuzzica buco,* literally "pick-a-hole." This ingenious implement is not available in America, but in its place a lobster fork will serve almost as well.

] To serve six or eight [

6–7 pounds shin of veal, sawed, not chopped, into
eight 2½-inch pieces
Salt
Freshly ground black pepper
¾ cup flour
6–8 tablespoons olive oil

4 tablespoons butter
1 cup finely chopped onions
½ cup finely chopped carrots
½ cup finely chopped celery
1 large leek (white part only), finely chopped
1 teaspoon finely chopped garlic

¾ cup dry white wine
½ teaspoon dried basil
½ teaspoon thyme
¾ cup brown beef or chicken stock, fresh or canned
1½ pounds ripe tomatoes, peeled, seeded, and
    coarsely chopped (about 2 cups of pulp)
    or a large can of Italian plum tomatoes,
    drained and chopped
A bouquet consisting of 6 sprigs parsley and 2 large
    bay leaves, tied together

GREMOLATA:

1 teaspoon finely chopped garlic
1 tablespoon grated lemon rind
3 tablespoons finely chopped parsley

When you order your shin of veal from the butcher (he may call it a knuckle or shank, but it's the same thing), be sure that he has left enough meat on the bone to make your labors worthwhile, marrow aficionados notwithstanding. Wipe the pieces of meat with a damp cloth, pat them dry, and season them well with salt and freshly ground black pepper. Coat the pieces heavily with flour, then shake off the excess accumulation.

To braise *osso buco* properly, choose two large cooking utensils: a heavy cast-iron or cast-aluminum frying pan in which to brown the veal; and a large shallow casserole with a tightly fitting cover, or a covered roaster, in which to brown the vegetable bed upon which the veal will ultimately rest. It is important that the casserole or roaster be only large enough to hold the veal pieces tightly packed together in one layer.

Preheat the oven to **350°F.** In the large frying pan heat the 6 tablespoons of olive oil until it literally begins to smoke. Add a few pieces of the floured veal, and, over moderate heat, brown them on all sides as thoroughly as you can without burning them. As each piece is finished, transfer it to a large platter.

Meanwhile, over moderate heat, melt the 4 tablespoons of butter in the casserole. When the foam subsides, add the chopped onions, carrots, celery, leek, and garlic, and cook them rather slowly, turning them frequently with a wooden spoon, until all the vegetables are lightly colored.

Then, carefully arrange the browned pieces of veal upright on the bed of vegetables, packing them together closely so that they will, in effect, prop each other up; this will prevent the marrow as it cooks and shrinks from falling out of the bone.

Pour off all but a tablespoon or so of the oil remaining in the frying pan, and deglaze the pan by adding to it ¾ cup of white wine. Bring the wine to a boil, meanwhile scraping into it all the brown sediment clinging to the bottom and sides of the pan. When the wine has boiled down to about ½ cup, stir in the ½ teaspoon each of basil and thyme and ¾ of a cup of brown beef or chicken stock. Stirring constantly, bring the mixture to a boil, then pour it over the meat in the casserole. Scatter over the top the chopped, drained tomatoes, and submerge in the stock the bouquet of parsley and bay leaves. The liquid in the casserole should come halfway up the sides of the meat; if it doesn't, add a little more stock.

On top of the stove, bring the casserole to a full boil, then cover it and place it on the lower-third shelf of the preheated oven. After 15 minutes or so, baste the veal thoroughly with the braising liquid, and add some salt and pepper if you think it needs it. The stock should barely simmer, and if for some reason (too thin a pot, perhaps, or a faulty oven gauge) it seems to be cooking too fast, turn the heat down to **325°F.** or even lower. The slower *osso buco* braises, the better. Baste the meat thoroughly every 15 min-

189

utes or so, until the meat is tender but not falling from the bones. This should take anywhere from an hour and 15 minutes to an hour and a half, depending upon the quality of the veal.

To serve, remove the *osso buco* from the oven and raise the oven temperature to **475°F.** Carefully transfer the pieces of veal from the casserole to a large ovenproof platter, and try not to lose any of the marrow in transit. Glaze the veal on the upper-third shelf of the oven for 5 or 10 minutes, turning the heat down if the meat shows any sign of burning.

Meanwhile, strain the casserole juices and all the vegetables through a fine sieve into a small saucepan and, with a large spoon, press down hard on the vegetables to extract all their juice before throwing them away. Bring the sauce to a rapid boil and continue to boil until it has reduced to a little more than half its original quantity. It should then be lightly thickened and quite intense in flavor; if it isn't, boil it down even further.

Remove the platter of veal from the oven (the meat should have a light, brilliant glaze), and pour the reduced sauce over it, reserving a little to be passed separately if you wish. Sprinkle each piece of veal copiously with the *gremolata* and serve the *osso buco* with its traditional accompaniment, RISOTTO MILANESE (see p. 285). However, any kind of pasta dressed simply with butter and cheese would do almost as well.

AFTERTHOUGHTS:

✳ You may cook the *osso buco* hours in advance and reheat it slowly on top of the stove before serving. If you plan to do this, undercook the veal somewhat, for it will continue to cook as it cools and will cook a bit more when you reheat it.

✳ If you are pressed for time, you may serve the *osso buco* directly from its casserole and by-pass the glazing of the veal and the reduction of its juices, though the meat and sauce will both lack something in refinement.

✳ Cook the veal entirely on the top of the stove if you must, but make sure the pot is a heavy one and the cover secure. Keep the heat as low as possible.

✳ If you have the time and patience, before cooking the veal, tie each piece securely with kitchen cord. This will prevent the meat from coming away from the bone. Remove the strings carefully before serving.

✳ The *gremolata* may be omitted and chopped parsley alone used in its place. In that event, add a 3-inch strip of lemon peel to the casserole before it goes into the oven.

ROAST LARDED RACK OF VEAL

HERE is a spectacular roast of veal, little known, seldom served, and yet so easy to prepare and carve for the most elegant small dinner party. The rack consists of one side of the rib section of the calf, left in one piece. A knowing and skillful butcher will trim and shape it so that the exposed or "frenched" rib bones will stand up and away from the roast in straight formation, ready for their paper frills after the roast is done. The lardoons, strips of salt pork inserted through the center of the roast, supply the necessary fat to keep the normally lean veal moist and tender.

] To serve six or eight [

An 8-chop rib rack of veal weighing about 3½
    pounds
2 strips larding pork cut ⅛ inch wide and length of
    the rack
Optional: ½ teaspoon finely chopped garlic
    2 tablespoons finely chopped parsley
    ½ teaspoon freshly ground black pepper

Barding fat
½ cup thinly sliced onions
¼ cup thinly sliced carrot
¼ cup coarsely chopped celery
Salt

191

Freshly ground black pepper
1 cup dry white wine

1½ cups chicken stock, fresh or canned
¼ teaspoon lemon juice

A butcher who takes any pride in his work will have his own special way with a rack of veal and he will insist that his way is the best. Be that as it may, ask him firmly to saw off the backbone, or chine, as it is called, if he hasn't done so already. This will enable you later to carve the rack without having to hack through any bone. The end of each rib bone should be carefully "frenched"—that is, cleared of all fat, gristle, and meat, and cut down so that only about an inch of the bone still shows.

You may, if you like, have the butcher lard the veal for you. Ask him to insert the two lardoons about half an inch apart through the center of the meat. In that event you will have to omit the chopped garlic, parsley, and pepper. But if you own a larding needle, lard the meat yourself. Follow the directions for doing this on page 165 in the recipe for BEEF À LA MODE; before chilling the lardoons, roll each one in the mixed garlic, parsley, thyme and black pepper.

Finally, the meat itself should be covered with a thin sheet of barding fat, tied securely in several places along the length of the roast.

Preheat the oven to **450°F.** Choose a shallow roasting pan just about large enough to hold the veal, and do not use a rack in it. Lay the meat in the pan, and sear it in the hot oven for about 15 minutes, or until it is lightly browned all over. Remove the pan from the oven and turn the heat down to **350°F.**

Scatter around the veal the sliced onions, carrots, and celery. Insert the meat thermometer, if you are going to use one, lengthwise into the widest part of the meat, and make sure the tip doesn't touch any bone. Pour into the pan ¼ cup of the white wine, sprinkle the veal with salt and some freshly ground black pepper, and return the pan to the center shelf of the oven.

192

Roast the veal uncovered, basting it every 15 minutes or so with the drippings in the pan. Pour another ¼ cup of wine into the pan after each basting until the whole cup has been used, and baste with the drippings thereafter. The veal should take about an hour and 40 minutes to reach an internal temperature of **170°F.**, indicating that it is fully cooked. Don't allow the veal to cook much beyond this or it will be dry and stringy.

When it is done, remove the veal to a board and cut away the strings and any stray bits of fat. Then transfer the rack to a large heated platter and cover each exposed rib bone with a paper frill. Let it rest for 5 minutes to make for easier carving and meanwhile prepare the sauce.

Pour into the roasting pan the 1½ cups of chicken stock. On the top of the stove, bring it rapidly to a boil, and scrape into it all the brown crust on the bottom and sides of the pan. Boil furiously for 2 or 3 minutes, or until the sauce has reduced to about half its original quantity. Then strain it through a fine sieve into a small saucepan, and press down hard on the vegetables in the sieve before throwing them away. Skim most, but not all the fat off the sauce, add the lemon juice, taste for seasoning, and heat once more before pouring it into a sauceboat.

Carve the rack into chops at the table and moisten each chop with a small spoonful of hot sauce before you serve it; pass the rest separately.

AFTERTHOUGHTS:

✳ A colorful accompaniment to the veal would be TOMATOES NIÇOISE (page 271) if you haven't used the chopped garlic on the lardoons; or broiled tomatoes if you have. Surround the rack with a circle of alternating tomatoes and sprays of water cress.

✳ You may omit larding the veal altogether if it is impracticable. But be sure, then, to baste the meat constantly and thoroughly.

✳ You might ask the butcher to wrap the rack in a caul instead of barding fat. The likelihood is that the butcher won't know what you are talking about, but if he does he can probably get one for you from a slaughterhouse. Without going into anatomical detail, the caul is a membrane that will seal in all the veal juices and, moreover, will have a wonderful flavor and crisp texture of its own.

GALANTINE OF VEAL

THERE are few culinary constructions, in any cuisine, quite as ingenious as the French galantine. Ordinarily made of a boned domestic or game bird, stuffed and shaped into a sausagelike cylinder, it is an intricate and demanding creation. This galantine of veal is considerably less complex and well within the range of an adventurous or even average cook. A shoulder of veal is boned and trimmed, and the opening is filled with a savory stuffing of ground veal and pork, cubes of ham and tongue, and truffles and pistachio nuts. In classical galantines, the solid meats are arranged in the ground stuffing in such a way as to form precisely composed designs when the galantine is sliced. In this version, the meats, truffles, and nuts are scattered throughout the stuffing at random, and the arbitrary patterns they create in each slice are, in fact, more interesting and colorful than the more formal arrangements.

Galantines are usually poached, but here the veal galantine is braised to give it more flavor. It makes its dramatic appearance, finally, masked with a golden, jellied *chaud-froid* sauce composed of the braising liquid, eggs, heavy cream, and gelatine.

] To serve ten or twelve [

A boned shoulder of veal, weighing about 5 pounds
    after boning

STUFFING:

½ pound veal (trimmings from the shoulder), ½
    pound fresh pork, and ½ pound fresh pork fat,
    all ground together twice

194

4 tablespoons butter
½ cup chopped onions
¼ cup chopped shallots
1 teaspoon chopped garlic
¼ cup cognac

1½ tablespoons salt
Freshly ground pepper
1 teaspoon thyme
2 tablespoons finely chopped parsley

2 egg whites
½ cup heavy cream

¼ pound boiled ham and ¼ pound cooked tongue,
    cut into ½-inch cubes
2 or 3 canned black truffles, coarsely chopped
2 tablespoons shelled whole pistachio nuts

FOR BRAISING:

¼ pound fresh pork fat, diced
    or 3 tablespoons vegetable oil and 2 tablespoons
    butter
3 tablespoons butter
2 medium onions, 2 medium carrots, and 3 stalks
    celery, all thickly sliced
½ cup dry white wine
1½ cups beef stock, fresh or canned
1 teaspoon salt
Freshly ground pepper
1 bay leaf

CHAUD-FROID:

1½ cups braising sauce (from the braising casserole,
    above)
1 tablespoon plus 1 teaspoon gelatine
1/3 cup cold water

3 egg yolks
1 cup heavy cream
Salt
⅛ teaspoon cayenne
1 egg white

Garnishes (see p. 200)

The ease with which you are able to stuff and shape the shoulder will depend in great measure on how skillfully your butcher has boned and trimmed it. Ask him to avoid tearing the surface of the meat when he removes the bones and to trim each side of the shoulder by cutting off the shank meat on the wider end and the blade bone on the other. In this way the meat should finally approximate the shape of a long rectangular muff, open on both short ends. Ask the butcher then to enlarge the pocket as much as he can by cutting, inside the meat, to within about half an inch of the surface along the long sides of the muff. This should give you a pouch large and secure enough to hold all the stuffing.

Plan on stuffing and braising the shoulder of veal a day before you intend to serve the galantine so that it can be properly chilled.
Start, with a large needle and strong white thread, by sewing up the blade or narrow end of the shoulder, darning along the way any rents in the body of the meat through which the stuffing might conceivably escape.

Despite the number of ingredients, the stuffing (called more properly, in this case, a meat mousse) is easy to make. Begin by putting the ground veal, pork, and pork fat in a large mixing bowl. In a small frying pan, melt the 4 tablespoons of butter and cook in it, over moderate heat, the chopped onions, shallots, and garlic until they are soft but not brown. Then pour the cognac into the pan and boil it for a couple of minutes; it should all but cook away. With a rubber spatula scrape the entire contents of the pan into the mixing bowl with the ground meat. Add the 1½

196

tablespoons of salt, a little freshly ground pepper, the thyme, and the chopped parsley.

Beat the mixture vigorously for about a minute with a large spoon (or in an electric mixer with a pastry-arm attachment). Still beating, add the egg whites, one at a time. When both are absorbed, beat in by spoonfuls the ½ cup of cream. At this point the stuffing should have a smooth, creamy look. Now mix, don't beat, the cubes of ham and tongue, the truffles, and the pistachio nuts into the mousse, stirring them gently until they are evenly dispersed.

To stuff the shoulder, salt and pepper the inside of the meat pocket. Then, dipping your hands occasionally in cold water, put in as much of the stuffing as the pocket will comfortably hold. The stuffing will expand as it cooks, so it is unwise to pack it in too tightly, great as the temptation may be.

With the needle and thread, sew up the open end of the veal as neatly and securely as possible, then pat the stuffed shoulder into as symmetrical a shape as you can. So that the galantine will keep its shape while cooking, tie it up with heavy white cord— once or twice lengthwise, and at intervals of an inch and a half or so all along it crosswise. Be sure to leave the strings the slightest bit slack so that the meat has room to expand as the stuffing swells.

Preheat the oven to **325°F.** To braise the veal you will need a heavy covered casserole or Dutch oven just about large enough to hold the meat and vegetables comfortably. And to give the veal its initial browning, you will need a large heavy frying pan.

Render the diced pork fat first by frying it slowly in the frying pan until the pieces turn crisp and brown, then remove them with a slotted spoon. Heat the rendered fat until it begins to smoke. Add the stuffed veal, and regulate the heat so that the meat browns fairly quickly without burning. Brown it thoroughly on all sides, turning it frequently with a clean towel or two large spoons. In the meantime, or, if you like, after the veal is browned, melt 3 tablespoons of butter in the casserole, and over moderate heat sauté the cut-up onions, carrots, and celery until they color lightly.

Carefully lift the browned veal out of the frying pan and place it on the bed of vegetables. Pour off most of the fat in the frying pan, and to the remaining drippings add the ½ cup of white wine and 1½ cups of stock. Bring this to a boil, meanwhile scraping into it all the brown sediment clinging to the bottom and sides of the pan. Let the stock boil a minute or two, then pour it over the meat in the casserole, salt and pepper the veal, and add the bay leaf.

Bring the casserole to a boil on top of the stove. Lightly drape a piece of aluminum foil over and around the meat inside the casserole (this is to concentrate the moisture over the meat). Cover the casserole, and place it on the lower-third shelf of the oven.

Baste the meat thoroughly every ½ hour with the braising liquid. At the end of about 1½ hours, remove the cover and the foil. For another and last ½ hour, baste the meat every 10 minutes until it is brightly glazed.

Now, with two large spoons or, better still, a thick clean kitchen towel, lift the galantine to a cake rack set in a large pan. Let it cool to room temperature, then add any drippings that accumulate in the pan to the braising liquid. Wrap the meat loosely in waxed paper and chill it.

Pour the entire contents of the casserole—braising liquid and vegetables—into a fine sieve set in a small bowl. Press down hard on the vegetables to extract every bit of their juice before throwing them away. Chill the braising liquid.

When you are ready to make the *chaud-froid,* some hours later or the next day, remove the layer of solid fat which will have formed on top of the chilled braising sauce. Dissolve the sauce in a saucepan over low heat, then measure it; you will need about 1½ cups. If there is too little, add more stock; if too much, either reduce the sauce by boiling it down to the proper amount, or remove the excess and use it for other sauces or gravies.

Sprinkle the 1 tablespoon plus 1 teaspoon of gelatine in 1/3 cup of water. While it softens, mix together the 3 egg yolks and 1 cup of heavy cream in a small bowl.

Bring the 1½ cups of braising sauce to a boil, and stir into it

198

the softened gelatine. Simmer a moment or two until the gelatine has thoroughly dissolved. Then add some of the hot sauce, a table-spoon at a time, to the egg-and-cream mixture. After the fourth tablespoon, reverse the process, and pour the now heated cream into the sauce remaining in the saucepan.

Cook this over low heat, stirring constantly until it thickens lightly; in no circumstances allow the sauce to boil, or it will most assuredly curdle. Remove it from the heat at once, add salt and cayenne to taste, and continue to stir the finished *chaud-froid* to cool it a bit. Then set the pan in a larger pan filled with ice cubes or crushed ice.

Remove the veal from the refrigerator and place it again on the cake rack set in the large flat pan. Beat 1 egg white in a small bowl with a fork or whisk until it froths lightly, then spread it thinly over the meat with a pastry brush. This will prevent the chilled *chaud-froid* from coming away from the galantine when the meat is sliced.

Now, with a large metal spoon, stir the *chaud-froid* over the ice until it begins to thicken. This will take less time than you think. When it becomes syrupy and falls sluggishly from the spoon, pour it quickly over the veal, spoonful by spoonful, until the entire sur-face of the meat is lightly coated.

Should the sauce thicken too much or lump up unmanageably during this process, set the pan back over the heat briefly to warm it, and with a wire whisk beat the *chaud-froid* until it dissolves and smooths out again. Don't add any liquid to it! Set it over the ice again, if necessary, and proceed as before.

Place the veal in the refrigerator and, when the first coat of *chaud-froid* is set (only a matter of minutes), coat the veal again in the same manner, then refrigerate it again. You may continue this process indefinitely or, more realistically, until the sauce gives out. When the last coat is on, press lightly into the still soft *chaud-froid* whatever decorations (see AFTERTHOUGHTS) you think suita-ble, and return the galantine to the refrigerator to set for at least an hour or several hours before you serve it.

Don't attempt to transfer the galantine to its serving platter until the *chaud-froid* is absolutely firm. Surround the galantine with a wreath of chilled water cress if you wish, or one or several VEGETABLES À LA GRECQUE (page 26). For that matter, you may use any garniture that suits your fancy. But do accompany the galantine with a bowl of FRENCH POTATO SALAD (page 299) and hot, crusty French bread.

AFTERTHOUGHTS:

✳ Remove the thread from the chilled galantine before you coat it with the *chaud-froid*. It should come out easily but, if it doesn't, leave it be and remember when you slice the galantine to avoid serving the sewn ends to your guests.

✳ Decorate the galantine with cut slices of truffles arranged in fleur-de-lys patterns (truffle cutters in many such fanciful shapes are available in stores that specialize in foreign kitchen utensils); or with sprays of parsley, dill, or watercress, small dots or circles of pimientos, hard-cooked whites of egg, and the like.

✳ The jelled *chaud-froid* that has spilled down into the pan under the galantine during the coating process may be chopped and arranged around the meat to mask any unevenness along the bottom of the *chaud-froid* coating.

✳ Another simple decorative device is to mash a couple of hard-cooked egg yolks and a teaspoon of soft butter together to a paste, and to force this through a pastry bag fitted with a small plain or fancy tip. With this you can create all manner of floral arrangements, using parsley for stems and leaves.

✳ The braised galantine may be served hot if you wish, and it makes a most impressive dish. Let it rest for about 10 minutes or even longer after you remove it from the casserole, and serve it with a clear sauce made of the simmered and strained casserole juices, augmented, if necessary, with ½ cup or more of hot beef or chicken stock.

*

VITELLO TONNATO

THE ITALIAN notion of marinating cold cooked veal in a tuna-fish sauce is indeed a unique one. You will not easily forget the savor of *vitello tonnato* experienced for the first time on a warm summer day. Although there are definitive recipes for the dish in Italian cookbooks, its preparation is by no means consistent throughout Italy. Frequently, the veal is cooked with the tuna fish, either fresh or canned; more often, the ingredients are prepared separately and then combined. The following recipe is an unusual one. The veal is highly flavored and the sauce is smooth, creamy, and delicate.

] To serve eight [

3 pounds boneless veal, in one piece and securely tied
3 anchovy fillets, cut into 1-inch lengths
1 small clove garlic, cut into thin slivers

1 quart chicken stock, fresh or canned
2 cups dry white wine
2 cups cold water, or more
2 bay leaves
2 small carrots, cut up
3 stalks celery, cut up
2 medium onions, quartered
1 leek, white part only
5 sprigs parsley
10 whole peppercorns
Salt

SAUCE:

¾ cup olive oil
1 egg yolk
One 3-ounce can Italian tuna in olive oil

4 anchovy fillets, cut up
2 tablespoons lemon juice
⅛ teaspoon cayenne
¼ cup heavy cream
¼ cup cold veal stock (above), more or less
2 tablespoons capers, washed and drained

GARNISH:

2 tablespoons finely chopped parsley
1 small bunch green onions (scallions), sliced into
    thin rounds
4 ripe tomatoes, peeled, sliced, and chilled
2 lemons, quartered or sliced
2 hard-cooked eggs, quartered or sliced
Black Italian or Greek olives

Traditionally, *vitello tonnato* is made with a boned leg of veal. But like all boned and rolled meats, this tends to fall apart when it is sliced and is difficult to serve. A more practical though much more expensive cut is a solid, boneless piece of meat taken from the round. Get it if you can. Whatever cut you buy, be sure that every bit of the outer skin and fat is removed and that the meat is securely tied.

Make small incisions along the length of the meat with a small pointed knife, and in each one insert a piece of anchovy and a thin sliver of garlic. Blanch the veal by covering it with cold water and bringing it to a full boil, let it cook a moment or two, then pour off the water and the accumulated scum. Rinse the meat quickly in cold water and wash the pot.

Now start all over again, but this time cover the veal with the quart of chicken stock, fresh or canned, 2 cups of dry white wine, and 2 cups of water—or more if the meat isn't quite covered. Add the remaining ingredients: bay leaves, carrots, celery, onions, leek, parsley, peppercorns, and salt. Naturally, the amount of salt you use will be determined by the saltiness of the chicken stock.

Bring the pot to a boil, reduce the heat, and simmer slowly, partially covered, for about an hour and 40 minutes, or until the meat is tender but still firm. Remove the pot from the stove and cool the veal in the stock.

Meanwhile, prepare the tuna-fish sauce. It can be made in a matter of minutes if you own an electric blender; if you don't, with a little more effort it can be done almost as well with an electric mixer, or, if you must, by hand.

With the blender: Combine in the container the olive oil, egg yolk, tuna fish, anchovies, lemon juice, and cayenne, and blend only long enough to reduce this to a smooth purée. Transfer the mixture to a small bowl and slowly stir in the heavy cream. The sauce will still be rather thick. Thin it further by adding the cool veal stock, a couple of tablespoons at a time, mixing well after each addition. Use as much stock as you need to give the sauce the consistency of heavy cream; it should be just fluid enough to run off the spoon. If the sauce is too thick, it will not penetrate the veal while it is marinating but will merely coat it.

Wash the capers by running cold water through them in a small sieve. Drain well and mix them into the sauce.

With the mixer, or by hand: Shred and chop the tuna fish and anchovies, and force them through a fine sieve with the back of a large spoon. Beat the egg yolk until it is quite thick, then stir into it the tuna-anchovy purée, the lemon juice, and the cayenne. Beating all the while, add ¼ cup of the olive oil, a scant teaspoon at a time; then, still beating, slowly pour in the remaining ½ cup of oil, and beat vigorously until the sauce is smooth and thick. Mix in the cream and enough cool stock to thin the sauce as described before, and add the washed capers.

Remove the cooled meat from the stock and carve it into thin, even slices. Trim off any fat or gristle. Spread the bottom of a large shallow platter with a thin layer of the tuna fish sauce, and in it lay the slices of veal, side by side. Pour the rest of the sauce over them, spreading it carefully with a spatula so that each piece of meat is thoroughly masked. Cover the platter tightly with Saran wrap or waxed paper (this is important; any prolonged exposure to air will turn the sauce a dark, unattractive brown), and refrigerate overnight, or longer if possible.

Two or 3 hours before serving, remove the veal from the refrigerator and let it stand in a cool place until it reaches room temperature. If it is served too cold, most of its distinctive flavor will be dulled.

Arrange the slices of veal, slightly overlapping, down the center of a large platter, cover them with the sauce remaining on the first platter, and sprinkle with the parsley and green onions. Surround with the sliced chilled tomatoes, the lemon, hard-cooked eggs, and black olives, arranging them as decoratively as you can. Serve the *vitello tonnato* as a luncheon, dinner, or buffet dish, with hot garlic bread and a chilled Italian white wine, perhaps a dry Orvieto.

AFTERTHOUGHTS:

✻ The stock in which the veal was cooked has many uses. It can be reduced, clarified with egg whites, and, with the addition of gelatine, used as an aspic garnish for the platter of *vitello tonnato* or any number of other cold dishes. To do this, for each 2 cups of reduced veal stock use 1 beaten egg white and 1 teaspoon of gelatine softened in 2 tablespoons of cold chicken broth or water; follow the method described in the recipe for fish aspic on page 94, but do not use the additional seasonings listed there, as they are intended to produce an aspic of quite a different flavor.

✻ Or, you can use the strained veal stock as a base for the VEAL SOUP BAGRATION on page 56 or in any recipe calling for a strong, highly flavored white stock. A veal stock used in chicken dishes calling for stock is a luxury but not an uncommon ingredient in classic cooking.

✻ The stock will have still more flavor if you add to it, when you first cook the veal, a cut-up veal knuckle or any stray chicken parts or giblets you may have on hand. When the cooled veal is removed, simmer the veal knuckle and/or chicken bits in the stock an hour or two.

✻ *Vitello tonnato,* if properly covered and refrigerated, will keep for a week. Use leftovers as a first-course hors-d'oeuvre; or, as a cocktail accompaniment—cut the meat into small cubes, roll them first in the sauce, then in finely minced parsley and chives, then spear each one with a toothpick.

Lamb

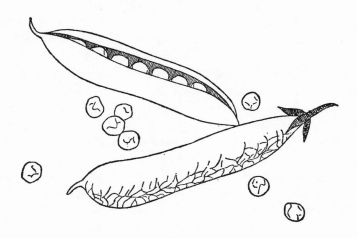

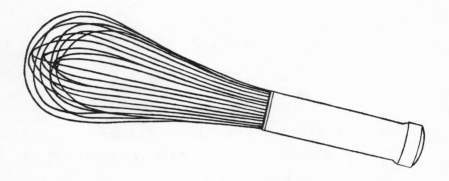

Most of the basic ways of cooking meats apply to lamb—broiling, pan broiling, roasting, stewing, or braising. The BROILED LEG OF LAMB is essentially a lamb steak, which you can cook with equal success in your kitchen or at an outdoor barbecue. The leg is boned, and instructions are given for doing this, though any good butcher should be willing to do it for you. For the BRAISED LEG OF LAMB À LA CUILLÈRE the meat should also be boned or it will be difficult to fit into the braising pot and difficult to carve. This is one of the five recipes for braised meat in this book (the others being BEEF À LA MODE, OSSO BUCO, GALANTINE OF VEAL, and BRAISED HAM; see Index); and, though all give quite different results, the essential process of cooking the browned meat with stock on a bed of sautéed vegetables recurs in each one.

The NOISETTES OF LAMB are small, boned, pan-broiled chops— very simple but an exercise in timing as the meat must be brown but lightly pink in the center. This is much easier to do in a skillet than in a broiler. With the *noisettes* is served the great classic egg-and-butter sauce, *sauce béarnaise,* which more usually accompanies beef *tournedos* and filets mignons. *Béarnaise* is not as difficult to make as most people think, but the present recipe includes special instructions to make it absolutely foolproof.

The NAVARIN is a delicate "brown stew" (see page 175) of spring lamb and another exercise in timing, this time in the handling of the several spring vegetables that are added to it. The ROAST SAD-DLE OF LAMB is a dinner-party showpiece; technically the most interesting thing about it is the way the fillets of the saddle are carved lengthwise with the grain, yielding handsome slices despite the comparatively small size of the cut of lamb.

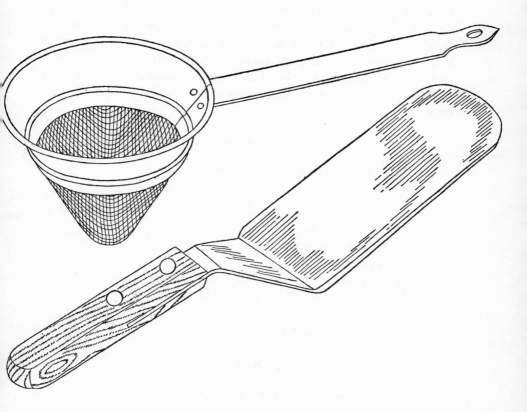

AVGOLEMONO SAUCE, the Greek egg-and-lemon sauce that is served with the broiled leg of lamb, has many other uses—notably for vegetables (asparagus, broccoli, artichokes, new potatoes) and any plain broiled or poached fish or chicken.

*

BROILED LEG OF LAMB WITH AVGOLEMONO SAUCE

ONCE YOU have broiled a boned leg of lamb, it is safe to predict that you won't want to cook it any other way again, at least for a while. Because it is subjected to rapid, continuous searing, the meat emerges literally bursting with its own juices. And you don't have to worry about it being too pink for one person or too well-done for another. Unlike a steak, the surface of a boned leg of lamb is uneven, varying in thickness from half an inch to three or four inches. When it is broiled, the meat will be simultaneously pink, medium, and well done, depending on the section you are carving.

] To serve six or eight [

6- to 7-pound leg of lamb, boned

MARINADE:

2/3 cup olive oil
3 tablespoons lemon juice
1 teaspoon salt
½ teaspoon freshly ground black pepper
2 tablespoons coarsely chopped parsley
1 teaspoon dried orègano
3 bay leaves, coarsely crumbled
1 cup thinly sliced onions
3 cloves garlic, thinly sliced

2 teaspoons coarse salt or 1 teaspoon ordinary salt

SAUCE:

3 egg yolks
1 tablespoon lemon juice
1 level teaspoon arrowroot
1 teaspoon salt

⅛ teaspoon cayenne
1 cup chicken stock, fresh or canned
1 tablespoon finely chopped parsley

Most butchers will bone a leg of lamb for you but, if for some reason you can't get it done, turn to page 227 and follow the directions for boning the leg yourself. It's not at all difficult and worth learning to do.

When the leg has been boned, it will be a fairly compact piece of meat with a large empty pocket. With a sharp knife cut down lengthwise through the thinnest side of the pocket and spread the leg out flat, fat side down. Cut away any clumps of exposed fat, then turn the meat over. If the butcher has not already done so, peel off the parchmentlike covering of the leg called the fell, and slice away most of the fat beneath it. The leg, in its present state, will be an unprepossessing sight indeed, ragged and uneven; but don't waste any time attempting to make it more presentable. It will look fine after it is marinated and broiled.

Marinate the lamb for at least 12 hours, preferably 24. Combine in a large shallow baking dish the olive oil, lemon juice, salt, pepper, parsley, orègano, and crumbled bay leaves. Mix them together thoroughly, then add the onions and garlic. Lay the meat in this and spoon some of the marinade over it. Every few hours turn the meat over. The marinade works best at room temperature, but if your kitchen is too warm, the meat will have to be refrigerated at least part of the time. In that case, remember to let the lamb come to room temperature before broiling it.

From start to finish, a 6-pound leg of lamb should take about 30 minutes to broil properly, after allowing 15 minutes to preheat the broiler to its maximum heat. It is well to be precise about this, for the lamb must be served as soon as it is done.

Without drying the meat, lay it, fat side down, on the hot broiler rack placed about 4 inches below the heat. Sprinkle the meat with about a teaspoon of coarse salt or ½ a teaspoon of ordinary salt,

209

and broil it for about 15 minutes. Don't baste it, but watch it carefully. If, at any point, the lamb shows signs of burning (some broilers are unpredictably hotter than others), turn the heat down a few degrees. At the end of 15 minutes, the surface of the lamb should be quite brown and charred attractively here and there.

With a pair of large tongs—not a fork—turn the meat over and moisten it with a few tablespoons of the marinade. Sprinkle the remaining salt over it, and broil for about 12 minutes. Now if you have any doubt about the state of the lamb before you remove it from the broiler, with a small sharp knife make a tiny incision in the thickest part; if it is too red, broil it a few minutes longer. Ideally, when it is sliced, the lamb should be a pale pink rimmed with a dark brown crust; there should be the slightest suggestion of red in the center. But this is really a matter of taste. The thinner areas of the leg will be quite well done, and there will be enough of it to take care of those who prefer it that way.

Have ready a hot serving platter when you remove the meat to a carving board. Carve the leg against the grain into quarter-inch slices, and lay them overlapping on the hot platter. Moisten the slices with whatever juices have collected on the board, and serve at once on warmed plates. Pass the following sauce separately.

✳ *The* avgolemono *sauce may be made while the lamb is broiling, or earlier if you prefer. Combine in the top of a double boiler the 3 egg yolks, the tablespoon of lemon juice, the level teaspoon of arrowroot, and the salt and cayenne. Beat together lightly with a wire whisk, then slowly stir in the cup of chicken stock. Stirring constantly, cook the sauce directly over moderate heat until it begins to thicken. In no circumstances let it come anywhere near the boil, or you will end up with lemon-flavored scrambled eggs. When the sauce has thickened sufficiently to cling to the back of a spoon, remove the pot from the heat and set it over hot, but not boiling water in the lower part of your double boiler. This will keep the sauce warm until you are ready to use it. Stir the chopped parsley into the sauce just before pouring it into a hot sauceboat.*

210

AFTERTHOUGHTS:

✳ If a 6- or 7-pound leg of lamb is too much for your immediate use, cut off the shank end and all the irregularly shaped pieces of the boned meat. Marinate these with the leg itself but cook them another time as shish kebob. Let them remain in the marinade as long as you like, and when you are ready to use them, cut them into small uniform cubes. String them on small skewers, brush each cube with marinade, and broil close to the heat for no more than 3 or 4 minutes on each side.

✳ Left-over broiled lamb may be cut into thin slices, spread lightly with mustard, and then coated with fine bread crumbs. Fry the slices quickly in clarified butter (page 81) or in a mixture of equal parts of butter and vegetable oil. *Avgolemono* sauce is good with this, too.

✳ If you can get it, add a few leaves of chopped fresh mint to the sauce along with the parsley.

NOISETTES OF LAMB ON CROUTONS
WITH BÉARNAISE SAUCE

UNFAMILIAR to many Americans, *noisettes* of lamb are less mysterious than they sound—they are merely boned loin lamb chops, trimmed of all fat and gristle and tied into small compact rounds. Obviously not for the budget-minded, these make a royal dish indeed and well deserve the homage of that aristocrat of sauces, *sauce béarnaise,* a shallot- and tarragon-flavored hollandaise.

] To serve six [

12 boned loin lamb chops
3 tablespoons butter
2 tablespoons vegetable oil

211

CROUTONS:

12 crustless rounds white bread
6–8 tablespoons clarified butter

SAUCE BÉARNAISE:

¼ cup tarragon vinegar
¼ cup dry white wine
2 tablespoons finely chopped shallots
2 small cloves garlic, unpeeled
½-inch piece bay leaf
1 tablespoon finely chopped fresh tarragon
    or 1 teaspoon dried crumbled tarragon
6 whole peppercorns
Pinch of thyme

3 egg yolks
1 tablespoon cold butter
1 tablespoon heavy cream

¼ pound unsalted butter, melted
Salt
Cayenne
Lemon juice
1 tablespoon finely chopped fresh tarragon
    or 1 tablespoon finely chopped parsley

Ask your butcher to prepare lamb *noisettes* for you from the loin, to trim them well, and to cut them no more than an inch thick; if they are thicker, you will have difficulty pan-frying them. Then have a thin strip of larding fat—lamb, beef, or fresh pork—tied securely around each one. The *noisettes* will take only about 10 or 12 minutes to cook; it is wise, therefore, to have the croutons and *béarnaise* made ahead of time and either kept warm or ready to reheat just before serving.

With a fluted or plain cooky cutter, the rim of a glass or an empty can, cut out crustless rounds of good white bread approximately the same size as the *noisettes*. Pour enough clarified butter (turn to page 81 if you have any doubts about this) into a large heavy frying pan to film the bottom lightly. Heat until sizzling, add the croutons, and fry them briefly until they are lightly browned on each side, adding more butter as it is needed. Drain the croutons on paper towels.

✳ *For the sauce, combine in a small enamel or stainless steel saucepan the vinegar, wine, shallots, garlic, bay leaf, tarragon, peppercorns, and thyme. Bring this to a boil, then reduce the heat, and simmer it slowly, uncovered, until the liquid in the pan has reduced to about 2 tablespoons or a little less. Strain this through a fine sieve into a cup, pressing down hard on the herbs with the back of a spoon. If you end up with more than 2 tablespoons of liquid, return it to the pan and boil it vigorously to reduce it further. Let it cool.*

Meanwhile, cut the quarter pound of butter into small pieces, and melt it slowly in a saucepan without letting it brown. In another small enamel pan, preferably a heavy one, beat the 3 egg yolks with a wire whisk until they are thick, then beat in the 2 tablespoons of reduced wine and vinegar.

Place the pan over moderate heat, add the tablespoon of cold butter and, with a whisk, stir constantly until the eggs begin to thicken and the butter is absorbed. Lift the pan off the heat every few second to cool it. If the eggs get too hot, they will curdle and the sauce will be ruined irretrievably, but if you proceed slowly and deliberately, this is not likely to happen. When the eggs have thickened enough to cling to the whisk, remove the pan from the heat and beat in a tablespoon of cold heavy cream.

Still off the heat, immediately start beating in the hot melted butter, pouring it over the eggs first in drops, then in a slow steady stream—the slower the better. It isn't essential, but you will have a better sauce if you don't beat in the milky substance or whey remaining on the bottom of the pan of butter. (In other words, you will be making the sauce with clarified but-

ter.) By now the sauce should be smooth, shiny, and thick. Stir in as much salt and cayenne as you think it needs, a few drops of lemon juice, and finally the chopped fresh tarragon or parsley.

If the béarnaise *is not to be used immediately, set the pan in a bowl of warm, not hot water, and cover it tightly with Saran wrap. It can remain this way safely for at least an hour. As the water cools, change it from time to time so the temperature remains fairly constant. Don't ever attempt to serve the* béarnaise *hot or it will most assuredly separate. Serve it warm in a heated sauceboat.*

Noisettes of lamb are best pan-fried rather than broiled. In a large heavy frying pan, heat the 3 tablespoons of butter and 2 tablespoons of vegetable oil until the fat sizzles. When the foam subsides, add the *noisettes* and cook them a minute on each side to sear them, then reduce the heat to moderate and cook them about 5 minutes on each side. At the end of this time they will be brown and crusty on the outside and slightly pink within. If you intend to leave the outer rings of fat on the *noisettes* when you serve them, turn them on their sides like cartwheels and brown the edges all around before removing them from the pan.

You will, meanwhile, have reheated the croutons and heated an ovenproof platter in a slow oven. When the *noisettes* are done, remove the strings and place each *noisette* on its individual crouton. Top each one with a spoonful of *béarnaise,* and decorate the platter with sprigs of crisp water cress. With it, serve small sautéed potato balls, hot French bread and a dry red wine. Pass the remaining *béarnaise* separately.

AFTERTHOUGHTS:

✳ Although this is not suggested with much enthusiasm, the flap of the boned chop may be left attached to the *noisette* for greater economy. Before he winds it around the kernel of meat, have the butcher trim it thoroughly of all fat and gristle or it will be tough and unpalatable.

✳ *Noisettes* may also be made with rib chops if the circle of meat is large enough.

✳ If the *béarnaise* sauce is too thick for your taste (there are thick and thin schools), thin it to the consistency you like with spoonfuls of warm, not hot heavy cream, stirring it in a little at a time.

✳ You may vary the flavor of the *béarnaise* by stirring into it when it is finished a teaspoon or more of commercial meat essence (BV) dissolved in a tablespoon of warm stock or water.

✳ *Sauce béarnaise* is appropriate on any broiled or pan-fried steak. The Belgians serve it also with broiled or roast chicken. And it is delicious on any fish that can be broiled, such as salmon, swordfish, or tuna.

ROAST SADDLE OF LAMB PERSILLÉ

IF A RIB roast of beef is the king of roasts, as has often been said, then a saddle of lamb is certainly the queen. It has all the necessary qualifications, ranging from its delicate flavor to its rather formidable cost. For those of you who love lamb and have never tasted the saddle, the only way to describe it adequately is to imagine the pleasure, exquisitely prolonged, of eating a thick loin lamb chop served to you in long, pink, succulent slices. And, in effect, that is what the saddle is—the two sides of the loin connected by the backbone left in one piece. The long slices result from carving the meat lengthwise, with the grain.

] To serve six [

8-pound saddle of lamb
2 tablespoons softened butter
Salt
Freshly ground pepper

2 medium carrots, cut into 1-inch pieces
2 stalks celery, cut into 1-inch pieces
2 medium onions, sliced

1 cup bread crumbs
¼ pound sweet butter
1 teaspoon finely chopped garlic
¼ cup finely chopped parsley
1 teaspoon salt
½ teaspoon freshly ground pepper
1 tablespoon lemon juice

1½ cups chicken stock, fresh or canned

Water cress

Don't let your butcher or anyone else talk you into having the saddle of lamb boned. Although it makes for easier carving, boning the saddle destroys much of the special flavor and character of the roast.

The most effective way to dress a saddle for roasting is the simplest: Have the butcher trim off the flanks if they are too long, so that they just meet when they are tucked under the loins. The kidneys and almost all the fat inside the saddle should be removed and only a thin layer of fat left on the outside. Have the meat tied in three or four places, but not too tightly.

The meat should be brought to room temperature before you roast it. Preheat the oven to **475°F.** Rub the meat all over with the 2 tablespoons of softened butter and place it, unseasoned, in a shallow roasting pan just about large enough to hold it. A rack under the roast in this case is not only unnecessary but undesirable. However, a meat thermometer is a must; the chance of error with approximate timing per pound is too great and the saddle must *not* be overcooked. Insert the thermometer as far as it will go into the exposed meat at one end of the saddle, and don't let the tip touch any bone.

Put the meat in the oven and let it cook undisturbed for 15

216

minutes. Now lower the heat to **425°F.** Salt and pepper the meat, scatter the cut-up carrots, celery, and onions around it, and baste the vegetables with the accumulated fat in the pan. Return the meat to the oven and roast it uncovered, basting it occasionally with the drippings, until the thermometer reads **140°F.** This should take approximately 1 hour and 10 minutes, but don't count on it. It may take a little less or a little more time, depending on the thickness of the loins. Check the thermometer after the saddle has cooked for an hour.

In the meantime, prepare the bread-crumb mixture. Avoid if you can commercially prepared bread crumbs; they are almost totally lacking in flavor and, for this purpose, too finely ground. Make your own, preferably from hard French or Italian bread. Grate it in the electric blender or with a hand grater, then shake the crumbs through a not too fine sieve.

Cream the ¼ pound of butter by mashing it against the sides of a small bowl with a large wooden spoon until it is soft and pliable. Mix into it the cup of bread crumbs, the lemon juice, garlic, parsley, salt, and pepper, and stir gently until everything is well combined.

When the meat thermometer does read **140°F.** remove the saddle from the oven, and raise the oven temperature to **500°F.** Now coat the saddle with the bread crumbs: Start by removing the meat thermometer and the strings tied around the meat. Place the saddle on a rack you can fit onto a baking sheet; a large cake rack is fine for this if you have one. Carefully spread the crumb mixture all over the surface of the lamb, patting it on firmly with your fingers or a spatula so that it will stick. It doesn't matter much if it is not evenly applied—it will spread out as it cooks.

Return the saddle to the **500°F.** oven. In a short time the coating will begin to color lightly. Watch it carefully after the first 5 minutes, for it burns easily. When the crumbs have become a golden brown all over, remove the saddle from the oven and transfer it cautiously to a heated platter; try not to dislodge the crumbs in the process, though you are bound to lose a few. Surround the saddle with fresh crisp water cress. It should rest for 5 minutes or more before you bring it to the table.

Meanwhile, make a clear gravy in the roasting pan. Remove most, but not all of the fat from the pan, and pour over the vegetables left in it the 1½ cups of chicken stock. Bring this to a boil over high heat, meanwhile scraping into it all the brown crust clinging to the bottom of the pan where the saddle rested. Boil this steadily until the liquid is reduced to about a cup. Taste the sauce for seasoning, then strain it through a fine sieve into a sauceboat, pressing down hard on the vegetables with a large spoon to extract all their liquid before throwing them away.

Carve the saddle at the table, and have ready a second heated platter. Steady the roast with a fork plunged into the center of the back, and, with the sharpest possible carving knife, locate the ridge on either side of the backbone. At this point, cut down through the meat holding the flat of the knife against the bone; follow the bone's contours until the whole eye of the loin is detached. Lay this on the extra platter, and proceed in similar fashion on the other side.

Now turn the saddle over on its back. Here, tucked into the cavities on either side of the backbone will be the two small fillets. Carve them each out carefully in one piece, again remembering to hold the flat of the knife against the bone as a guide. Then carve the meat into long, not-too-thin slices, and sprinkle each portion with some of the crumb mixture that will have fallen onto the platter.

Pass the clear gravy separately. POTATOES ANNA (see page 278) and artichoke bottoms filled with buttered peas would be worthy accompaniments, and a red Bordeaux the ideal wine.

AFTERTHOUGHTS:

✳ Since the carving may take more time than you anticipate, it is wise to have the platters, plates, and clear gravy as hot as possible. In any case, warm plates are a good idea, particularly for carved meats of any kind.

✻ Vary the bread-crumb coating by adding to it either tarragon, rosemary, or thyme—1 teaspoon of a dried herb or 1 tablespoon of the fresh.

✻ The *persillé* coating may be left off the saddle altogether if you prefer. In that event, roast the saddle until the meat thermometer reads **150°F.** for medium rare.

✻ The flanks of the saddle are not usually served, but you may do so if you wish. Or reserve them for another meal: Cut them into small squares, paint each one with a little mustard, coat them lightly with bread crumbs (either the same *persillé* mixture or plain buttered crumbs), and broil or sauté them to a golden brown. Accompany with melted butter seasoned with a little lemon juice and chopped parsley.

NAVARIN OF LAMB

HERE again is an example of the French genius for transforming the simplest ingredients into a dish of extraordinary individuality and flavor. To describe a *navarin* flatly as a lamb stew does it scant justice, for its quality is such that all stews might well be measured against it. And not least among its virtues is its low cost. Although the cooking procedures are demanding, the *navarin* may be prepared hours or even a day ahead and reheated very successfully. Moreover, it may be served directly from the casserole for informal dinners or, with no change in its composition, presented elaborately on more formal occasions.

] To serve six or eight [

3 pounds boned shoulder of lamb, ½ pound breast
   of lamb, ½ pound neck of lamb, all cut into
   2-inch chunks
½ pound fresh pork fat, cut into small dice

1 teaspoon salt
Freshly ground pepper
1 teaspoon thyme
3 level tablespoons flour

½ cup finely chopped shallots
1 teaspoon finely chopped garlic
3 cups fresh brown beef stock
    or 2 cups condensed canned beef bouillon and
    1 cup canned chicken stock
¾ pound ripe tomatoes, peeled, seeded, and coarsely
    chopped *or* 1 cup drained canned tomatoes
1 teaspoon tomato paste
A bouquet consisting of 2 celery tops, 4 sprigs parsley,
    1 large leek (white part only), a large bay leaf,
    all tied together

VEGETABLES:

6 tablespoons butter (¾ stick)
16 small white onions, all approximately 1 to 1½
    inches in diameter, peeled and left whole
6–8 small white turnips, about 2 inches in diameter
    or 3 large turnips, quartered
16 two-inch lengths of carrots about 1 inch thick
16 small new potatoes
    or larger potatoes, quartered or cut into 2-inch
    dice
1 pound fresh peas
    or ½ box frozen peas
½ pound fresh string beans, cut into 1-inch pieces
    or ½ box frozen cut string beans

2 tablespoons finely chopped parsley

The fat in which the lamb is browned will determine to a noticeable degree the flavor and color of the *navarin* when it is done.

220

Fresh pork fat is decidedly worth making the effort to render; because it takes heat well, you can brown the lamb in it thoroughly without burning it. And, even more important, pork fat forms a dark, delicious glaze on the bottom of the sautéing pan.

Render the diced pork fat by frying it in a large heavy frying pan over moderate heat. Stir it with a wooden spoon until most of the solid fat has dissolved, then scoop up the brown bits with a slotted spoon and throw them away. Pour the rendered fat into a small bowl.

Wipe the pieces of lamb with a damp cloth, and pat them dry with paper towels; they won't brown well if they are damp. Simultaneously, preheat the oven to **500°F.** In the large frying pan, heat enough pork fat to film the bottom of the pan until it is almost smoking. Sauté the lamb in this, four or five pieces at a time (more than that will reduce the heat of the pan too much), adjusting the heat so that the lamb browns quickly but doesn't burn. Each piece of lamb should have a fine, dark crust on all sides before you remove it with kitchen tongs to a 6- or 8-quart casserole or Dutch oven.

When all the lamb has been browned, pour off and discard all but about a tablespoon of the fat from the frying pan, and let the pan cool a bit. Meanwhile, sprinkle over the lamb in the casserole the teaspoon of salt, a few grindings of black pepper, a teaspoon of thyme (rub it between your fingers), and the 3 level tablespoons of flour. With a large spoon turn the lamb over and over until it is thoroughly coated with the flour and seasonings.

Place the casserole, uncovered, on the center shelf of the oven, and let the floured lamb brown for about 10 minutes, until the flour forms a light brown crust on the meat. Watch carefully for any sign of burning and reduce the heat if necessary. After 5 minutes or so, turn the meat up from the bottom with a large spoon to expose the pieces underneath to the heat. Remove the casserole from the oven, and immediately turn the temperature down to **325°F.**

While the lamb is in the oven, stir into the tablespoon of fat remaining in the frying pan the ½ cup of chopped shallots and the teaspoon of garlic. Cook over moderate heat for about 3 minutes, scraping up the brown glaze from the bottom of the pan with a large spoon or metal spatula. When the shallots are a delicate brown, pour over them the 3 cups of stock and bring it to a boil. Continue to scrape the bottom of the pan until all the glaze has dissolved in the stock, turning it a deep russet brown. Stir in the tomatoes and tomato paste, bring the stock once more to a boil, then lower the heat and simmer slowly for 3 or 4 minutes.

Now pour the entire contents of the frying pan over the meat in the casserole, and with a large spoon gently mix all together. Push the herb bouquet down into the stock. Bring the casserole to a boil on top of the stove, cover it tightly and slide it onto the center shelf of the oven. It should now simmer for about 45 minutes, or until the lamb is about three quarters done.

Melt 6 tablespoons of butter over moderate heat in a large frying pan. When the foam subsides, add the onions, carrots, turnips, and potatoes, all of which should be wiped bone dry if you want them to brown attractively. Sprinkle them with a little salt, and cook the vegetables briskly for about 7 or 8 minutes, stirring them or shaking the pan almost constantly. When you remove the pan from the heat, each vegetable should be glistening with melted butter and lightly colored here and there.

The fresh peas and string beans may be cooked at the same time. Bring a saucepan of cold water to a rolling boil, salt it lightly, and throw in the shelled peas and the beans. Boil them briskly, uncovered, until the string beans are tender but still quite firm (the peas will be done at the same time). Drain them immediately in a sieve, then plunge the sieve into a bowl of cold water; this will stop their cooking and leave them a bright fresh green. Drain the vegetables again and put them aside until later.

If you intend to use frozen peas and string beans, they needn't be cooked, but simply defrosted. They will be heated through and cooked briefly before you serve them.

Remove the lamb from the oven at the end of its 45 minute cooking time. Set a large fine-meshed sieve or colander over a big mixing bowl, and carefully pour the lamb and all its juices into it. Let the gravy drain into the bowl while you scrub the casserole thoroughly.

Put the sautéed vegetables (but not the peas and string beans) in the bottom of the clean casserole. With tongs, pick the lamb out of the sieve, piece by piece, and arrange it on top of the vegetables. With a large spoon, skim the gravy of most of its fat, add some salt if you think it needs it, and pour it over the meat and vegetables in the casserole.

Bring the stew to a boil on top of the stove, then cover it and return it again to the oven. In about half an hour, or perhaps 40 minutes, the vegetables should be tender and the *navarin* done. Ten minutes before that time, stir into it gently the peas and string beans.

If you intend to serve the *navarin* directly from the casserole, merely sprinkle it with the chopped parsley, and serve it on hot plates, with plenty of hot French or Italian bread. If you want to present it more dramatically, have ready a large, fairly deep heated platter. Mound the pieces of lamb in the center, and surround them with the various vegetables. The variety of colors make a gratifying display. Moisten the meat and vegetables with about half the gravy, put the rest in a heated gravy boat, sprinkle the meat with the chopped parsley, and serve immediately.

AFTERTHOUGHTS:

✳ If the gravy seems too thick (it should coat a spoon lightly) when the *navarin* is done, thin it with a few tablespoons of hot stock.

✳ The supreme test of a good *navarin* is how perfectly you have cooked the vegetables. Your diligence will be repaid if you remove any vegetable (turnips are the likely ones) which may be cooked before the others. Put them aside and reheat them with the peas and string beans before you serve the *navarin*.

✱ The 2-inch lengths of carrot are particularly attractive if you shape each one into oval pieces (*en olive*) with a sharp paring knife. If you are perfectionist enough to carry this further, smooth the rough edges with a vegetable peeler. Pieces of turnip may be treated in the same fashion.

✱ Made ahead, the *navarin* may be reheated by bringing it to a simmer on top of the stove, then placing it in a preheated **325° F.** oven for about 10 minutes. In that event, do not add the peas and string beans until you reheat the stew. Furthermore, the potatoes will taste fresher if they are cooked simply in salted water sometime before dinner and combined with the *navarin* a few minutes before serving.

✱ The choice of cuts of lamb for this *navarin* is dictated by American tastes. Actually, a more traditional *navarin* is made with the shoulder which has not been boned and with more breast and neck meat. Each of these cuts contributes its flavor and texture to the dish and for some palates makes it far more interesting. But, if you are doubtful even about serving the small amounts of breast and neck pieces specified here, use 3½ to 4 pounds boned shoulder in all instead.

✱ If, you do not use the fresh pork fat to brown the meat, use vegetable oil or equal parts of oil and butter.

BRAISED LEG OF LAMB À LA CUILLÈRE

FOR THOSE unregenerate souls to whom "pink" lamb is anathema, here is a classical version of lamb cooked so thoroughly that it may, as its name indicates, be eaten with a spoon. This is by far the best way to cook well-done lamb. The long, slow braising process keeps the meat moist and succulent, which would certainly not be the case were the leg to be roasted for a comparable period.

BRAISED LEG OF LAMB À LA CUILLÈRE

] To serve eight [

7-pound leg of lamb, boned and trimmed of all but
  ¼ inch of fat
¼ pound fresh pork fat, diced
  or 4 tablespoons vegetable oil

4 tablespoons butter
3 medium onions, thinly sliced
2 large carrots, cut into 1-inch pieces
3 stalks celery, cut into 1-inch pieces
1 teaspoon finely chopped garlic

3 cups brown beef stock in all, fresh or canned
1 teaspoon thyme
2 medium tomatoes, peeled, seeded, and coarsely
  chopped *or* 1 medium can solid-pack tomatoes,
  strained and coarsely chopped
A bouquet consisting of 4 sprigs parsley, 1 large leek
  (white part only), and a bay leaf, all tied
  together

2 tablespoons finely chopped parsley

You should have no difficulty getting your butcher to bone a 7-pound leg of lamb; but if you do, bone the leg yourself. There is a detailed description of the process in the AFTERTHOUGHTS following this recipe. After the leg is boned, whoever does it, the flaps of meat at each end should be tucked back into the openings left by the bones, and the meat tied securely into a neat oblong package—once or twice lengthwise and four or five times crosswise.

Preheat the oven to **325°F.** Choose a large heavy skillet in which to brown the lamb; and, to braise it, a heavy casserole, with a tightly fitting cover, just about large enough to hold the lamb and vegetables comfortably but no larger.

225

Brown the leg in rendered fresh pork fat if you can; apart from its flavor, it will give the meat a beautiful brown glaze almost impossible to achieve with any other fat. Render the pork fat by cutting it into small pieces and frying them over moderate heat in the large skillet. When the solid scraps are brown and crisp, remove them with a slotted spoon and throw them away.

Heat this fat almost to the smoking point, then turn the heat down to moderate, and add the leg of lamb. Brown it on all sides, turning it with two wooden spoons every 5 minutes or so. Allow 20 minutes to a half hour to do the job thoroughly, and regulate the heat so that the lamb browns evenly without burning.

Simultaneously, over fairly low heat, melt the 4 tablespoons of butter in the casserole and, when the foam subsides, stir in the sliced onions, carrots, celery, and chopped garlic. Stir from time to time, and cook until the vegetables soften and color lightly. This should take about the same time, roughly, as the browning of the lamb.

Now remove the browned lamb from the skillet and place it, fat side up, on the vegetables in the casserole. Deglaze the skillet by pouring into it 1½ cups of the beef stock; bring it to a boil, meanwhile mixing into it all the brown particles you can scrape up from the bottom and sides of the pan. Let the stock boil a minute or two, then pour it over the meat. If by some mischance the fat in the skillet seems badly burnt, don't deglaze it; merely pour the stock, hot or cold, directly into the casserole.

Add the thyme, the tomatoes, and the bouquet, and sprinkle the meat generously with salt and freshly ground black pepper. Drape a sheet of aluminum foil lightly over and around the meat, cover the casserole, and bring it to a boil on top of the stove. As soon as you hear the stock bubbling, transfer the casserole to the lower-third shelf of the preheated oven, and plan on having the lamb braise slowly for about 3½ hours. Turn the meat over every ¾ of an hour or so. After the first 1½ hours, heat the remaining 1½ cups of stock, and add it to the casserole.

The lamb is done when it can be easily pierced with a fork and the sauce is dark and rich. If the meat seems too firm, cook it 15 minutes to ½ hour longer.

───────────────

To serve, lift the lamb carefully from the casserole with two large spoons—a fork would be disastrous—and place it on a carving board. Cut away the strings and let the lamb rest for a few moments while you strain the entire contents of the casserole into a fine sieve set in a small saucepan. Press down on the vegetables with the back of a large spoon before throwing them away.

When all the fat rises to the surface of the sauce, as it will in a minute or two, tilt the pan and, with a large spoon, skim off as much of the fat as you can. Reheat the sauce, taste it for seasoning, and pour it into a heated sauceboat.

Slice the lamb cautiously with a long, thin, sharp knife—though you can, if you will, scoop out portions of the lamb with a spoon—and lay the slices, slightly overlapping, down the center of a heated platter. Moisten each slice with a spoonful of the hot sauce, sprinkle with a little chopped parsley and serve. Pass the remaining sauce separately.

AFTERTHOUGHTS:

✳ *To bone a leg of lamb, you will need a narrow 5- or 6-inch pointed knife, ground to razor sharpness. Special boning knives are available in most cutlery stores, but any knife fitting these specifications will do. The boning process itself is comparatively simple if you know where to begin and how to proceed from there.*

Fortunately, the structure of a leg of lamb is clearly defined. Starting from the top of the leg, it has four bones: the rump, middle, shank, and leg bones. First dispose of the leg bone, if it is still attached, by cutting it off at the shank. Then, using your knife, pry and peel off the outside skin of the leg, called the fell, and remove all but a quarter-inch layer of the exposed fat from both the upper and under sides of the meat.

Start boning the leg by inserting the knife between the meat and the rump bone at the top of the leg. Hold the flat of the knife firmly against the bone; this bone is full of nooks and crannies,

227

but if you remember always to use the point of the knife as a probe and the flat of it against the bone as a guide, you should have no trouble cutting the meat cleanly from the bone, no matter where it leads. Use short incisive strokes as you cut and, when you have exposed the rump bone completely (don't be concerned if the meat looks ragged), cut the ligaments holding it to its socket and twist the bone out.

Now switch to the shank end. Most of the shank meat is on one side of the bone and presents no special difficulty. Again, using the flat of the knife as a guide, slice the meat from the bone. When the shank flap hangs free, sever the ligaments at the socket, and ease the bone out.

The middle bone which follows is shaped literally like a dumbell. Once you've skirted the rounded socket, cut around and around the straight end of the bone beyond with short exploratory strokes, pushing and forcing the detached meat back like a glove as you proceed. Work from both ends of the bone if you like—most butchers do.

When you have finally removed the middle bone, pat the leg back into a reaonable facsimile of its original shape and, as explained at the beginning of the recipe, tuck the flaps of meat at both ends back into the openings left by the bones.

✻ A traditional and effective accompaniment to braised lamb *à la cuillère* is dried beans—pea, marrow, or Great Northern—presoaked according to package directions, and simply cooked in simmering salted water until tender. Moisten them with the braising sauce and serve them sprinkled with a little chopped parsley.

✻ The lamb may be braised hours ahead, the sauce strained and degreased, then the meat and sauce returned to the casserole to be reheated on top of the stove. In that event, the beans may be reheated too in the strained sauce, and scooped out with a slotted spoon when you are ready to serve them.

✻ Taste the sauce before serving it; if it seems to lack character, boil it rapidly until it reaches the flavor you prefer. The sauce may also, if you wish, be thickened by adding to it ½ teaspoon of arrowroot powder per cup or sauce; first stir the arrowroot to a paste with a tablespoon of Madeira or cold water, combine it with the degreased sauce, and **cook** until the sauce is thickened and clear.

CHAPTER VIII

Pork & Ham

Braised Pork Chops with Mustard Cream
Roast Loin of Pork à la Boulangère
Braised Smoked Ham with Tarragon Cream

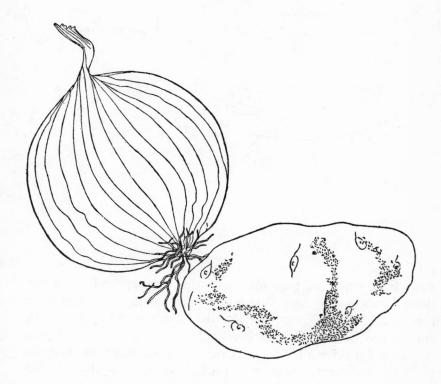

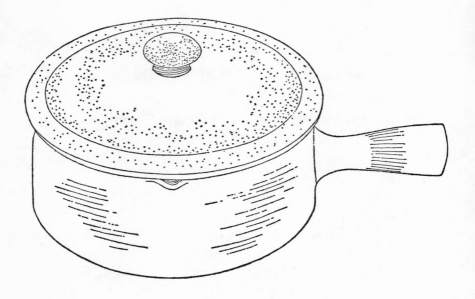

PORK is in general of high quality in this country, and it is a particularly succulent meat. But it rarely comes to our tables at its best, first because we have been panicked into cooking it too long and second because it is seldom cooked correctly. Though pork can indeed survive a longer cooking time than other meats, it displays its true worth when it is cooked by moist heat—in other words, when it is braised—even if your final objective is a roast. The ROAST LOIN OF PORK is here partially cooked by braising be-

fore it is roasted in a second pan, which also conveniently eliminates excess fat in the potatoes and onions that are roasted with
it. How long pork should be cooked and why is explained in the
AFTERTHOUGHTS to this recipe. And the BRAISED PORK CHOPS may
look like ordinary pan-broiled chops, but they are far better and
their MUSTARD SAUCE is rich but perfectly simple. Precisely the
same treatment could be given to veal chops.

The recipe for BRAISED SMOKED HAM may also end up with all
the appearances of a roast glazed ham if you wish, and it will be
all the better for having been braised instead. Merely glaze it
after braising, by whatever method you prefer or as indicated in
the AFTERTHOUGHTS. The braised ham's TARRAGON CREAM sauce is
a provincial variation on a simple *jambon à la crème*. From the
same point of departure, you can also arrive at *jambon, sauce madère,* another familiar and simple minor classic.

✳

BRAISED PORK CHOPS WITH MUSTARD CREAM

PORK CHOPS are not known for their glamor, and with good reason. They are almost always pan fried or broiled—usually to a
crisp—and served with the inevitable dish of applesauce. But when
pork chops are sautéed and braised, then masked with a piquant
mustard sauce, they can hold their own as the main course of an
elegant dinner party.

] To serve four or six [

    6 pork chops, 1 inch thick
    Salt
    Freshly ground black pepper
    ½ cup flour
    2 tablespoons butter
    2 tablespoons vegetable oil

231

1½ cups thinly sliced onions
½ teaspoon finely chopped garlic
2 tablespoons white wine vinegar
1 large bay leaf

1 cup heavy cream
1 tablespoon Dijon mustard
¼ teaspoon lemon juice
1 tablespoon finely chopped chives or parsley

Costly as they are, pork chops cut from the center of the loin are by far your best buy. There is very little waste and the texture of the meat is fine and evenly grained. Have them cut one inch thick, and ask the butcher to leave at least a quarter of an inch of fat on each chop.

Season the chops liberally with salt and freshly ground black pepper, dip them in flour, then shake each one vigorously to dislodge as much excess flour as you can. Preheat the oven to **325°F.** In a large heavy frying pan, heat the 2 tablespoons each of butter and oil. Add the chops, two or three at a time, and sauté them about 3 minutes on each side until they are golden brown. Transfer them to a shallow casserole, large enough, if possible, to hold all six chops in one layer.

When the last chop has been browned, pour out of the frying pan all but about 2 tablespoons of fat, and cook the sliced onions and garlic in the pan rather slowly until they color lightly. Remove the pan from the heat, and add the 2 tablespoons of white-wine vinegar. With a metal spatula or spoon, quickly scrape up all the brown crust you can find on the bottom and sides of the pan, then spoon the onions and drippings over the chops.

Crumble in the bay leaf, and heat the casserole on top of the stove until you hear it bubble. Then cover it tightly, and place it on the center shelf of the oven. After about 10 minutes, baste the chops with the casserole juices (if little or no juice has accumulated, add a couple of tablespoons of hot stock), and 10 minutes later turn the chops over. They should bake, in all, for about 30 minutes to be cooked through. Try not to overcook them or they will be dry and stringy. If you have any doubts, cut into a chop near the bone; if there is no trace of pink, the chops are done. With a pair of tongs, transfer the chops to a heated platter, and keep them warm in the turned-off oven while you complete the sauce.

Tip the casserole slightly and skim from the juice as much fat as you can; what little remains will contribute flavor to the sauce. Pour into the casserole the cup of heavy cream and bring the sauce to a boil over high heat, meanwhile scraping into it every speck of brown crust in the casserole. Turn off the heat when the sauce has reduced to about half, then mix into it the tablespoon of mustard and a few drops of lemon juice. Taste for seasoning, and strain the sauce through a fine sieve directly over the chops. Sprinkle with the minced chives or parsley, and serve with sautéed potato balls or, more elaborately, with POTATOES ANNA (page 278).

AFTERTHOUGHTS:

✳ Although the chops are not at their best cooked ahead of time and reheated, they may be kept warm directly after they are cooked. Return them to the casserole, pour the sauce over them, and keep the casserole warm either in a pan of hot water on top of the stove or in the turned-off oven. If you must heat the sauce again, don't let it boil.

✳ Try sprinkling the finished chops with chopped fresh fennel tops in place of the chives or parsley.

✳ You may braise the chops on top of the stove instead of in the oven, but your casserole must be heavy and the cover must fit tightly. The cooking time will be approximately the same.

ROAST LOIN OF PORK À LA BOULANGÈRE

MORE a family than a festive dish, a loin of pork roasted *à la boulangère*, or in the style of the baker's wife, is essentially a simple preparation. The pork is anointed first with the lightest touch of garlic and a breath of thyme, then roasted in two stages to emerge finally, glazed and succulent, resting on a bed of browned potatoes and onions.

Since there is no agreement on the derivation of the term *à la boulangère,* one might reasonably conjecture that it stems from the old French custom of having joints of meat roasted at the *boulangerie,* or local bakery, when there was no oven at home, which was often the case. How the baker's wife became involved in this is anybody's guess, but we could assume it was she who first created the potato and onion garniture which now bears her name.

] To serve six [

3-pound loin of pork, center cut
1 small clove of garlic, cut into thin slivers
Juice of 1 small lemon
2 teaspoons salt
1 scant teaspoon freshly ground pepper
1 teaspoon thyme

1 large onion, cut up coarsely
1 large carrot, cut up coarsely
2 stalks celery, cut up coarsely

7 large potatoes, sliced ¼ inch thick
2 tablespoons butter
2 medium onions, thinly sliced
Soft butter
Salt
Freshly ground black pepper
2 cups brown beef stock, in all
    or 1 cup each canned bouillon and canned
    chicken stock, combined

2 tablespoons finely chopped parsley

When you purchase your loin of pork, you need to be concerned primarily with the youth of the animal from which it was taken.

234

Young pork is easily recognized. The flesh is greyish pink and finely textured, the covering fat pure white and firm; older pork is noticeably redder.

Avoid the temptation to buy the cheaper ends of the loin, useful as they may be for other purposes. Apparently composed of solid meat, they frequently conceal large pockets of fat, disconcerting, to say the least, when you discover the six portions you had counted on reduced to barely three or four, and not very attractive portions at that. The center cut of the loin, admittedly costly, is yet in the long run the better buy. Ask your butcher to saw through the backbone, or chine, but to leave it attached to the loin like a hinge. This will enable you later to carve each chop neatly without having to hack your way through bone. Have the loin tied crosswise in three places to keep the chine in place. Though you won't serve it, the bone will lend its flavor to the potatoes and onions upon which it will later rest.

Remove the pork from the refrigerator at least an hour before you intend to cook it so that it reaches room temperature. Preheat the oven to **500° F.**; remember this will take at least 15 minutes and the oven must be hot.

With the point of a small, sharp knife, make four or five incisions along the length of the loin, and in each of them insert a thin sliver of garlic. Sprinkle the meat on all sides with the lemon juice, or, more easily, spread it on with a pastry brush. Mix together in a small dish the salt, pepper, and thyme, then with your fingers pat this into the moistened meat.

In the following procedures, it is practical to use two roasting pans. The first should be a casserole, with a tightly fitting cover, just about large enough to hold the meat; the second doesn't need a cover but should be attractive enough to bring to the table. An oval enameled pan about 12 inches long and 1½ inches deep would be ideal.

Place the seasoned loin, fat side up, in the casserole and slide it, uncovered, onto the center shelf of the hot oven. Sear the meat for about 20 minutes, turning it over every now and then. When

235

the pork is browned, scatter around it the coarsely cut onion, carrot, and celery, and cover the casserole. Reduce the oven heat to **350°F.**, and roast the meat for 40 minutes longer, basting it three or four times with its own drippings.

While the meat is cooking, peel and slice the potatoes. Drop them into a bowl of cold water to prevent them from discoloring. Slice the onions as thinly as possible. In a small frying pan, melt the 2 tablespoons of butter and, when it foams, add the onions and fry them over moderate heat until they are transparent and lightly colored. Stir them frequently with a wooden spoon.

Ten minutes or so before the 40 minutes roasting time is up, prepare the uncovered roasting pan. Brush the bottom and sides with a little softened butter. Pat the potato slices dry with paper towels, lay them in the buttered pan, and season them well with salt and freshly ground pepper. On the top layer scatter the sautéed onions, then pour into the pan ½ cup of hot stock.

When the pork has cooked its alloted 40 minutes, remove the casserole from the oven. Carefully lift out the pork with two large spoons, and place it dead center on top of the potatoes and onions. Moisten the exposed potatoes and onions with a couple of tablespoons of pork fat skimmed from the drippings in the casserole.

Return the pork in its new guise to the oven (still **350°F.**), but this time place the pan on the shelf one notch above the oven floor. Let it cook undisturbed for an hour and 15 minutes. At the end of this time the dish will be fully cooked, the pork crusty and glazed on the outside yet moist within, and the potatoes tender and brown. However, if at any point the meat seems to be getting too brown, cover it lightly with a piece of buttered brown paper or aluminum foil.

Sometime during the second roasting, make a clear gravy in the first casserole: Pour the remaining 1½ cups of stock into the brown drippings and bringing it to a boil. With a large spatula or spoon, scrape up all the hardened glaze on the bottom of the casserole and mix it into the boiling stock. Cook the stock briskly for 5 minutes or so, then strain it through a fine sieve into a small pan, pressing down hard on the vegetables to extract all their liquid. Let the gravy rest long enough for the fat to rise to the surface, then skim off most but not all of it. Taste for salt, and put the finished gravy aside to be reheated later.

To serve, remove the pork from its potato bed and carve it in the kitchen. You should have no trouble slicing through each chop neatly if you cut between the exposed rib bones. Lay the separated chops, slightly overlapping, in one line on top of the potatoes and onions, and moisten each one with a teaspoon of the reheated gravy. Pour the remainder of the gravy into a sauce boat to be passed at the table. Dust the potatoes around the chops with the chopped parsley, and serve at once. Cold beer, cider, or a chilled rosé would be a fitting accompaniment to this simple and hearty dish.

AFTERTHOUGHTS:

✳ The only problem confronting the cook in this recipe is to have the pork and potatoes finished at the same time. Some types of potatoes take longer to cook than others. If, at the end of the specified cooking time you find the potatoes still firm (test them with a cake tester or the point of a sharp knife), remove the pork from the pan and keep it warm on a hot platter. Raise the oven heat to **450°F.**, and cook the potatoes until they are done. The pork will not suffer a bit if it is allowed to stand outside the oven 10 or 15 minutes; if anything, you will find it easier to carve and the meat will be juicier.

✳ While it is true that pork must be thoroughly cooked to destroy any lurking trichina parasites, it can also, alas, be overcooked, which it usually is. The result is a dry, tasteless meat, difficult to carve. Since it was proved many years ago that trichinae are destroyed at a temperature of **137°F.**, there is no danger whatsoever unless you serve the pork really rare. For this small roast, a reliable timetable is approximately 30 minutes of cooking to the pound at **350°F.**, plus the initial 20 minutes searing at **500°F.** If you plan to cook a whole loin (12-15 pounds) reduce the roasting time to 15 minutes per pound, still allowing the same searing time.

Should these arithmetical formulae confuse or depress you, use a meat thermometer and insert it in the fleshy part of the meat at the beginning of the second roasting period. When it reaches a temperature of **185°F.**, the pork is done; much beyond that, it is hardly worth eating.

❋ For variety, try using different herbs when you first season the meat. In place of the thyme, use rosemary, marjoram, or sage, the last with discretion.

❋ Thicken the gravy if you like with a paste made of 1 scant teaspoon of arrowroot power and 2 tablespoons of cold water. Mix this into the clear gravy and boil a minute or two.

❋ Should you wish to prepare the second roasting pan earlier, blanch the sliced potatoes by covering them with cold water and bringing it to a boil. Let the potatoes cook a minute or two, then drain and dry them. Set up the pan as described in the recipe, scatter the sautéed onions on top, cool, and cover tightly with Saran wrap. The potatoes may remain this way for hours without discoloring. Moreover, you may do the first roasting earlier, too, if you wish, and complete the cooking just before dinner.

BRAISED SMOKED HAM WITH TARRAGON CREAM

AMERICAN smoked hams are among the best in the world, but they are so persistently served baked and glazed that it is difficult to imagine them cooked any other way. But other, and better, ways there are. Once you have tasted a ham braised slowly in a wine-flavored stock, it is unlikely that you will ever bake one again. And, if you insist, the braised ham can still be glazed.

The accompanying tarragon cream sauce is an unusual version of *jambon à la crème* and uses the braising liquid of the ham as its base.

] To serve six or eight [

Half a ham, about 4 pounds

3 tablespoons butter

238

½ cup coarsely chopped onions
½ cup coarsely chopped carrots
¼ cup coarsely chopped celery
½ teaspoon thyme

1 cup dry white wine
6 cups beef stock, fresh or canned
    or canned bouillon and canned chicken broth,
    mixed half and half
A bouquet consisting of 4 sprigs parsley, 1 leek
    (white part only), and a large bay leaf, all tied
    together

SAUCE:

1/3 cup finely chopped shallots
½ cup white-wine vinegar
1 tablespoon finely chopped fresh tarragon
    or 1 teaspoon dried tarragon, crumbled
½ bay leaf
5 whole black peppercorns
3 sprigs parsley

¾ cup braising liquid from ham, above
3 egg yolks
½ cup heavy cream
Salt
1 tablespoon finely chopped fresh tarragon
    or 1 tablespoon finely chopped parsley

2 tablespoons soft butter

Confronted by the dizzying variety of hams available today, you may find a choice is difficult to make. A mildly cured, precooked ham is best for your purposes here. And buy the best brand you can afford; too often cheaper hams lack texture and flavor and are disappointing no matter how well you cook them. Ask the butcher to remove the rind and most of the fat.

Preheat the oven to **350°F.** while you prepare the vegetable base, or *mirepoix*, which forms the usual base for braising. Melt the 3 tablespoons of butter in a heavy covered casserole or roaster large enough to hold the ham comfortably. When the foam subsides, add the onions, carrots, celery, and thyme, and cook the vegetables over moderate heat until they have colored lightly.

Place the ham, fat side up, on the *mirepoix,* and pour the wine and stock around it. The liquid should come about half way up the sides of the meat; if it doesn't, use more stock. Add the bouquet and bring the stock to a boil on top of the stove. Then cover the casserole, and slide it onto the middle shelf of the oven where it should cook slowly for about an hour. Baste it thoroughly every 15 minutes or so with the braising liquid, and regulate the heat so that the stock barely simmers.

Start the sauce at any time while the ham is cooking. In a small enamel or stainless-steel saucepan, combine the vinegar, shallots, tarragon, bay leaf, peppercorns, and parsley, and bring this to a boil. Then reduce the heat to the barest simmer and let the liquid cook down to about 2 tablespoons. Strain it through a fine sieve into a small cup, and press down hard on the shallots and herbs before throwing them away.

When the ham is done (it should offer almost no resistance when pierced with the point of a knife), remove 2 cups of the braising liquid from the casserole and strain it into a small saucepan. Boil it vigorously until it has reduced to precisely ¾ cup. Meanwhile keep the ham warm in the oven, either turned off or with the door slightly ajar.

Beat the 3 egg yolks in a small bowl just long enough to break them up, then slowly mix in the ½ cup of cream. Into this stir the hot reduced stock a tablespoon at a time (in no circumstances may you do this the other way around). Pour the combined mixture into the top of a double boiler and add the 2 tablespoons of reduced vinegar.

Stirring constantly with a whisk, cook the sauce directly over moderate heat until it begins to thicken. At the first sign of thickening, raise the pan off the heat every few seconds to cool it, and continue to stir; this is to prevent the sauce from coming anywhere near the boiling point, which would assuredly make it curdle. When the sauce has thickened sufficiently to coat the back of a spoon heavily, taste for salt, then stir in the tablespoon of chopped tarragon or parsley.

Until you are ready to serve it, keep the sauce warm over tepid, not hot, water; stir it every now and then, particularly around the bottom and sides.

Remove the ham from the casserole, and strain some of the remaining liquid. With a long sharp knife, carve the ham into quarter-inch-thick slices. Arrange them, slightly overlapping, down the center of a heated serving platter, and moisten each slice with a few drops of the strained braising liquid. Decorate the platter with sprigs of parsley.

Now, before pouring the sauce into a hot sauceboat, beat into it, a little at a time, the 2 tablespoons of soft butter. Send it to the table to be passed separately. A purée of spinach and POTATOES ANNA (page 278) would be the approved and colorful accompaniments to the ham, and the wine should be a young, not too robust red such as Beaujolais.

AFTERTHOUGHTS:

❋ The braised ham may be served with sauces other than the tarragon cream. The braising liquid alone may accompany it, either with or without the *mirepoix* of vegetables. Or, 2 cups of the liquid, strained, may be brought to a boil with 1 tablespoon of arrowroot first dissolved in 2 tablespoons of Madeira. Then pour in another ¼ cup of Madeira and simmer the sauce slowly until it thickens. The addition of a chopped truffle, should you have one around, and a tablespoon of soft butter beaten into the sauce before serving will give you a beautifully finished sauce. Ham served in this manner is called *jambon, sauce madère,* and a spinach purée is almost always served with it.

❋ The simplest way to glaze a ham after it is braised: Place it on a rack set in a baking sheet and sprinkle it heavily with confectioners sugar. Place the ham on the center shelf of a preheated **500°F.** oven, and bake it until the sugar melts to a light but brilliant glaze, a matter of 8 minutes or so.

✳ A whole ham, of course, may be braised in the same fashion if you have a covered pan large enough to hold it. Increase the vegetables, wine, and stock proportionally, and cook the ham about 2 hours. Or, if you're in doubt, use a meat thermometer; it should read between 130°F. and 140°F. when the ham is done.

✳ If you wish to make the tarragon cream sauce for slices of cooked leftover ham and have no braising liquid available, use ¾ cup of canned condensed stock, undiluted.

CHAPTER IX

Casseroles

Swedish Meat Balls

Tripes à la Mode de Caen

Paella Valenciana

Cassoulet

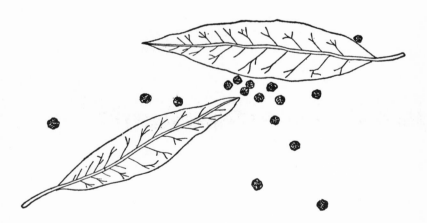

THESE four great European specialties, far from belonging to the *haute cuisine,* are down-to-earth peasant dishes. They are not difficult to make, but the many recipes you can find for them can be mystifying, as they require ingredients and procedures many cooks are not accustomed to. And each of these dishes has a characteristic quality that must be achieved in a particular way. The SWEDISH MEAT BALLS, for instance, are not made merely of ground meat but of finely ground mixed meats and beef marrow beaten to a smooth paste that gives the finished meat ball an extraordinary texture. TRIPES À LA MODE DE CAEN is cooked almost interminably not only because the tripe would otherwise be tough but also because the sauce must be magnificently rich. Neither the tripe nor the calves' feet it is cooked with are in the least difficult to handle, as you will see.

The rice in a Spanish PAELLA VALENCIANA absolutely must be light and fluffy. The surest way to do this is to cook the traditional chicken, sausage, and rice separately, and to combine them and add the seafood at the last for a final blending of flavors. The rice is cooked in the Mediterranean manner, somewhat like a PILAF (see Index). The many ingredients of a CASSOULET are always cooked in separate installments and combined at the end to be baked all together. There is no other way to achieve the right combination of textures and blending of flavors. Though it is time consuming, the recipe for *cassoulet* is satisfyingly logical and you should not be tempted by shortcuts, though a good dish can still be made without including every one of the meats specified.

✳

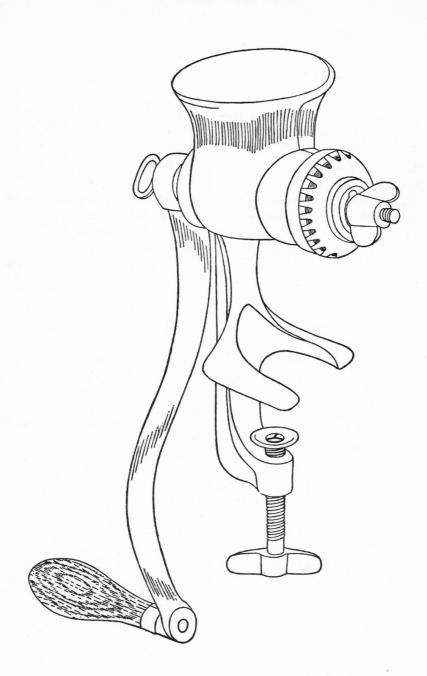

*

SWEDISH MEAT BALLS IN SOUR-CREAM SAUCE

RANGING in size from a pea to an orange, ground-meat balls can be found in almost every part of the civilized world. Called *bitki* in Polish, *fricadelles* in French, *ballekens* in Flemish, *polpette* in Italian, their names are as varied and colorful as the ingredients that compose them. And certainly, among the most famous are *frikadellar*, the Swedish meat balls. In the following version, uncooked beef marrow is combined with three kinds of ground meat to produce a meat ball with a texture unlike any you have ever tasted. These tiny morsels make excellent hors d'oeuvres served from a chafing dish, do equally well as a main course for dinner, and reheat perfectly for whatever purpose you use them.

] To serve six [

½ pound each beef chuck, lean fresh pork, and veal,
      all fat removed, and ground together twice
2 tablespoons bread crumbs
¼ cup cream
4 tablespoons finely diced beef marrow
2 tablespoons butter
½ cup finely chopped onions
1 tablespoon finely chopped shallots
½ teaspoon finely chopped garlic
1 teaspoon grated lemon rind
2 tablespoons finely chopped parsley
1 tablespoon salt
½ teaspoon freshly ground black pepper
½ teaspoon thyme
2 eggs

3 tablespoons butter
2 tablespoons vegetable oil

246

SAUCE:

2 tablespoons flour
1 cup brown beef stock or canned bouillon
½ cup sour cream
2 tablespoons finely chopped fresh dill
   or 1 tablespoon dry dill weed
¼ teaspoon lemon juice
Salt
⅛ teaspoon cayenne

Ask the butcher to split a few marrow bones lengthwise and extract the marrow for you. Have the beef, pork, and veal ground together in front of you, for unless you see it you can't be certain that it will be free of fat.

So that they can be chilled, prepare the meat balls at least an hour before you plan to cook them. They are less likely then to crumble and lose their shape when they are fried.

Soak the bread crumbs in the four tablespoons of cream for 5 minutes, then put them in a large mixing bowl with the marrow and ground meat. Melt the 2 tablespoons of butter in a small frying pan, and in it cook the chopped onions, shallots, and garlic over moderate heat for about 5 minutes, until they soften and color lightly. Add them to the mixing bowl, and at the same time add the grated lemon rind and the parsley, salt, pepper, and crumbled thyme. Beat the 2 eggs lightly with a fork, and pour them over the meat.

With a large spoon, beat this mixture together vigorously until the ingredients are thoroughly combined and the meat loses its granular texture. If you own an electric mixer with a pastry-arm attachment, the beating operation will be much easier. But don't attempt to use an ordinary beater attachment; it won't work.

Form the meat into small balls about an inch in diameter. The simplest and most efficient way to do this is to place a heaping teaspoon of the meat in the palm of one hand and, after moistening the other hand with cold water, roll it lightly over the meat until

247

you have shaped it into a sphere. Don't fuss with this too much; when the balls are chilled, you can reshape them easily if you wish. Place the meat balls, as you finish them, on a baking sheet or platter lined with waxed paper. Cover them with another sheet of waxed paper, and chill for at least an hour.

When you are ready to cook the meat balls, melt the 3 tablespoons of butter and 2 tablespoons of oil over high heat in a large heavy frying pan. When the fat begins to sputter, lightly drop into the pan enough meat balls to cover the bottom about three quarters full. At once slide the pan back and forth over the burner so that they roll around in the hot fat; this will help them to keep their shapes and to brown evenly.

After a couple of minutes, turn the heat down to moderate, and cook the meat balls 6 or 7 minutes longer, or until they are a crisp brown all over and cooked through. Make sure by breaking one open; there should not be the slightest indication of pink in the center. With a slotted spoon transfer the finished meat balls to a shallow casserole, and continue with the remaining meat balls until they are all cooked.

Make the sauce in the same frying pan. If the fat remaining in it is a good deep brown, pour off all but 3 tablespoons of it. If, however, it is black and badly burned, scrape it all out and in its place melt 3 tablespoons of fresh butter. Off the heat, with a wooden spoon, stir into the pan 2 tablespoons of flour and mix it to a smooth paste with the fat. Return the pan to a low heat, and cook this *roux* slowly for a minute or so, stirring all the while.

Then pour in, all at once, the cup of stock. Raise the heat to moderate and, with a wire whisk, beat this sauce together until it boils, thickens, and becomes quite smooth. Then turn the heat down to the barest simmer. Still using the whisk, stir the sour cream into the sauce, about a tablespoon at a time. Use more than ½ cup if you like the sauce fairly thin. At the last, add the fresh dill, lemon juice, salt to your taste, and the cayenne. Pour the sauce over the meat balls in the casserole.

When you are ready to serve them, reheat the meat balls slowly without letting the sauce boil. Serve them directly from the casserole, sprinkled with a little extra fresh dill if you have it. Buttered rice, noodles, or pasta of any kind go well with this.

AFTERTHOUGHTS:

❋ If you can't get any beef marrow, in its place beat into the meat-ball mixture 3 tablespoons of soft butter.

❋ For more firmly crusted meat balls, roll them each lightly in flour just before frying them.

TRIPES À LA MODE DE CAEN

FREQUENTLY in culinary history, a city becomes almost exclusively identified with a particular dish; in this case the city is Caen, in Normandy, and the dish is tripe. Like many great and enduring creations—the recipe can be traced back to the fourteenth century —*tripes à la mode de Caen* is a dish of surprising simplicity, its only extravagance the length of time necessary to cook it. And a minimum of twelve hours is absolutely essential. Staggering as the thought may be in these days of instant cooking, the actual labor involved in preparation is negligible. Moreover, tripe may be cooked days ahead, if you want, and reheated without any loss of flavor or texture.

] To serve eight or ten [

5 pounds honeycomb tripe
4 calves' feet, cut into 3-inch pieces
3 large onions, peeled and halved
3 large carrots, scraped and cut into 4-inch pieces
4 large leeks (white parts only), split and carefully
    washed

> 5 cloves garlic and 15 whole black peppercorns, tied
>   in a square of cheesecloth
> A bouquet consisting of 6 sprigs parsley, 2 large bay
>   leaves, 2 celery tops, all tied together
> 1½ tablespoons salt
> 1 teaspoon thyme
> 3 cups dry white wine
> 3 cups chicken stock, fresh or canned
> ½ cup aged Calvados or American applejack
> ½ pound beef fat, sliced in sheets ⅛ inch thick
>
> 2 tablespoons finely cut chives
> 2 tablespoons finely chopped parsley

Honeycomb tripe, the most delicate variety, comes in large sheets, already blanched or parboiled; so all you need do is cut it it into 1½- or 2-inch squares, and wash it thoroughly before you cook it. To make sure the tripe is absolutely clean, place the squares in a large bowl, and let a thin trickle of cold water from the tap run over them for as long as it takes the water in the bowl to become absolutely clear.

In the meanwhile, blanch the calves' feet by covering them with cold water in a large pot and bringing it to a boil. Let the feet boil for about 30 seconds, then drain them in a colander and run cold water over them to stop their cooking.

Preheat the oven to **250° F.** Although there are special narrow-necked tripe pots available in restaurant-supply houses, a heavy 6- or preferably 8-quart casserole will do quite as well. Arrange in the bottom of it all the cut-up vegetables—the onions, carrots, leeks, the bag of garlic and peppercorns, and the bouquet. Lay the tripe over them, and sprinkle it with 1½ tablespoons of salt and a tea-spoon of crumbled thyme. Scatter the cut-up calves' feet over the tripe, and pour into the casserole the 3 cups each of white wine and chicken stock. If, after you have added the apple brandy, the combined liquids don't quite cover the calves' feet, add more stock. Place the thin sheets of beef fat on top of the stock like a tarpaulin,

250

spreading them out so that they cover as much of the surface as possible.

It is traditional, at this point, to seal the pot hermetically with a rope of paste made of flour and water, but heavy-weight aluminum foil does the job quite as well. Spread a double thickness of foil over the top of the casserole, fold it down against the sides, and tie it as tightly as you can. When you are quite satisfied that not a drop of steam can escape, cover the foil with the lid of the casserole.

Over high heat, bring the casserole to a boil on top of the stove. As soon as you hear it bubble, transfer it at once to the center shelf of the oven and, to be on the safe side, place under the casserole a shallow baking pan or jelly-roll pan. It is not impossible, despite your precautions, that some of the fat may escape and overflow. Allow the tripe to cook in the slow oven for at least 12 hours; even 14 to 16 hours is not too much. And at this point, possibly you will worry about the cost of the fuel, but the tripe will take care of itself.

When the tripe is done, remove the casserole from the oven, peel off the foil and, with a pair of tongs, pick out of the pot and throw away the calves' feet, vegetables, cheesecloth bag, and bouquet— in fact, every bit of solid matter but the tripe; the shreds of meat clinging to the calves' feet may be removed and returned to the pot if you like.

Set a large fine-meshed sieve over a deep mixing bowl, and pour the tripe and all its sauce into it. Let the sauce drip through and, meanwhile, using the tongs, transfer the pieces of tripe to another and smaller casserole.

The best way to remove the fat from the sauce (there will be a lot of it), is to cool and then chill the sauce until the fat hardens into a solid piece. But if you want to serve the tripe at once, simply tip the bowl, and, with a large spoon, remove as much of the fat as you can. Pour the cleared sauce over the tripe in the casserole, heat it to the boiling point, and taste it for seasoning. Then let it simmer until you are ready to serve it.

It cannot be stressed too strongly that the tripe must not only be served boiling hot but the serving plates themselves must be hot.

The gelatine in the sauce is so concentrated that at the slightest sign of cooling it will begin to solidify. In France, tripe cooked in this fashion is served in individually heated pots, or in small earthenware *terrines* set in bowls of boiling water, or even over tiny individual charcoal braziers. However you manage it, serve the tripe hot, sprinkled with the mixed chives and parsley, and accompanied by buttered boiled potatoes. Chilled cider is traditional with tripe, but beer is almost as good.

AFTERTHOUGHTS:

❋ For those of you who care, honeycomb tripe is the muscular lining of a cow's second stomach—the second of four stomachs, that is.

❋ Old recipes for *tripe à la mode de Caen* call for an ox hoof rather than calves' feet. If you have any influence with your butcher, you can probably persuade him to get one for you from his slaughterhouse. One whole ox hoof is the equivalent of the 4 calves' feet specified in this recipe. The flavor makes it well worth a determined effort to find one.

❋ A practical way to keep the tripe hot while you serve it is to place the casserole over an alcohol lamp. Or, transfer the tripe and its sauce to a chafing dish, and keep it hot over direct heat.

❋ Unless you have a really fine old Calvados, the apple brandy of Normandy, use applejack; inferior Calvados is not good enough.

❋ You may stop the cooking of the tripe at any time and continue cooking it later if you wish.

PAELLA VALENCIANA

FOR MANY people the very word *paella* conjures up a nightmare of odds and ends mired in overcooked, glutinous rice. But when *paella* is knowingly and lovingly prepared, it is a creation of elegance as befits one of the great national dishes of Spain. There are, of course, many versions of *paella Valenciana*, some simple, others complex. In the one following, all the carefully considered ingredients—

chicken, sausages, shrimp, clams, and saffron-flavored rice—disparate as they may sound, confront the eye and palate finally with a series of colorful and delightful surprises, intensely flavored to be sure, but not overpoweringly so.

] To serve six [

6 small sausages—*chorizos* or fresh Italian sausages, sweet or hot
2½-pound chicken, cut into 6 pieces (see p. 106)
4 tablespoons olive oil
2 tablespoons butter

½ cup finely chopped onions
¼ cup finely chopped shallots
1 teaspoon finely chopped garlic
1 medium green pepper, finely chopped (about ½ cup)
1 cup raw rice
¾ pound fresh ripe tomatoes, peeled, seeded, and coarsely chopped (about 1 cup)
    or 1 cup drained canned tomatoes, coarsely chopped
1–1½ cups chicken stock, fresh or canned
¼ teaspoon powdered saffron
Salt
Freshly ground black pepper

12 large uncooked shrimp, shelled and deveined
2 dozen small cherrystone clams, carefully scrubbed

1 tablespoon finely chopped parsley

Chorizos, Spanish sausages, are hard to find except in Spanish neighborhoods; fresh Italian sausages, sweet or hot, are more generally available and will do very well indeed. In any case, the sausages, Spanish or Italian, must be precooked to rid them of excess fat.

Place them in a small pan and cover them with cold water. Bring the water to a boil, then reduce the heat and slowly simmer the sausages, uncovered, for about 20 minutes. Remove them from the water with tongs and, while they are still hot, pierce them in three or four places with the point of a small sharp knife. The fat will spurt out in small geysers. If the sausages are more than 3 inches long, cut them into 2- or 3-inch lengths. Lay them on a double thickness of paper toweling to drain until you are ready to use them.

Wash the pieces of chicken, dry them thoroughly, then salt and pepper them quite heavily. In a large heavy frying pan, heat the 4 tablespoons of olive oil and 2 of butter until the butter dissolves and the fat begins to sputter. Starting with the dark meat, skin side down, fry the chicken rapidly, three or four pieces at a time, turning them over when the skin has browned. When they are a uniform brown all over, remove them to a baking dish. Continue with the remaining chicken and cook the white meat ever so briefly, just long enough to brown it lightly.

Then fry the sausages in the fat remaining in the pan, turning them constantly until the sausage casings have a light brown crust. Add them to the chicken in the baking dish. Preheat the oven to **350° F.**

Pour all the fat out of the frying pan into a small Pyrex bowl, then return 2 tablespoons of it to the pan. In this, fry the ½ cup of minced onions over moderate heat for 3 or 4 minutes, until they color lightly. Stir them constantly with a wooden spoon and scrape up and into them whatever brown crust may have formed earlier on the bottom and sides of the pan. Add the shallots, garlic, and green pepper, and cook about 3 minutes longer or until the pepper is soft. Into this aromatic vegetable base, stir a cup of unwashed rice.

There are many schools of thought about the type of rice to use for a *paella*. However, most authorities are agreed that almost any good white rice will do except the precooked or converted varieties. Long-grained Carolina rice is the most accessible here, but if you live near a foreign food store, try Patna, Persian, or the short stubby rice imported from Italy.

Whatever rice you finally use, cook it slowly in the fat with the vegetables, stirring constantly until each grain begins to turn slightly opaque or milky white. Don't in any circumstances allow the rice to brown; the total process should take about 5 minutes, possibly a little less.

Now turn the entire contents of the frying pan—rice, vegetables, and fat—into a heavy 4-quart casserole equipped with a heavy tightly fitting cover. Stir in the fresh tomato pulp, or drained canned tomatoes, and the cup of boiling chicken stock in which you have first dissolved the $\frac{1}{4}$ teaspoon of powdered saffron. Season rather highly with salt and freshly ground pepper.

Bring the rice to a boil on top of the stove, then cover the casserole tightly, and transfer it to the lower-third shelf of the preheated oven. At the end of 15 or 20 minutes the rice will have absorbed all the liquid and be almost, but not quite cooked through. If, at any point during the cooking, the liquid has cooked away too fast—and that will happen if the casserole is a light one or the heat is too intense—add another $\frac{1}{2}$ cup of hot stock.

Remove the casserole from the oven, and reduce the oven temperature to **325° F.** Fluff up the rice with a couple of forks (never a spoon, which would mash it) and add to it the sautéed chicken and sausages and their accumulated juices. Stir together gently so that the meats and liquid are distributed evenly throughout the rice, and taste for seasoning.

Cover the casserole tightly and return it to the center shelf of the oven. Cook the *paella* undisturbed for about 10 minutes, then quickly add the shelled raw shrimp and thoroughly scrubbed clams. Push them gently beneath the surface of the rice, cover the casserole, and cook for another 10 minutes, or until the shrimp have turned a rosy pink and all the clams have opened. Discard any clams that don't open, but first give the recalcitrant ones a little more time to cook.

Although it is customary to serve the *paella* directly from its casserole, it is far more effective and easier to handle if you arrange the rice on a heated platter and imbed the other ingredients in it. Be as fanciful as you like about this, for you will certainly have enough color and variety to work with. When you finish, dust lightly with finely chopped parsley and serve with hot French or Italian bread.

AFTERTHOUGHTS:

✳ Many substitutions or omissions are possible in this *paella*: The sausages may be omitted and cubes of ham added instead. Scrubbed mussels will do as well or better than clams or you can use both. Lobster, green peas, mushrooms, squid—the choice is limitless—but whatever variants you choose to use, remember that the various ingredients must complement each other, not cancel each other out.

✳ The quality and intensity of the chicken stock you use will determine to a large degree the successful flavor of your *paella*. If you use canned stock, improve it as suggested on page 38.

✳ Most of the *paella* may be made successfully hours ahead of time. Ideally, the best way to do this is to cook everything up to the point where the meats are to be combined with the rice. A half hour before dinner, combine them, heat the casserole to sizzling on top of the stove, then cover, place in the oven, and proceed as described before. If, for some reason the *paella* must wait after it is done, turn the oven down to **250° F.** Remove the cover from the casserole, and drape a kitchen towel loosely over the rice. The *paella* may remain this way for 20 minutes or so without coming to any harm but much longer will toughen the clams.

✳ For large buffet dinners, the chicken may be boned after it is sautéed and cut into small pieces. This will make it much easier to serve.

*

CASSOULET

ONE OF the great regional dishes of southwestern France, the *cassoulet*, like the Spanish *paella*, takes its name from the clay utensil in which it was originally cooked, a capacious casserole called a *cassole d'Issel*. Undoubtedly, its devotees will quarrel forever about where the *cassoulet* itself originated, but at least they are agreed that it must have been one of three places—Toulouse, Castelnaudary, or Carcassonne. Lest you be seduced by these lyrical names into imagining that *cassoulet* is an esoteric creation, be assured that the true *cassoulet* is a rough, homely, country dish. It is composed of beans, goose or duck, lamb, pork, and sausage, highly flavored with stock, aromatic herbs, garlic, and tomatoes. Because of the number and diversity of its ingredients, a *cassoulet* is not a dish to be whipped up on the spur of the moment. Nor, for practical reasons, should it be made for less than ten or twelve people. But it can all be put together at least a day or two before you plan to serve it without any loss of freshness or flavor.

] To serve ten or twelve [

BEANS:

2 pounds small white beans—Great Northern,
    marrow, or pea beans
1 pound fresh or smoked garlic sausage
1 pound lean salt pork, in one piece
½ pound fresh pork rind, if available
2½ quarts chicken stock, fresh or canned

3 whole medium onions, peeled
1 teaspoon finely chopped garlic
1 teaspoon thyme
A bouquet consisting of 4 sprigs parsley, 2 large bay
    leaves, 1 leek (white part only), 3 celery tops, all
    tied together

257

Salt
Freshly ground pepper

DUCK:

4- or 5-pound duckling, quartered and broiled
    (see pp. 138-140)

PORK AND LAMB:

1 pound boned loin of pork, cut into 2-inch chunks
1 pound boned shoulder of lamb, cut into 2-inch
    chunks
¼ to ½ pound fresh pork fat (trimmed from the
    loin, above)

1 cup finely chopped onions
½ cup finely chopped celery
1 teaspoon finely chopped garlic
1 cup dry white wine

1½ pounds ripe tomatoes, peeled, seeded, and
    coarsely chopped (about 2 cups pulp)
        or 1 large can solid-pack tomatoes, drained of all
        liquid
Large bay leaf
Salt
Freshly ground black pepper

1½ cups coarsely grated bread crumbs
Duck fat (from broiled duck, above)

½ cup finely chopped parsley

The best way to prepare a *cassoulet* is to go about it at your leisure. Don't try to make everything in one fell swoop (though it can be done), but stagger the various procedures—boiling, broiling, braising and baking—to suit your convenience. As each thing is cooked, put it aside to cool, then refrigerate it until you assemble the *cassoulet*.

258

Prepare the beans for cooking in one of two ways—either soak them overnight covered with cold water, or use a short cut: An hour before you plan to cook them, cover the beans with cold water in a large pot and bring the water to a boil. Turn off the heat at once, and let the beans soak in the hot water for about an hour. The beans will ferment if they are oversoaked, so cook them as soon as possible thereafter, whatever method you have used.

Drain the beans and put them in a 6- or 8-quart pot or casserole. Add the sausage, salt pork, and pork rind, then pour in the stock, and bring it to a boil. Carefully skim off all scum and foam as it rises to the surface. When the stock is boiling and fairly clear, add the 3 whole onions, and the minced garlic, thyme, bouquet, salt, and pepper. Turn down the heat so that the surface of the liquid barely moves; the beans will burst if they are cooked too fast.

Simmer the beans, uncovered, for about an hour and 15 minutes, or until they are tender but not falling apart. At the end of 40 minutes remove the sausage and, with the point of a small sharp knife, prick it in three or four places to release the fat, and put it aside until later. When the beans are done to your taste (if you have any doubts, undercook them), remove the salt pork and pork rind, and put them aside also until later. Throw away the onions and bouquet. Strain the beans through a large strainer set over a mixing bowl, and let the bean stock drip through until every bit of it is safely deposited in the bowl. Skim it of all the fat when it rises to the surface. Store beans and stock separately.

The duck may be broiled at any time. Follow the directions on page 138 for BROILED DUCKLING WITH ORANGES, but omit the sauce. Marinating the duck is not absolutely essential but will give the *cassoulet* added piquancy. When the broiled duck has cooled, trim the quarters of all extraneous fat and gristle, and with poultry shears cut them into small neat serving pieces. Pour all the fat and drippings out of the broiling pan into a small bowl, scraping up all the dark sediment on the bottom and sides of the pan. When the fat rises to the surface, remove it, with a kitchen syringe or a large spoon, to another bowl and save it. Pour the dark duck drippings into the bowl of bean stock.

The braising of the pork and lamb may also be done at any time. First preheat the oven to **325° F.,** and render the fresh pork fat: Cut the fat into small dice, and fry these slowly in a large heavy frying pan. When the pieces have crisped, throw them away, and heat the rendered fat in the pan to smoking. In this, a few pieces at a time, brown the cubed pork and lamb over moderate heat, transferring them, when they are a dark mahogany color on all sides, to a 4-quart casserole or Dutch oven.

Pour off all but 3 tablespoons of fat from the frying pan, and now cook slowly in the pan the cup of chopped onions for about 5 minutes, scraping into them any dark crust clinging to the bottom and sides of the pan. After the onions have colored lightly, stir into them the ½ cup of celery and teaspoon of garlic. Cook 2 or 3 minutes longer, then pour in the cup of dry white wine, bring it to a boil, and cook rapidly until it has reduced to about half.

With a rubber spatula, transfer the entire contents of the frying pan to the casserole with the meat. Add the tomato pulp, bay leaf, salt, and pepper. Mix everything together gently, and bring the casserole to a boil on top of the stove. Cover the casserole tightly and place it on the center shelf of the preheated oven. Let it cook undisturbed for about an hour, but give it a glance every now and then to make sure all the liquid hasn't cooked away; if it has, add only enough stock (or water) to keep it moist.

When the meat is tender but still somewhat firm, remove the casserole from the oven. Lift the cubes of meat out with tongs and put them aside in a bowl or baking dish. Skim the casserole juices of all fat and add the juices, tomato pulp and all, to the bean stock.

All you need to do now is put the *cassoulet* together. That may be done, if you prefer, hours or even a day before you plan to cook it. Check back. You should have arrayed before you: the drained beans; the sausage, salt pork, and pork rind; the broiled duck and the duck fat; the cubes of braised pork and lamb; and finally, the bean-stock mixture. Before you proceed to combine them, peel the sausage and slice it into quarter-inch rounds; and cut the salt pork and pork rind into approximately 1-inch squares.

The best pot in which to cook the *cassoulet* is a large heavy 6-quart casserole at least 5 inches deep. It will just about hold all the ingredients easily, though there may be a few beans left over. Begin by spreading an inch-thick layer of beans in the bottom of the casserole. On top of them arrange half the sausage, duck, pork, lamb, salt pork, and pork rind. Cover this with more beans, then the rest of the meat, and finally a last layer of beans. If you have a few slices of sausage left, spread them over the top.

Taste the bean stock for seasoning; it should be very definite in flavor and quite highly salted. Pour it over the beans slowly, so that it may seep down to the bottom of the casserole. As it rises, the stock should eventually come almost to the top of the beans; if there isn't enough, supplement it with a little chicken stock. Spread the bread crumbs in a thick layer over the beans, and moisten them with 3 or 4 tabespoons of the duck fat or dot them with bits of soft butter. If you don't intend to bake the *cassoulet* immediately, refrigerate it until you do.

An hour and a half before dinner, preheat the oven to **350° F.** Heat the casserole on top of the stove until the stock begins to bubble, then slide the pot onto the upper-third shelf of the oven. Bake for about an hour and 15 minutes, or until the crumbs have formed a firm, dark crust. Sprinkle the *cassoulet* with chopped parsley and serve immediately, with hot French bread and a simple green salad.

AFTERTHOUGHTS:

✳ The choice of sausage for the *cassoulet* may present something of a problem. The traditional sausage is, of course, the *saucisse de Toulouse*, impossible to get here. The Italian garlic sausage called *coteghino* is excellent but Polish sausage, more generally available, will do almost as well.

✳ Any left over *cassoulet* may be reheated the next day, but it will be merely a pallid reflection of itself. A far better alternative is to transform it into a thick hearty bean soup. Purée the beans in the electric blender, or force them through a sieve. Thin the purée with some stock, canned or fresh, and serve it with a dusting of parsley. Bits of left-over sausage may be floated on top.

✳ *Cassoulets* are frequently made with left-over meats. Certainly, half a roast duck or the leg of a goose could be used to advantage this way, but a *cassoulet* made up entirely of left-over meats will have little character and seems hardly worth the effort.

✳ In France, it is customary to break up the crust of the *cassoulet* as it bakes by pressing the crumbs into the simmering liquid three or four times with the back of a large spoon, and then allowing a final crust to harden and brown. A good deal of the stock is absorbed in this manner and the result is a somewhat drier *cassoulet*.

✳ An important ingredient of a true *cassoulet* has unfortunately had to be left out of this recipe because it is both expensive and difficult to find. This is *confit d'oie*, goose preserved in its own fat, which fine food stores do sometimes carry in cans, imported, of course, from France. If you are so fortunate as to find some, the goosemeat is fully cooked and may be substituted for the pieces of broiled duck when you assemble the *cassoulet*. Use some of the goose fat on top of the coating of crumbs.

Vegetables

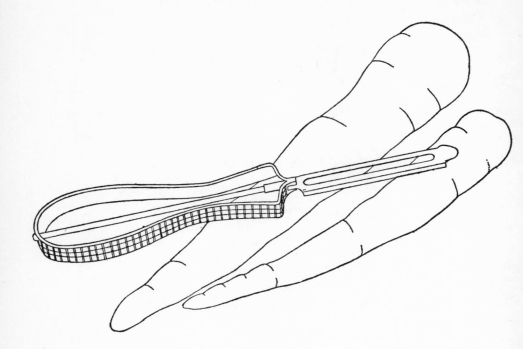

WE ARE so obsessed with the nutritional value of vegetables that we forget frequently how good they can taste. It is a little late in our culinary history to start serving hot vegetables as separate courses in the French or Italian manner, and there is really little reason we should. But there is every reason to stop underboiling or overboiling the vegetables we consume nationally in such staggering amounts. On the one hand, we have the nutritional faddists who will cook a vegetable for a minute or two in a few drops of water, then serve it, unbuttered and unsauced, in limbo as it were, in a half-cooked, half-raw state. In restaurants, on the other hand, those kitchen purgatories known as steam tables do so thorough a job of keeping cooked vegetables warm that when they are finally served, they have, literally, been cooked to death. Vegetables carelessly cooked at home can be equally uninteresting.

BOILED FRESH VEGETABLES:

In fact, the cooking of vegetables is a simple affair and, barring a few more complex braising and baking procedures, rather a matter of timing than anything else. Commonly used vegetables such as peas, string beans, lima beans, corn on the cob, broccoli, asparagus, Brussels sprouts, cauliflower, and a few others should, ideally, be cooked uncovered in plenty of boiling salted water, drained, and served immediately, dressed with melted butter or a sauce of your choice. Vegetables cooked in this fashion preserve their color, freshness, and flavor to a remarkable degree. But they must be served at once; they will taste as if they had been subjected to the restaurant steam table if they are not.

FROZEN VEGETABLES:

Interestingly enough, frozen vegetables, before being packaged, are prepared in very much the same way. Technically known as blanching, the process is to plunge the vegetables briefly into boiling water, then into cold water to stop their cooking, then to freeze them immediately.

If you must use frozen vegetables, for the best results they should be wholly, or at least partially defrosted before being cooked. Frozen peas, thoroughly defrosted, need only be heated for a few minutes with a little butter in a covered saucepan, seasoned with salt and pepper, and served without further ado. Cooking them in liquid for any length of time will destroy what little character they have. Frozen, defrosted spinach, should be treated similarly.

Most other frozen vegetables, however, do require further cooking. Bring the vegetable to a boil in a little chicken stock or water and with at least 1 tablespoon of butter, cover the pan, and cook it over moderate heat until it is barely tender. Any liquid that remains in the pan should be boiled away rapidly with the pan uncovered; shake the pan constantly to keep the vegetable from sticking or burning.

A wise precaution is to cook all frozen or, for that matter, fresh vegetables in enamel, Pyrex, or stainless-steel saucepans, skillets, or casseroles. Many vegetables pick up a metallic taste from aluminum or iron pans, and some, particularly asparagus and artichokes, tend to discolor badly.

BRAISED VEGETABLES:

We are not much given to braising fresh vegetables—that is, cooking or, more literally, half steaming them in a little stock and butter in a covered pan, and then using the braising liquid, somewhat reduced, as a sauce. Although the braising process can hardly be compared in simplicity to tossing a vegetable into a pot of boiling water, there is still much to recommend it. Since the vegetables are cooked rather slowly, they are less likely to overcook. Moreover, they needn't be rushed to the table the moment they are done; and they may be kept warm for a reasonable length of time or, when cold, reheated, even a day later with little if any loss of flavor. Onions, carrots, turnips, celery, leeks, and endive take particularly well to this kind of preparation.

BRAISED ENDIVE

] To serve four [

To BRAISE 8 heads of endive, enough for four people, trim the heads carefully of all discolored leaves, and slice away as much of the root as you can without cutting loose the leaves. If you like the bitter taste of cooked endive, do not blanch them. However, if you prefer a milder flavor, blanch the endives by immersing them in a 2-quart enamel pot of boiling water seasoned with 1 tablespoon of salt and 2 tablespoons of lemon juice. Simmer the endives over moderate heat for about 10 minutes. Then remove them from the water with kitchen tongs, and lay them side by side in a heavily buttered enamel or Pyrex baking dish just about large enough to hold them.

Sprinkle them lightly with salt, dot each one with a little soft butter, and pour into the pan ½ cup of chicken stock, fresh or canned, and 1 teaspoon of lemon juice. The endives should be half immersed in the stock; add some more if they are not. Bring the stock to a boil on top of the stove, then cover the baking dish with a piece of buttered waxed paper, and braise the endives in a preheated **325° F.** oven for an hour, more or less. They should be tender and lightly browned when they are done.

To serve, remove the endive carefully to a hot serving dish, reduce whatever liquid is left in the pan to 2 tablespoons, and pour it over the endive. Sprinkle lightly with finely chopped parsley.

———

MOST BRAISED vegetables are cooked in this way, but with certain individual departures. Carrots, for example, are braised with butter and a little sugar without first being blanched, and the entire cooking operation takes place on top of the stove instead of being finished in the oven. The result is a brightly glazed carrot, its natural sweetness enhanced by the extra sugar needed to glaze it. Glazed carrots are often called . . .

CARROTS VICHY

] To serve four [

Scrape, wash, and cut into 1½-inch lengths enough young carrots to make 2 cupfuls. If you have the time and patience, trim the carrots into small, olive-shaped cylinders (*carottes en olive*).

In a large enamel frying pan you can cover, melt 2 tablespoons of butter in ½ cup of water or chicken stock. Stir in 1 tablespoon of granulated sugar and ¼ teaspoon of salt, and bring to a boil. Add the carrots, turn them about in the liquid a bit, cover the pan tightly, and reduce the heat to the barest simmer. Cook slowly, shaking the pan occasionally and checking to see if the liquid has evaporated, in which event add a couple of tablespoons of stock or water.

The carrots should be tender within 20 minutes to half an hour and the liquid reduced to a syrup. If it seems too thin, boil it down before pouring it over the carrots in a serving dish. Sprinkle with a little finely chopped mint, if you can get it, or finely chopped parsley. These go particularly well with roasts and broiled meats.

———

BRAISED ONIONS

LITTLE WHITE ONIONS may also be braised so that they emerge whole and brown, slightly crusted on the outside and tender within. Here we come to the classic use of vegetables as a garniture. Onions braised in this fashion are spoken of as cooked *à brun,* and they are braised in the oven in rendered salt-pork fat. Detailed instructions for cooking them are given on page 160 in the recipe for BEEF BOUR-GUIGNON where, with the addition of mushrooms and salt pork scraps, they constitute a *garniture à la bourguignonne.* They are, naturally enough, also added to COQ AU VIN À LA BOURGUIGNONNE, and are the traditional garnish for VEAL MARENGO. In short, they are appropriate for most brown stews, and in addition are excellent, sprinkled with chopped parsley, with any roasted or broiled meat.

Little onions are also cooked *à blanc,* which does not mean that they are boiled but rather that they are stewed, not browned, in butter. This is the garnish for white stews, including *blanquettes* of lamb or veal (instructions for cooking the onions are given with this recipe, on page 181) or a chicken fricassee (page 35).

Finally, brown braised onions are also cooked with carrots, again in rendered salt-pork fat, and without adding sugar to the carrots. The combination then becomes a *garniture bourgeoise.* Directions are given for this on page 166 in the recipe for hot BEEF À LA MODE, which is always served with this garniture. On the whole, a *garniture bourgeoise* is usually reserved for braised meats. You may give the onions and carrots their initial browning together before braising, but it can be more convenient to brown them separately.

THE WHITE TURNIP, usually relegated to a supporting role in soups and stews, is quite able to stand proudly alone when it is braised. In fact, when properly prepared, it has an extraordinarily subtle flavor, particularly good with duck, pork, or ham. Although braising a turnip is quite similar to braising a carrot, turnips may be blanched to tame their intense flavor a bit.

BRAISED TURNIPS

] To serve four [

Trim and peel about 1½ pounds of small young white turnips; if they are very small, leave them whole, but cut larger ones into halves or quarters. They may also be trimmed into olive shapes, but don't make these too small; as they become tender and absorb the braising liquid, they tend to fall apart.

To blanch the turnips, bring them to a boil in enough salted water to cover them, and let them boil steadily for about 7 minutes. Drain at once, and arrange them in one layer in an enamel casserole or frying pan you can cover.

Pour in enough fresh or canned chicken or beef stock to almost, but not quite submerge the turnips—three quarters of the way up should be about enough. Add 3 tablespoons of butter, some salt, and a little pepper. Bring the stock to a boil, then cover the pan tightly and cook the turnips on top of the stove at the barest simmer for about 20 minutes, more or less, until they are tender but not falling apart.

With a slotted spoon, transfer them to a hot serving dish. Boil down almost to a glaze whatever liquid remains in the pan, and pour it over the turnips. Season with a few drops of lemon juice, if you like, and dust with a little finely chopped parsley.

ONE OF THE most famous of all braised vegetables is *petits pois à la française,* or fresh peas braised in the French manner. Fresh, preferably young peas are cooked with shredded lettuce, little white onions, parsley, butter, and only a sprinkling of water, and the result can only be described as magical.

BRAISED PEAS À LA FRANÇAISE

] To serve four [

Have ready about 2 cups of freshly shelled young peas—approximately 2½ pounds in the pod. Combine them in a 2-quart pan with a small head of carefully washed and shredded Boston lettuce, 8 very small peeled white onions (no more than ¾ inch in diameter), four sprigs of parsley with their stems (tied in a bouquet), ½ teaspoon of salt, ¼ teaspoon of sugar, and 4 tablespoons of butter. Stir gently together and moisten with 1/3 cup of cold water.

Bring this slowly to a boil, then cover the pan tightly and cook over moderate heat for about half an hour, or until the peas and onions are tender and the liquid has all but cooked away. If it hasn't, cook briskly, uncovered, shaking the pan constantly, until the liquid has entirely evaporated. Remove the parsley, gently stir into the peas a couple of tablespoons of soft butter, taste for salt, and serve.

*

TOMATOES:

Although there are a few classic tomato recipes which effectively use the tomato in its entirety, the majority of tomato dishes requires that the tomato be peeled, seeded, and drained. These are not the precious, over-refined procedures they may at first glance appear. Whatever its nutritional value, the watery center of the tomato has little if any flavor when cooked, and the seeds and the outer skin have even less. Together, they merely dilute and weaken the flavor of any dish to which they are added, be it a soup, stew, or fondue. However, broiled and stuffed tomatoes should not be peeled or they will lose their shape and collapse. But, if you neglect to seed and drain the tomatoes you stuff, your stuffing will be a sodden mess indeed.

TOMATOES *niçoise,* one of the great tomato dishes of Provence, is perhaps the best model for all stuffed-tomato recipes. Seeded and drained tomato halves are filled with a simple stuffing composed of dry bread crumbs, garlic, herbs, and oil, then baked until tender and served either hot or cold. Hot, they make colorful, aromatic accompaniments to roast such as LARDED RACK OF VEAL. But they do equally well teamed with sautés such as VEAL SCALOPPINE MARSALA.

270

Cold (really at room temperature), they make fine hors d'oeuvres, sprinkled with parsley and served with a slice of lemon and hot French bread.

TOMATOES NIÇOISE

] To serve six [

CUT IN HALF crosswise 8 ripe but firm tomatoes, preferably about 4 inches in diameter. With the handle of a teaspoon, a small rounded knife, or the tip of your finger, carefully scoop the seeds from each tomato half, removing as little of the sectional walls as possible. Sprinkle the inside of each tomato half rather generously with salt, and turn them over to drain on a double sheet of paper towelling.

Meanwhile, prepare the stuffing: Combine in a small bowl 1 cup of bread crumbs, made preferably from hard French or Italian bread, 1 teaspoon of finely chopped garlic, ½ cup of finely chopped parsley, 1 tablespoon of chopped fresh basil or 2 teaspoons of crumbled dry basil, a scant teaspoon of salt, a little coarsely ground pepper, and, finally, enough olive oil—anywhere from 1/3 to ½ cup—to give the crumbs the consistency of damp sand when the oil is mixed into it.

Fill each tomato half with this mixture, arrange them side by side in a large lightly oiled baking dish, and dribble a little olive oil over each one. Bake the tomatoes in a preheated **375° F.** oven for 20 minutes to half an hour, or until they are soft but not falling apart and the stuffing is lightly browned. If you like, you may slide the tomatoes under the broiler for a few seconds before serving them.

TOMATO FONDUE

IT MAY come as a surprise to you to learn that fondues are not always made of cheese. In classical French cooking the term refers as well to special vegetable preparations, of which the most useful is probably the tomato fondue. Fresh ripe tomatoes are peeled, seeded,

271

and drained, the pulp cut into julienne strips and rapidly cooked in butter. Simple to prepare, it makes a colorful and freshly flavored accompaniment to dishes cooked *à la provençale,* as in the recipe for SAUTÉED SEA SQUABS where directions for making the fondue are given, on page 81. And it is equally successful as a garnish for an omelette or scrambled eggs.

Depending on how you plan to use it, all manner of additional ingredients may go into tomato fondue: minced onion or garlic, fresh herbs, and even the barest pinch of powdered saffron.

✳

POTATOES:

Perhaps because it is the most popular of all vegetables, the potato suffers the greatest number of culinary assaults upon it. That it survives them, its popularity unimpaired, is a testimony to its durable and universal appeal. Almost all our main dishes are accompanied by potatoes in one form or another, yet for the most part these are carelessly or indifferently prepared and unimaginatively served. With a little effort and knowledge, any cook can lift the potato out of its commonplace role as a "starchy vegetable" and transform it into a true delicacy.

Potatoes can be boiled, steamed, baked, broiled, sautéed, or fried; they can be served hot, tepid, or cold, and with equal success become an hors d'oeuvre, soup, salad, main dish, and even, in some forms, a dessert. Not only are potatoes economical and always available, but contrary to popular misconception, they are considerably less fattening than bread. It is time, then, to rediscover the potato and cook it with the respect it deserves.

WHAT BETTER place to begin than with mashed potatoes, at once the most difficult and simple of all potato dishes? Not the dreary restaurant version, or the synthetic-tasting dehydrated ones, but the real thing: honest, old-fashioned, freshly cooked potatoes, beaten to velvety smoothness with lots of sweet butter and heavy cream, and rushed to the table as if this were a soufflé on the verge of collapsing.

MASHED POTATOES

] To serve four [

To insure the proper texture and density of your mashed potatoes, choose a mealy baking potato in preference to any of the firmer varieties. Two pounds should do nicely for four people. Peel the potatoes and cut them into halves or quarters, but no smaller or they will absorb too much water and crumble as they cook. Drop them into a couple of quarts of salted boiling water and, with the pot uncovered, let them boil steadily until they are tender. Cooking charts notwithstanding, it is impossible to say how long this will take; your best gauge is to pierce the potatoes periodically with a small pointed knife. When the pieces are no longer resistant at the center, they are done.

Drain the potatoes at once in a colander, return them to the pan, and shake them over moderate heat until they are mealy and dry. Don't be tempted to ignore this step, for the success of the mashed potatoes will largely depend on how dry the boiled potatoes are before you purée them.

An electric mixer (not a blender), will do the puréeing most easily and effectively, but if you don't own one, use a ricer or potato masher and sieve. In any case, mash the potatoes into a bowl which you have first rinsed in very hot water and then thoroughly dried. Beat the purée until it is completely free of lumps, then beat into it a little at a time at least ¼ pound of soft butter. Sometime earlier, you will have heated and kept hot ½ cup of heavy cream (or light cream or milk, if you must). Beat this into the mashed potatoes a tablespoon at a time, using more or less of the cream to give the potatoes the consistency you prefer. Ideally, the purée should be neither wet nor dry and should hold its shape lightly when scooped up in a spoon.

Now beat into it as much salt and white pepper as you think it needs, and serve the potatoes at once in a heated serving dish. Garnish them with whatever you like: chopped parsley, chives, dill, or basil—fresh, of course; or float a small well of melted butter in the center. But whatever you do, serve the potatoes the moment they are ready. If it is absolutely necessary, they may be kept warm for a few minutes in a pan set over barely simmering water, but then the first bloom will be gone and the potatoes, though certainly edible, will never taste quite the same.

IDEALLY, baked potatoes demand the same split-second timing as mashed potatoes if they are to be savored at their peak, the moment they are done. As a potato bakes, its inner moisture is converted into steam which gives the potato pulp its characteristic puffy texture. But if the potato is allowed to languish for too long after it is cooked through, the steam turns to water, the pulp becomes soggy, and the potato skin (for some tastes, the whole point of baking a potato in the first place) becomes wizened as old parchment.

BAKED POTATOES

For perfect baked potatoes, use only mealy potatoes, commercially referred to as "baking" potatoes no matter what part of the country they come from: Maine, Idaho, Oregon, California, and elsewhere. How long you bake them will, of course, depend on the size and type of the potato and the heat of the oven.

Before baking the potato, many potato-skin fanciers like to rub the scrubbed, thoroughly dried skin with soft butter and then roll the potato lightly in coarse salt. As the potato bakes, the salt sticks to the skin and gives it a most unusual texture and appearance.

Potatoes bake best set on a grill or cake rack placed in a shallow pan or on a cooky sheet. This allows for a free flow of heat under the potatoes and insures even cooking. As for the oven heat, a preheated **425° F.** oven is the perfect temperature to bake the potato through quickly without burning it. At this temperature, a ½-pound Idaho potato should be done in about 40 minutes. However, if you have other food in the oven at the same time, bake the potatoes at whatever *lower* temperature the oven may be set for; they will simply take longer to cook.

Choose potatoes approximately the same size so that they will be done simultaneously, and start testing them after they have been in the oven about 20 minutes. Don't pierce them full of holes with a fork or knife but, instead, press them gently between your thumb and forefinger. When the potatoes yield to the pressure quite readily on all sides, they are done.

With a small knife, cut a cross in the top of each potato. Squeeze the potato gently, forcing up some of the pulp and thus allowing the steam to escape. Place a generous lump of soft butter in each opening and serve at once. All manner of garnishes may accompany baked potatoes: more butter, a bowl of sour cream, crumbled crisp bacon, freshly grated Parmesan cheese, or any fresh herb such as minced chives, dill, basil, or parsley. If by chance you have some Italian PESTO (page 290) around, use it in place of butter.

NEW POTATOES are in a class by themselves. Because they remain firm after they are cooked, it is not absolutely necessary to rush them from the kitchen to the table the minute they are done. They may be kept warm for reasonable lengths of time without becoming soggy and, in a pinch, they may even be reheated. But like most young fresh vegetables, the new potato is unquestionably at its best simply boiled, bathed in butter, and served with salt, pepper, and a sprinkling of fresh chopped parsley, dill, chives, or basil. As an accompaniment to a poached fish such as the BOURRIDE on page 87, boiled new potatoes are difficult to surpass.

BOILED NEW POTATOES

Choose firm red, or white, small new potatoes all approximately the same size. Peel or scrape them; or, if you are concerned with preserving their nutrients, cook them in their jackets and peel them later. Peeled or unpeeled, plunge them into a kettle of boiling salted water, and boil them steadily, uncovered, until they are done, testing them periodically with a small pointed knife. Drain them at once, and if they must be peeled, peel them while they are still hot. Hold them in a kitchen towel if they are too hot to handle comfortably.

If the potatoes were previously peeled, return them to the pot, or a dry skillet, after draining them, and shake them gently over moderate heat until they are absolutely dry. Transfer them to a heated casserole or serving dish in which you have previously melted, without browning, a generous amount of butter, and roll the potatoes around in the butter until they are thoroughly coated on all sides. Salt and pepper them, and serve them as they are or garnished with the herb of your choice.

If the potatoes must be kept warm for any length of time (even these are really at their best served immediately), place the casserole, covered, in a **250° F.** oven, and baste them occasionally with the melted butter. Add the herb, if any, just before serving. And remember that with certain sauced dishes the potatoes are as good or better *without* butter.

Sautéed potatoes are indispensable garnishes for many roast or broiled meats, for example the NOISETTES OF LAMB on page 211. New potatoes are ideal for sautéing, though you may of course use winter potatoes if you wish. Although they may be parboiled first, they are far better if they are sautéed raw. The French have a variety of names for sautéed potatoes, each determined by the shape of the cut potato: *château* if the potatoes are small enough to sauté whole or are cut into olive shapes; *noisette* if they are scooped into small balls with a melon cutter; *Parmentier* if they are cut into 1/4- or 1/2-inch dice; or plain *pommes sautées* if they are sliced. Whatever their shape, the sautéing process is the same, though the cooking time varies with the size of the pieces of potato.

SAUTÉED POTATOES

] To serve six [

Peel and cut into whatever shape you wish 3 pounds of new (or old) potatoes. Make certain that all the pieces are the same size, and drop them into a bowl of cold water as you proceed. When the potatoes are all prepared, drain them and dry them thoroughly in a kitchen towel.

In a large heavy frying pan at least 10 inches, preferably 12 inches in diameter, heat until almost smoking either 6 tablespoons of clarified butter (see page 81) or 3 tablespoons each of butter and vegetable oil. Drop the potatoes in all at once, and cook them briskly over high heat, shaking the pan almost continuously until the potatoes have browned lightly on all sides.

At that point, if the potatoes are large, lower the heat and cover the pan and, again shaking the pan periodically, cook them until they are evenly brown all over and can be pierced easily with the point of a knife. Potatoes cut into small dice or ½-inch balls needn't be covered and may be cooked somewhat more quickly. However, it is necessary to turn them frequently or to shake the pan lest they burn. The test for doneness is the same.

Of course, sautéed potatoes are at their best served the moment they are done. But if they must wait, transfer them to a baking dish lined with a paper towel to absorb the fat, and let them rest in a preheated **250° F.** oven for as long as 15 minutes but definitely no longer. When you serve them, drain off any excess fat, and sprinkle the potatoes lightly with salt, pepper, and a couple of tablespoons of chopped parsley.

ALL KINDS of masterful tricks are possible with the adaptable potato and the French seem to have explored them all. Their recipes run into the hundreds. One of the most practical and useful is the famous potatoes Anna. There are so many possible versions of this remarkable dish that it might be well to understand the process in its simplest form before attempting any of its variants. Ostensibly invented in the nineteenth century by a famous Parisian chef in honor of some mythical Anna, it is a method of cooking thin slices of potato arranged in layers in a circular baking dish. The potatoes are steeped in butter and baked until they have absorbed as much butter as they can hold. In the process, a thick outside crust is formed, encasing the soft potato slices within. The potatoes, in a compact cake, are turned out onto a platter to be served.

The whole procedure is essentially simple and reliable if a number of possible pitfalls are avoided: First, use firm potatoes—old or new—rather than mealy ones, and slice them no more than a six-teenth of an inch thick. Even more important is the choice of baking dish. Theoretically, potatoes Anna may be made in almost anything from the special potatoes Anna pan of earlier days to a frying pan, cake pan, or what have you. In reality, however, the dish that works best is a rounded quart-size Pyrex baking bowl. Its round form shapes the potatoes attractively and prevents them from coming apart when they are unmolded. Moreover, the transparent glass allows you to check periodically on how fast the potatoes are browning.

It should be pointed out that a bowl larger than one quart is not effective. The crisp, brown outside crust of potatoes Anna is all important, and a larger baking bowl will produce less crust per serving. Therefore it is more practical to use two separate quart-size bowls for making a larger quantity.

POTATOES ANNA

] To serve six [

Peel about 2 pounds of medium-sized firm, old or new, potatoes and as each one is peeled drop it into a bowl of cold water. Slice them into rounds a sixteenth of an inch thick, with a vegetable slicer if you have one, otherwise with a thin sharp knife. Return the slices (there should be 5 to 6 cups) to the bowl of water, and run cold water over them until the water in the bowl is absolutely clear.

Drain the potatoes thoroughly, lay them side by side on sheets of paper towelling, and pat each slice dry. Preheat the oven to **450° F.**

Meanwhile, clarify ¼ pound of butter: Melt it slowly, skimming off the surface foam. Turn off the heat, and pour the clear butter into a small bowl, discarding the milky solids, or whey, which will have settled at the bottom of the pan.

With a pastry brush, heavily coat the bottom and sides of a 1-

quart Pyrex bowl with the clarified butter. Then lay the potatoes out in a neat circle, each slice slightly overlapping the next, around the bottom of the bowl. Continue to arrange slices in concentric rings until they completely cover the bottom of the bowl. Salt and pepper the potatoes, and brush them with a tablespoon or so of the butter. Build up the next layer of potatoes in the same fashion but don't bother to arrange them so meticulously.

Now place a row of potatoes carefully around the sides of the bowl, and again have them overlap slightly. Continue to build up the dish with the remaining potatoes, from the bottom and the sides, spreading each layer heavily with butter and seasoning each well with salt and pepper. Don't be afraid to pack the bowl as tightly as you can, for the potatoes will shrink considerably as they cook.

After spreading the top layer of potatoes with the last of the butter, cover the bowl with a heavy lid (which needn't fit precisely), and bake the potatoes on the center shelf of the hot oven for about 50 minutes, or until the potatoes barely resist the point of a sharp knife.

Now remove the cover, turn the oven heat down to **425° F.,** and move the bowl to the floor of the oven, directly over the source of heat. Bake the potatoes another 15 or 20 minutes, or long enough to brown without burning the overlapping potato slices on the bottom and sides of the bowl. Then remove the bowl from the oven, and let the potatoes rest for 3 or 4 minutes. Turn the oven down to **250° F.**

Have ready a heated ovenproof platter. Slide a flexible metal spatula around the inside rim of the bowl, carefully freeing any potato slices that may be sticking to the sides. Then gently force the spatula as far down as you can, and move it under the potatoes without disrupting the design.

When you are reasonably certain no slices are sticking, place the heated platter upside down over the bowl and, grasping bowl and platter together securely, quickly reverse them, rapping the platter once sharply on the table. The potatoes should emerge in a round compact mass. If any of the slices do stick to the bowl, carefully remove them, and replace them where they belong on the unmolded potatoes.

With a basting syringe, remove any butter that collects on the serving platter, sprinkle the potatoes Anna with some chopped parsley, and serve. If they must wait, simply place the platter in the slow oven where they will stay hot for 10 minutes or so without coming to any harm.

AFTERTHOUGHTS:

✳ It is not possible to cook potatoes Anna ahead and reheat them, but you may, if you like, arrange the potatoes in the buttered bowl early and set them aside until you are ready to bake them. In that event, the slices must first be blanched to prevent discoloring. To do this, drop them into boiling salted water and boil them briskly for 2 minutes. Drain them at once, run cold water over them to stop their cooking, and pat them dry with paper towels. Proceed to fill the bowl as described before, then cover it tightly with Saran wrap. The potatoes can remain this way for hours without discoloring. Cook exactly as before.

✳ Potatoes Anna may be varied in any number of interesting ways: Sprinkle each layer of buttered potatoes with freshly grated Parmesan cheese; or arrange lightly sautéed onion rings over them; or, more discretely, spread the layers with a few finely chopped and lightly sautéed shallots; fresh herbs, such as chives, dill, or basil, lend to the potatoes an interesting aromatic flavor. But probably the ultimate in garnishes consists of chopped truffles scattered at random over each layer of potatoes.

Rice, Pasta & Kasha

RICE:

Rice is probably as old as any food known to man. The staple diet of millions, it has no social or economic boundaries and is equally relevant in a coolie's rice bowl or accompanying a dish of LOBSTER L'AMÉRICAINE. Yet the cooking of it remains a problem for many cooks.

Modern food technology has taken the mystery out of rice by converting or precooking it. Now, with no effort at all, it is possible to serve perfectly cooked rice and have each grain separate and dry. But it is also rubbery and tasteless. Far more interesting are the many varieties that have not been tampered with—the short, fat-bellied Piedmontese rice from northern Italy, our own long-grained Carolina rice, and Patna rice, among others, each with its particular texture and flavor. And learning to cook them well and predictably is less difficult than you might think. The following recipes describe in detail three useful and different methods: the simple boiled rice, indispensible to rich sauced dishes such as BLANQUETTE DE VEAU; the Middle-Eastern PILAF, a moist, highly flavored rice suitable for meats such as BROILED LEG OF LAMB; and the classic, creamy Italian *risotto,* a superb dish by itself or the perfect and necessary accompaniment to OSSO BUCO MILANESE.

BOILED RICE

] To serve four [

THIS METHOD of cooking rice is literally what the name says it is and foolproof if you don't let the rice overcook: Bring to a boil, in a large pot of any kind, 6 quarts of water. Add 3 tablespoons of salt, then slowly pour in 1 cupful of unwashed rice, letting it dribble in slowly enough so that the water never stops boiling. Lower the heat slightly, and allow the rice to boil undisturbed for about 15 minutes, at which point start testing it for tenderness. The grains should be soft but slightly resistant to the teeth—*al dente*, as the Italians say. Depending on the type of rice, you may have to cook it as long as 18 minutes, but whatever you do don't overcook it.

When the rice is done, drain it in a large colander, and pour over it enough boiling water to wash it free of any excess starch. Loosen and toss the rice in the colander with a couple of forks, transfer it to a heated serving dish or casserole, and serve.

If the rice must wait, cover the casserole loosely with a kitchen towel, and place it in a **250° F.** oven to keep warm. The towel will prevent the top layer of rice from browning and permit any excess moisture in the rice to evaporate.

To reheat the rice if it is cold, place it in a colander which will just about fit over a pot of rapidly boiling water without touching the water. Cover the colander loosely with a kitchen towel, and let the rice steam until it is hot enough to serve. With a fork, turn the rice up from the bottom of the colander every few minutes so that it heats through evenly.

AFTERTHOUGHT:

✳ Naturally, it is not necessary to double the quantity of water in order to cook twice the quantity of rice. Add 2 more quarts of water and a little additional salt to the original 6 quarts for another cup of raw rice.

RICE PILAF

] To serve four [

TECHNICALLY, this Middle Eastern method of cooking rice is a braise. In other words, the rice is lightly sautéed in fat, with onions, garlic, or what you will, covered with stock, and cooked slowly until the stock is absorbed. Sometimes a bouquet of herbs is added.

Melt 2 tablespoons of butter in a heavy 2-quart casserole equipped with an equally heavy cover. Add to the butter 2 tablespoons of finely chopped onion and, if you like, ¼ teaspoon of minced garlic, and cook slowly without browning for about 5 minutes. When the onions are soft and translucent, stir into them 1 cup of unwashed rice and, with a wooden spoon, mix until each grain of rice glistens with the melted butter.

Over moderate heat, sauté the rice for 2 or 3 minutes, but in no circumstances let it brown. Depending on the type of rice, some or all of the kernels will become opaque at the end of that time. Pour over them, then, 2 cups of hot strong chicken stock, fresh or canned, and bring the rice to a boil, stirring to dislodge any grains which may have stuck to the bottom of the pan. Add 1 teaspoon of salt, and cover the casserole.

Simmer the rice over the lowest possible heat, undisturbed, for 15 to 18 minutes. At the end of that time the rice will have absorbed all the stock. If it hasn't, cook it a moment or two longer. Loosen and toss the rice with a couple of forks and serve. If it must wait, drape a kitchen towel loosely over the uncovered casserole, and place it in a **250° F.** oven for as long as half an hour—much longer, the pilaf will dry out; one of its charms should be its slight degree of moistness.

RISOTTO MILANESE

] To serve six or eight [

UNLIKE a rice pilaf, a true *risotto* is a soft, creamy mixture, though the grains of rice still retain their shape. This requires a grain that will absorb an unusual amount of moisture. The ideal rice for the purpose is, of course, the short fat-bellied Piedmontese rice the Italians use. Now imported from Italy in considerable quantity, it is decidedly worth making an effort to find. Lacking it, however, Carolina rice will make tolerable *risotto,* but it must be watched carefully lest it overcook and turn into an unattractive mush. Don't attempt a *risotto* with converted rice; it simply won't work.

Bring 7 cups of well-seasoned chicken broth, fresh or canned, to a simmer in a small saucepan. Meanwhile, in a heavy 3- or 4-quart casserole, melt 4 tablespoons of butter over low heat. Add to it ½ cup of finely chopped onions, and cook them slowly without letting them brown for about 5 minutes. Stir in 1/3 to ½ cup of choppel uncooked beef marrow if you can get it (leave it out if you can't), and cook a moment longer. Then add 2 cups of unwashed rice.

Raise the heat a bit and, stirring constantly, sauté the rice for 2 or 3 minutes, or until it is thoroughly coated with the butter and becomes somewhat opaque. Immediately pour over it ½ cup of dry white wine, and bring this to a boil. The wine should be almost completely absorbed by the rice in a matter of seconds.

When the wine has all but disappeared and not before, pour over the rice 2 cups of the simmering broth. Stirring occasionally, let the rice cook, uncovered, over moderate heat until the broth is almost all absorbed. Add another 2 cups of hot broth, and cook at the same rate until it also is absorbed.

Meanwhile, steep in 2 cups of the hot stock about ⅛ teaspoon of powdered saffron, or saffron filaments rubbed to a powder with the back of a spoon. Pour this stock over the rice, and stir gently but thoroughly. Reduce the heat somewhat, for at this stage the rice has a tendency to stick; you should also stir it more often. When these 2 cups of saffron stock have been fully absorbed, the rice should be creamy and tender. If it isn't, add ½ cup more stock (and possibly still another ½ cup after that), cooking and stirring as before until the *risotto* is done.

Remove the pan from the heat and, with a fork, stir into it 4 tablespoons of softened butter, being careful not to mash the rice.

When the butter has been absorbed, stir into the rice in the same fashion anywhere from ½ to 1 cup of freshly grated Parmesan cheese. Taste for seasoning, and serve at once, with more cheese passed separately if you like.

The casserole of *risotto*, uncovered, and with a kitchen towel draped loosely over it, may be kept warm in a **250° F.** oven for 5 to 8 minutes but not a minute longer.

＊

PASTA:

Like so many foreign foods taken over wholeheartedly by Americans and the American food industry, Italian pasta is a much abused dish. Except for a few excellent restaurants in the larger cities, pasta, whether it is spaghetti, ravioli, lasagna, or anything else, is usually overcooked, oversauced, and overseasoned. And when one adds to that the commercial preparations lining the shelves of our stores—cooked pastas and pasta sauces of all descriptions, bottled, canned, frozen, and dehydrated—one is tempted in the interest of digestion alone to foreswear pasta altogether. But that would be a mistake, for in knowing hands pasta can be a delight indeed, and its preparation, at least in its simplest forms, is not at all demanding. In fact, a dinner composed of, say, *prosciutto* and melon, a dish of hot buttered pasta, a green salad, and some cheese can be made even by a novice cook in less time than it would take to open and heat a number of cans—to say nothing of how much less it would cost.

TO COOK PASTA

All pastas without exception are prepared initially in the same way: They are immersed in salted boiling water and cooked rapidly to the desired degree of tenderness. If you make it a practice always to cook a pound of pasta—any pasta—in at least 6 quarts of furiously boiling water and, after it has softened a bit, to test it every few minutes for tenderness, you need never eat a strand of overcooked pasta again. Exact timings are not possible, for each type of pasta must cook a different length of time. And timings suggested on boxes of pasta aren't much help; they are almost always too long.

The best gauge to follow is the size of the pasta. The standard varieties like the wiry *vermicelli,* the flat *linguine,* the thin tubular spaghettini and thicker spaghetti, vary enormously in their cooking times, *linguine* taking perhaps half as much time to cook as spaghetti. And the homemade noodles such as *fettuccine* or *tagliatelle* (if you know how to make them, or are lucky enough to find a store where you can buy them) take even less time. On the other hand, really thick macaroni, and lasagne and pasta shells, must be cooked for somewhat longer periods than are usually suggested on the boxes if they are to lose their tough rubbery texture. The Italian term *al dente,* slightly resistant to the teeth, expresses admirably and succinctly the point to which all pastas should be cooked.

And most important of all, the pasta must be drained thoroughly. You will ruin any sauce, no matter how perfectly prepared, if there is any water left in the drained pasta.

Of the innumerable sauces invented by the Italians to dress their pasta, perhaps the simplest—butter, cream, and grated cheese—is the best. Proceeding on the principle that the flavor and texture of a pasta sauce should be determined by the pasta itself, this delicate creamy butter sauce should be used on the most delicate of pastas; ideally, *fettuccine,* but *linguine* or spaghettini will do as well.

BUTTER AND CHEESE SAUCE

For 1 pound of pasta, enough to serve four as a separate course, cream ¼ pound of butter, either by hand or in an electric mixer, until it is light and smooth. Beat into it 3 tablespoons of heavy cream, and little by little ½ cup of freshly grated Parmesan or Romano cheese. Make this mixture ahead of time and put it aside.

While the pasta is cooking, heat a large serving bowl or casserole in a **250° F.** oven until it is too hot to touch. When the pasta has cooked *al dente,* pour it into a large colander, and lift the strands with a fork to make sure that every drop of water drains off. Immediately transfer the pasta to the hot serving bowl and, with two forks, mix into it the softened creamed butter, lifting the pasta up and over itself until every bit of it is coated with sauce. Taste it now for seasoning. It will need a great deal of salt; add it courageously, for there is nothing duller than undersalted pasta. A few gratings of freshly ground black or white pepper, and the pasta is ready to serve; on heated plates, of course.

AFTERTHOUGHTS:

✳ The white truffles discussed on page 23 in the recipe for BAGNA CAUDA make an unusual addition to this sauce. Slice one very, very thin, or mince it, and stir it into the pasta just before serving.

✳ When you place long pasta into the boiling water, *never* break it to make it fit in the pot; simply push it down gently until it softens and bends enough to slide under the water.

TOMATO SAUCE

A MORE robust sauce, particularly good on spaghetti or any of the heavier pastas, is this tomato sauce. For 1 pound of pasta, cook very slowly ¾ cup of finely chopped onions and 1 teaspoon of finely chopped garlic in ¼ cup of olive oil. When, after about 15 minutes, the onions are quite soft but not brown, pour the entire contents of the pan into a fine sieve set over a small heavy saucepan. Let all the oil drain through, and press down heavily on the onions to extract all their juices before throwing them away.

Add to the olive oil 1 medium can of Italian plum tomatoes and 2 tablespoons of concentrated tomato paste dissolved first in ¼ cup of dry red wine. Bring this slowly to a boil, then reduce the heat to the barest simmer, and add to the sauce 1 teaspoon of sugar (to cut the acidity of the canned tomatoes), 1 teaspoon of dry, or 1 tablespoon of fresh chopped basil, and a bouquet of 4 sprigs of parsley, a large celery top, and a bay leaf, all securely tied together. Season well with salt and coarsely ground black pepper, half cover the pan,

and simmer the sauce for a couple of hours or more until it is reduced to a purée. You may add to the sauce at this point 2 flat
drained and finely chopped anchovies, and simmer it a few minutes
longer.

Cook the pasta *al dente,* drain it through a colander with the utmost care, lifting up the strands with a fork to make sure all the
water is released, and transfer the pasta to a hot serving bowl. With
two forks, mix into it about 6 tablespoons of hot slightly browned
butter, and serve. Pass the sauce and a bowl of freshly grated Parmesan or Romano cheese separately.

IN THE Italian repertory of sauces, there is one which is particularly
inspired, *pesto genovese.* Traditionally, it is made in a mortar, of
fresh basil, garlic, pine nuts, and cheese all pounded to a paste and
moistened with olive oil, then served uncooked over hot pasta of
any type. But unless you grow your own or know special sources for
it, fresh basil is most difficult to come by. Also, the pounding process
takes a great deal of energy and presupposes that you own a large
mortar and pestle. So, more practically, the sauce can be made in
an electric blender, substituting parsley and a little dried basil for
the fresh basil, and substituting walnuts for the pine nuts when
these are not available. While this *pesto* lacks something of the aromatic distinction of the original, it is nevertheless a remarkable
sauce.

PESTO GENOVESE

For a pound of pasta, enough to serve four, make the *pesto* as follows: Strip enough washed and dried parsley from its stems to make
2 cups, quite firmly packed; naturally, if you can get the basil, all
the better. Place this in the jar of your blender with 1 tablespoon
of dry basil (if you're using parsley), 1 teaspoon of salt, ½ teaspoon
of freshly ground black pepper, 1 teaspoon of chopped garlic, 2
tablespoons of pine nuts or walnuts, and finally, ½ cup of olive oil.

Blend at high speed, pushing the herbs down with a rubber spatula, and adding more olive oil if necessary to make a smooth thick

purée. Turn off the motor, and add to the jar ½ cup of freshly grated Parmesan cheese. Blend just long enough to mix, and the *pesto* is ready. Stir it into a bowl of hot, thoroughly drained pasta and, with two forks, mix and mix until each strand of pasta is flecked with green. Taste for salt (add it generously), and serve at once, accompanied by a bowl of freshly grated Parmesan cheese.

AFTERTHOUGHTS:

✳ If you can find some Sardo cheese, the Sardinian cheese also used to make *pesto,* by all means substitute it, all or in part, for the Parmesan.

✳ Stir into the hot pasta 4 tablespoons of softened butter for a richer sauce, before adding the *pesto.*

✳

KASHA:

An unfamiliar grain to most Americans, *kasha* is as indispensible to a Russian or Pole as pasta is to an Italian. But national habit aside, kasha, or buckwheat groats, is worth knowing for its own sake and is now available in many supermarkets and specialty food stores. It is simple to cook, reheats perfectly, goes with almost anything, and is, if you care, a nutritional powerhouse. Serve it in place of potatoes or rice and, specifically, as an accompaniment to CHICKEN CUTLETS KIEV on page 133.

KASHA

] To serve four to six [

1 large egg
1 cup whole-grain brown buckwheat groats
1½ teaspoons salt
2 cups chicken stock, fresh or canned
2 tablespoons butter or rendered chicken fat

Make certain the groats you buy are the whole-grain type, or your kasha will end up a gruel. With a fork, beat the egg in a large bowl

291

only long enough for the yolk and white to combine. Pour over it the cup of groats and the salt, and stir thoroughly until all trace of the egg disappears. Transfer the groats to a small, heavy ungreased frying pan—enamel is best—and, over moderate heat, toast them until the grains begin to separate and give off a pleasant nutlike odor. Lift them frequently from the bottom of the pan with a spatula, for they are bound to stick during the first few minutes. Toast them as long as you like but make sure you don't burn them.

Meanwhile, in a heavy 2-quart casserole, bring the 2 cups of chicken broth to a boil. Stir into it slowly the toasted groats, add the butter or chicken fat, and cover the casserole tightly. Cook the *kasha* over the lowest possible heat for 15 to 20 minutes, or until the buckwheat has absorbed all the stock and each grain is dry and separate. If you like, the groats may be baked for about the same length of time in a **350° F.** oven, after you have brought the casserole to a boil on top of the stove.

However you have cooked it, when it is done, fluff it up with a fork and serve. If it must wait, drape the uncovered casserole lightly with a kitchen towel, and keep the *kasha* warm in a **250° F.** oven for as long as you like. As a matter of fact, the grains will be even drier and more separate after being subjected to this treatment, for the towel will allow any excess moisture to evaporate and yet prevent the surface of the *kasha* from browning.

AFTERTHOUGHTS:

✳ To reheat the *kasha,* place it in a colander which will just fit over a pan of boiling water. Cover loosely with a towel, and from time to time turn the *kasha* up from the bottom of the colander so that it will steam through evenly.

✳ Hot *kasha* makes a fine luncheon or supper dish when it is combined with lightly sautéed mushrooms and served with a bowl of cold sour cream sprinkled with fresh chopped dill. Or, stir some *kasha* into a clear soup as a garnish in place of rice.

CHAPTER XII

Salads

PLAIN SALADS

French Dressing
Spinach Salad
French Potato Salad
Mayonnaise

COMBINATION SALADS

Salade Niçoise
Caesar Salad
Salad of Cold Beef Vinaigrette
Mimosa Salad Fifi

Today, the word salad is used so loosely that it might be well to return to the orderly concepts of the French for whom salad making is a precise affair indeed. The French divide salads into two large categories: first, the plain salad, or *salade simple,* consisting of one or more fresh greens dressed with oil, vinegar, salt, and pepper, or a single cold cooked or uncooked vegetable similarly dressed; and second, the combination salad, or *salade composée,* a mixture of various cold cooked or uncooked ingredients, dressed more elaborately.

✳

Plain Salads:

The plain green salad is, of course, comparatively simple to prepare but because of its very simplicity can be exceedingly dull unless it is made with the utmost care. It should contain only the choicest greens. Today, with the word "seasonal" almost an anachronism and vegetable stands virtual jungles of greenery from the beginning of the year to the end, to find at least fresh and often unusual greens should present no problem at all. The next time you go marketing, pass by the crisp but flavorless Iceberg or Simpson lettuce, and instead, try romaine, Boston, escarole, chicory, or any other interesting green your vegetable man may have on hand. If he is an Italian and it is spring, he will probably suggest young dandelions, a salad delicacy still too little appreciated by most of us. And arugala or "rocket" salad, also, a slightly acrid leaf much beloved by the Italians, will when you can find it give your salads originality and distinction. Less frequently available are those aristocrats of the lettuce families, Bibb and field lettuce. Delicate and perishable, they are always expensive but worth every bit of their cost. They make memorable salads.

If you plan to serve more than one green, the choice is a matter of some importance. The so-called mixed-green salad, attractive as it can be, is usually too arbitrary a mixture to have much distinction. Far better to limit yourself deliberately to two or, at the most, three greens of contrasting color, flavor, and texture. Good examples might consist of pale green Boston lettuce paired with dark sprays of water cress; rough-textured romaine and delicate spears of endive. The possibilities are limitless.

Whatever you choose, make certain the greens are fresh, discard all imperfect outside leaves, and wash the greens thoroughly under cold running water. Shake them free of excess water, then dry them, literally leaf by leaf, with absorbent paper or kitchen towels. A French lettuce basket is useful to a point—if you have a back yard or terrace in which to swing it—but it never really dries the greens and finally is more effective as a tool of calisthenics than anything else. If you can spare a couple of old pillowcases, a fairly handy drying method is to wash the greens, shake off the excess water by hand in the kitchen sink, and then place them in one of the pillowcases and shake and pat them dry. Transfer the greens to the second pillow case, roll it up loosely, and refrigerate the greens, pillowcase and all.

The importance of having salad greens bone dry cannot be stressed too strongly, for no matter how fine your dressing, it can be ruined irretrievably by any extra moisture.

FRENCH DRESSING

THE CLASSIC dressing of plain salads is known as *sauce vinaigrette*, more commonly called French dressing. In its basic form, the recipe consists of 3 or 4 parts of oil to 1 part vinegar, seasoned liberally with salt and freshly ground pepper. However, the simple formula poses a number of questions: Should the oil be olive oil, vegetable oil, or a combination of both? Should the vinegar be wine vinegar, white or red? Or should there be no vinegar at all, only lemon juice? What about garlic? Should it be chopped, crushed, rubbed, or mashed? And mustard? And herbs—dried or fresh? These questions, and many more, are easily answered: What finally goes into a dressing must be determined by the salad itself.

Delicate, subtle greens like Boston, Bibb, or field lettuce should have a dressing which supports their flavor without overpowering it: lemon juice, perhaps, all or in part, in place of the vinegar, in the proportion of 1 tablespoon to 4 tablespoons of the lightest French olive oil; no garlic, but, if you like, a little finely minced shallot; salt and freshly ground black pepper, and finally a fresh herb—any herb—but it must be fresh. Dried herbs need heat or long marination to release their volatile essences. They add little to a fresh salad, and their texture when the dried leaves are used in appreciable amounts is coarse and unpleasant.

A salad of romaine, escarole, arugala, or chicory, on the other hand, should have a robust dressing, one that can stand up to these assertive greens and meet them on equal terms: a husky red-wine vinegar in the proportion of 1 tablespoon to 3 tablespoons of an olive oil with a decided bouquet, a touch of powdered mustard, and some finely chopped—never crushed or mashed—garlic, or garlic croutons. And finally, a small dash of lemon juice. Fresh basil or chopped Italian flat-leafed parsley would be fine, pungent, herb additions.

SPINACH SALAD

UNCOOKED SPINACH, not often thought of as a salad green, is, in fact, an excellent one, but the spinach should be young or the leaves may be coarse. Because spinach has a more pronounced flavor than romaine, escarole, chicory, and arugala, it needs an even more assertive dressing than they do. Here is a mustard-onion dressing, enough for about 1 pound of washed and dried spinach, the leaves stripped of their stems: Grate into a bowl about 2 teaspoons of onion, and mix into it 1 scant teaspoon of salt, 1/2 teaspoon of freshly ground pepper, and 2 teaspoons of prepared mustard, either the French or American variety, or a mixture of both. Moisten this paste with 2 tablespoons of wine vinegar. Then, with a wire whisk or a fork, beat into it gradually 8 tablespoons of oil—olive, vegetable, or a mixture of both combined to your taste. Continue to beat until the dressing reaches the consistency of a light mayonnaise. Stir in 1/4 teaspoon of lemon juice, and pour the dressing over the chilled spinach. Toss thoroughly and serve. Interesting variations for this unusual salad are the addition of strips of fresh chilled fennel or sections of oranges. (The oranges must be peeled with a knife right down to the flesh and the sections cut out from between the membranes; see page 329.)

When, in what, and how, to serve a salad is a subject of the greatest dissention among food enthusiasts, amateur or professional. In California, and other parts of the West Coast, salads are more often than not served at the beginning of the meal, taking the place of an hors d'oeuvre in the French manner. Other parts of the country have their own justifications for serving salads as an accompaniment to a hot or cold main course, or serving it directly after the main course with cheese.

No matter when you serve the salad, serve it cold. Ideally, not only should your glass or porcelain salad bowl be well chilled, but the individual salad plates should spend a few minutes in the refrigerator or its freezing compartment before being brought to the table.

Individual wooden salad bowls, apparently indispensible to restaurants of the fish-and-chips type, have no place on a well-appointed table. Since wood is a poor conductor of heat or cold, the bowls can't be chilled; moreover, they are difficult to clean and are, to say the least, clumsy and lacking in elegance. Large wooden salad bowls, we are so often and authoritatively told, become seasoned with constant use, particularly if they are never washed. But it must be pointed out that the bowl, sooner or later, will develop imperceptible cracks, oil and food particles will inevitably collect in the cracks and become rancid. However, if you find a wooden salad bowl absolutely necessary, it isn't a bad idea to scrub it thoroughly after each use.

The practice of tossing green salads with a flourish at the table has little to recommend it, aside from the flourish; the salads are usually undermixed, particularly if the bowl is small. A more practical approach is to toss the salad in the kitchen (in a large mixing bowl if necessary), so that every leaf is thoroughly coated with the dressing. If you are not overly fastidious, mix the salad the way

298

the chefs do, with your hands. Not only will the salad then be thoroughly mixed, but you are less likely to bruise tender greens with the sharp edge of a spoon or fork. And never serve a salad until you have tasted it first. You will find it is almost always undersalted. Surprisingly, that extra bit of salt, judiciously employed, can lift even the most ordinary salad to extraordinary heights.

AMONG THE other varieties of plain salads, French potato salad is perhaps one of the most useful to know. It may be combined successfully with other ingredients—cold vegetables, meat, or shellfish —and is equally at home on a buffet table or at a country picnic. Quite unlike potato salad as we are accustomed to it, the French version is almost always prepared with a *vinaigrette* dressing, highly seasoned with mustard and fresh herbs. Occasionally mayonnaise is also used and, of course, it is freshly made. For the best results, the salad must be prepared with freshly cooked potatoes and dressed while they are still warm. Only then will the potatoes be able to absorb the dressing and not have the characteristic stale left-over taste of most cold potato salads.

FRENCH POTATO SALAD

] To serve eight [

Peel and slice 1/4 inch thick enough old, or any variety of firm potatoes to make 2 quarts. Cook them in salted boiling water until they are tender but not falling apart. Drain them, then transfer them to a large heavy ungreased frying pan, and shake them gently over low heat until each slice is quite dry. (New potatoes of the waxy variety may be cooked whole in their jackets, then peeled and sliced. Drying them in the pan is unnecessary.)

Transfer the potatoes to a large mixing bowl and, while they are still warm, pour over them 4 tablespoons of hot beef or chicken stock, fresh or canned. Stir them gently with a rubber spatula until the stock is entirely absorbed. Mix together to a fluid paste 1 tablespoon of salt, 1/2 teaspoon each of dry and prepared mustard, and 4

299

tablespoons of white-wine vinegar. Add this to the potatoes and again stir together gently but thoroughly.

Let the potatoes rest to absorb the seasonings for a minute or two, then slowly pour over them 2/3 cup of olive oil. With the rubber spatula, turn the potatoes slowly in the oil until each slice glistens brilliantly, at which point sprinkle over them 2 or more tablespoons of thinly sliced scallions, green tops and all, and 2 tablespoons each of fresh dill and parsley, both finely chopped. Mix once more, taste for seasoning, and serve while still warm, or at room temperature. If the salad must be refrigerated for any reason, let it return to room temperature before serving it.

The surface of the salad may be spread lightly with mayonnaise if you wish. Or the warm potatoes, after their initial moistening with the hot stock, may be dressed wholly with mayonnaise and the suggested fresh herbs. In any case, make the mayonnaise yourself.

BEFORE YOU start the mayonnaise, it is well to remember that three factors will determine its success or failure: First, the egg yolks and oil must be at room temperature; second, the yolks must be beaten to a perceptible thickness before you add the oil; and finally, the oil must be beaten into the eggs as slowly as possible for the proper emulsion to take place.

Make the mayonnaise either in an electric mixer (*not* a blender) or by hand in a large bowl with a rotary beater or wire whisk.

MAYONNAISE

For approximately 2 cups of mayonnaise, you will need 3 large egg yolks (four, if they're small), 1 scant teaspoon of salt, ⅛ teaspoon cayenne, 1 tablespoon of vinegar or lemon juice and, if you like it, ½ teaspoon dry or prepared mustard. Decide on the oil you want to use. Although olive oil is the best, you may use vegetable oil in its place, or combine the oils in any proportion you wish. Have ready 1½ cups of it. And, a couple of tablespoons of boiling water or stock beaten into the mayonnaise after it is finished will make it creamier and lessen the danger of its separating if it must stand for any length of time.

Beat the yolks in a mixing bowl for a couple of minutes until they thicken and cling to the beater. Add the seasonings and vinegar or lemon juice, and beat a minute longer. Then, and only then, beat in ½ teaspoon of oil. When it is fully absorbed, beat in another ½ teaspoon, and, beating constantly, add the oil in ½-teaspoon amounts until you have used about ½ cup of it.

The mixture will by now have taken on the general appearance of mayonnaise. Beat in the remaining oil in larger amounts, a tablespoon at a time if you are doing the beating by hand; or, with the electric mixer set at moderate speed, pour the remaining oil into the bowl in a slow but steady stream. If, at any point, the oil is not being absorbed by the eggs, stop adding the oil, and beat the mayonnaise alone until it regains its creamy appearance. Then continue as before.

When all the oil is absorbed, the mayonnaise will be quite properly thick. Now beat into it first a little more lemon juice or vinegar if you think it needs it, then the couple of tablespoons of boiling water, or chicken or beef stock. If you prefer the mayonnaise thinner still, beat into it, one at a time, teaspoons of heavy sweet or sour cream.

COMBINATION SALADS:

Here is one area in which the imaginative cook, perhaps a little short on technique, can be as fanciful and creative as he likes without fear of sauces curdling, soufflés falling, or cakes collapsing. Even the great legendary chefs, from Carême to Escoffier, were not above a flight of fancy when they named their original salads Lorette, Isabelle, Suzette, Véronique, and the like. That the names bore no direct relation to the salad mattered not at all; a composed salad could be made of almost anything if its ingredients had a reasonable affinity for one another and the salad was presented colorfully and tastefully.

301

But the non-professional cook would do well, first to master the great traditional salads such as *salade Niçoise* or cold beef salad *vinaigrette*. These salads are prototypes, as it were, of what a composed salad should be and, once learned, all manner of original variations and departures are possible. The *niçoise* salad consists of lettuce, anchovies, tunafish, one or more cold cooked or raw vegetable, hard-cooked eggs, fresh tomatoes, olives, and fresh herbs. The dressing is the classic *vinaigrette* but, as the salad originated in the south of France, prodigal in its use of garlic.

SALADE NIÇOISE

] To serve six or eight [

HAVE READY a large head of romaine lettuce, washed, dried, and chilled; 4 medium tomatoes, peeled, seeded, and cut into 2-inch by ½-inch julienne strips (as described for TOMATO FONDUE on page 81); 2 large green peppers, seeded and cut into pieces the same size as the tomatoes; 1 medium can of tuna, packed in olive oil, if possible; 3 quartered hard-cooked eggs; 12 black olives, preferably the Italian or Greek type; 1 cup of garlic croutons (below); a can of flat anchovy fillets; and ¼ cup each of thinly sliced scallions and finely chopped parsley. If you prefer, omit the garlic croutons, and add 1 teaspoon of finely chopped garlic to the dressing instead.

For the dressing, stir into 3 tablespoons of good wine vinegar a scant teaspoon of salt, ½ teaspoon of freshly ground black pepper, and ½ teaspoon of powdered mustard. Then slowly beat in 2/3 cup of olive oil, and complete this *vinaigrette* with ¼ teaspoon of lemon juice.

Make the garlic croutons with day-old French or Italian bread cut into ½-inch cubes; not-too-fresh white bread will do if it must. In a large heavy frying pan, heat almost to smoking 1/3 cup of olive oil. Add the bread cubes and, over fairly high heat, brown them quickly, replenishing the oil as it is absorbed. Turn off the heat when the cubes are a golden brown, and immediately stir into the pan 1 teaspoon of finely chopped garlic; the heat remaining in the pan should be sufficient to brown the garlic without burning it. Turn the croutons out onto a few sheets of paper towelling, and let them drain until you are ready to use them. They will crisp as they cool. See page 41 for more detailed instructions.

Once the ingredients for the salad are assembled, putting it together is no problem at all. A large white porcelain bowl, somewhat wider than deep, would be the ideal setting in which to display the *niçoise* salad in all its Mediterranean brilliance. But, of course, any bowl will do if it is large enough.

Fill the bowl loosely with the romaine lettuce, gently torn, not cut, into manageable serving pieces. Over it spread the julienned tomatoes and, over them, the pepper strips, spreading them out so that the red of the tomatoes shows through. Drain the can of tuna and, after breaking it up slightly, arrange it in the center of the bowl. Around the edge, arrange alternately the egg quarters and olives. Either drape an anchovy fillet over each piece of egg, or place the anchovies spokewise around the tuna. Scatter the croutons about as you will.

Sprinkle the salad with the combined sliced scallions and chopped parsley, and refrigerate. Present the *salade niçoise* at the table in all its colorful splendor and, just before serving, pour the dressing over it. Toss together gently with two large wooden spoons.

AN INTERESTING variant on *salade niçoise* is the American Caesar salad. Although the derivation will be hotly denied by loyal Californians, in whose state the salad is said to have originated, its birthplace was certainly Nice. The family characteristics are unmistakable.

CAESAR SALAD

To make a Caesar salad, use the ingredients listed for the *niçoise* salad, but omit the green peppers, tuna fish, and olives. For the anchovies you may substitute ½ pound of bacon, cooked until crisp and crumbled. Add ½ cup of freshly grated Parmesan cheese. Also add to the original *niçoise* dressing another ½ teaspoon of dry or prepared mustard, and another ¼ teaspoon of lemon juice. And, at the last, stir into the dressing 1 raw lightly beaten egg. As with the *niçoise* salad, present the Caesar salad at the table before tossing it.

———

COMBINATION salads in which cold meat is the principal garnish are on the whole not very successful. The so-called chef's salad, with its bits of tongue, ham, chicken, cheese, and the rest is, understandably, a useful and thrifty way to use leftovers, but as a combination salad quite undistinguished. Most cold cooked meats have so dense and impregnable a texture that, unless they are marinated for an appreciable length of time, they tend to be dry and have little if any flavor.

The French way with cold beef is perhaps the best example of how to handle meat in a salad. This dish has such a diversity of names in France that it might be well to settle for the simplest one which describes what it is exactly—a salad of cold beef *vinaigrette*. Suitable beef for this purpose, should you have some on hand, is cold BEEF À LA MODE (page 163). Lacking that, the remains of any braised or boiled beef will do almost equally well.

The success of the salad depends wholly on how long the beef is marinated; you should plan on having the beef remain in its dressing for at least 2 hours, and even 6 hours is not too long. There are, of course, innumerable versions of this salad; some contain cold vegetables, others potatoes or rice. But finally, the simplest one in which the beef gets all the attention is really the best. Cold vegetables, potatoes, hard-cooked eggs, and whatever else you wish can and should be used as a garnish, rather than combined with the meat. Unlike most salads, cold beef *vinaigrette* has real substance, which makes it ideal as an important dish for a large buffet or for a main course on a hot summer day.

SALAD OF COLD BEEF VINAIGRETTE

The amount of dressing you prepare will depend, naturally, on how much meat you have. For each 8 slices, or for 3 cups of cubed beef, make the *vinaigrette* in the following proportions: 3 tablespoons of red-wine vinegar combined with 1 teaspoon of salt, ½ teaspoon of freshly ground black pepper, and 1 teaspoon of powdered or prepared mustard of the French type. Having dissolved the seasonings in the vinegar, beat into this 9 tablespoons of olive oil. Wash, dry, and chop coarsely 2 tablespoons of capers. Add them to the dressing along with ½ teaspoon of finely chopped garlic and 2 tablespoons of chopped parsley.

Trim the meat of all fat and gristle, and spread the slices or cubes in a shallow glass or enamel baking dish. Scatter over it ½ cup of thinly sliced onions, and pour in the dressing. Spoon it over the meat and onions, moistening them thoroughly. Do not refrigerate the salad, but allow it to marinate at room temperature as long as you can, turning the meat and onions over in the marinade from time to time. Like FRENCH POTATO SALAD, beef *vinaigrette* is at its best served at room temperature.

To serve, arrange the meat on a platter, scatter the onions rings over it, and sprinkle copiously with finely chopped parsley. Surround the salad with the garnish of your choice—tomatoes, cold vegetables, hard-cooked eggs—and moisten them with any dressing remaining in the baking dish. Serve with a bowl of FRENCH POTATO SALAD, if you like, and hot French or Italian bread.

MIMOSA SALAD FIFI

CREATING AN original combination salad is, in reality, more easily said than done. But occasionally there will appear a fresh new salad, delicate, colorful, and slightly outrageous. Such a salad was quite spontaneously created by a gifted young cooking student and out of deference to her, must certainly be named MIMOSA SALAD FIFI. It is simply and quickly prepared: Arrange on chilled individual salad plates a few leaves of chilled, dry, Boston lettuce. Place a few slices of chilled ripe avocado (sprinkled with a little lemon juice to prevent their darkening) on the lettuce and gently scatter on each slice a few grains of the best black caviar you can afford. And since you will use so little, this is not as extravagant as it may sound. Dust the caviar and avocado lightly with a little sieved yolk of hard-cooked egg, and refrigerate until ready to serve. Just before serving, moisten the individual salads with a tablespoon or so of French dressing, prepared with olive oil combined with fresh lemon juice in the proportion of four to one, and seasoned with salt and freshly ground black pepper and nothing else.

CHAPTER XIII

Desserts

Strawberries Narcisse

Pineapple Alexandra

Pêches Cardinal

Cassata alla Siciliana

Chocolate Torrone Loaf

Coconut Blancmange with Strawberries

Orange Ginger Bavarian Cream

Crêpes Suzette

Lemon Soufflé with Vanilla Custard Sauce

Crêpes Soufflées

Profiteroles au Chocolat

✳

A FINE repertory of desserts is the cook's pride and also, in surprising fashion, the student's way to create on the one hand quite sensational effects with a minimum of skill, or on the other hand to learn a number of advanced techniques.

Fruit desserts, of course, tend to be the easiest and by no means the least spectacular: STRAWBERRIES NARCISSE are unusual but simplicity itself; you only need to cut up fruit and whip cream to make the classic PINEAPPLE ALEXANDRA; and anyone surely can learn to peel and poach peaches and strain raspberries for PÊCHES CARDINAL. Only a little more laborious but just as easy are two splendid Italian creations, CASSATA ALLA SICILIANA and CHOCOLATE TORRONE LOAF, which are both assembled without cooking and chilled. Flavored whipped cream, wherever it appears, is called *crème Chantilly,* and the frosting on the *cassata* is the classic butter cream, or *crème au beurre.*

After these come a series of classic procedures: How to handle gelatine, first in the uncooked COCONUT BLANCMANGE (here, also, are directions for peeling a fresh coconut and preparing coconut milk which are seldom given in enough detail to make the process feasible). The somewhat more complex BAVARIAN CREAM begins with the standard dessert sauce, *crème à l'anglaise;* the addition of gelatine to this automatically adds the word *collée* to the name, as it does when added to several other sauces, for example the *mayonnaise collée* on page 95. Without gelatine, served warm or cold, we know the same sauce as plain custard sauce, a less rich version of which is used for the LEMON SOUFFLÉ.

The recipe for this soufflé is not the usual one, but once you have learned to make the cream-sauce and egg-yolk base and to beat and fold in the whites, you will be able to follow successfully any other soufflé recipe you wish. In the meantime, you have here a double-rising soufflé that can be cooked ahead and reheated—surely the most convenient soufflé ever devised. If you then proceed to the classic CRÊPES SUZETTE, you have the two techniques that are combined in a remarkable dish, CRÊPES SOUFFLÉES—crêpes stuffed with the airy double-rising batter of the lemon soufflé.

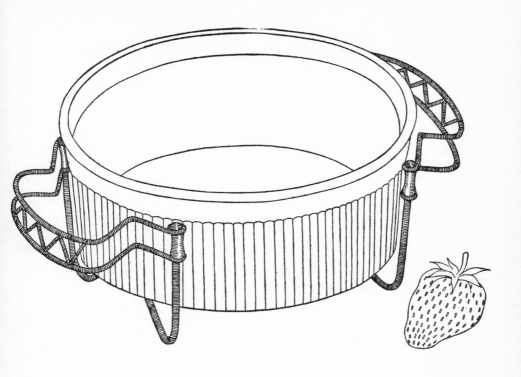

The famous PROFITEROLES AU CHOCOLAT involve the classic *pâte à chou* (first used in the GOUGÈRE on page 17), *crème Chantilly*, and a simple chocolate sauce. The cream puffs here are the *choux* that give this paste its name. Making them and stuffing them with the whipped cream are opportunities to use a pastry tube, though you do not necessarily have to. And note that the apricot glaze used for pineapple Alexandra could be used warm for *profiteroles*, instead of the chocolate sauce, and as a sauce for the CRÊPES SOUFFLÉES.

✳

STRAWBERRIES NARCISSE

As LYRICAL as their name, strawberries Narcisse are a delicate, fanciful dessert with a surprising juxtaposition of flavors: Fresh strawberries are brightly glazed with an orange syrup and served with an unusual Danish cheese, Hablé Crème Chantilly. Conceivably, another cheese might perform the accompanying role as well, but it is most unlikely. The nutlike flavor of this creamy cheese makes it worth every effort to find.

] To serve eight [

1 quart large fresh strawberries

1 cup best Seville-orange marmalade
½ cup Grand Marnier, or Cointreau, or Curaçao
¼–½ cup orange juice
1 teaspoon grated orange rind
½ teaspoon lemon juice

Two 6-ounce boxes of Hablé Crème Chantilly cheese

For the most effective presentation of this dessert, try to find large ripe strawberries with long stems. Naturally, if these are not available, any good strawberry will do, but in that event hull them carefully. Dip the strawberries briefly in cold water, dry them at once with a towel, and arrange them side by side on a cake rack. Refrigerate until ready to use.

The preparation of the dessert is simplicity itself. To make the glaze, mix the cup of marmalade with the ½ cup of orange liqueur, and stir until they are well combined. Now add the ¼ cup of orange juice. The thinned marmalade should run fairly easily off the mixing spoon; if it doesn't, continue to add orange juice, a teaspoon at a time, until it does. Now stir in the grated orange rind and the

310

½ teaspoon of lemon juice (more, if you prefer a tart flavor), and the glaze is ready. Do not refrigerate.

Be sure to remove the Chantilly cheese from the refrigerator at least 2 hours before using it so that it will soften to a creamy texture.

You may present strawberries Narcisse in one of two ways: Scoop up spoonfuls of cheese (minus the rind, of course) and place them in the center of small individual dessert dishes—the very small individual French soufflé dishes or ramekins would be ideal. Dip the berries one at a time in the glaze, turning them until they are well coated. If the berries have long stems, arrange them around the cheese stem ends up; if they have been hulled, arrange them in the dish hulled ends down. Pour some extra glaze over the berries if you like.

The other alternative is simpler but effective enough: Arrange the berries in a large attractive bowl and pour the glaze over them. Serve them directly from the bowl and pass the cheese separately.

PINEAPPLE ALEXANDRA

HERE is a dessert to end any dinner with a flourish: a mound of fresh pineapple and strawberries steeped in kirsch, masked with whipped cream, and surrounded with slices of pineapple burnished with apricot glaze. Although the actual ingredients of this classic dessert are simple enough, its construction is so cleverly contrived that it gives the illusion of a *tour de force* far more complex than it really is.

] To serve ten [

1 large ripe pineapple, 4½ to 5 pounds
    or two 2½-pound pineapples

311

1 quart fresh strawberries
Sugar to taste
½ cup kirsch

APRICOT SAUCE:

1 cup apricot preserves
½ cup cold water
1 tablespoon sugar
½ teaspoon lemon juice
2 tablespoons kirsch

1½ cups heavy cream
1 tablespoon confectioners' sugar
1 teaspoon vanilla extract

Try to buy the large Azores pineapple known as the Sugar Loaf; although expensive, it is usually the sweetest and most reliable fruit of its kind. Smaller pineapples will do, if they must, but they should be heavy for their size and perfectly ripe, with no soft pulpy spots or signs of decay at the base.

When you select your strawberries, make sure that at least 20 of them are bright red, uniform in size, free from blemishes, and preferably though not essentially long stemmed. These will decorate the dessert when it is assembled and should be cleaned with care: Dip each berry briefly in a dish of cold water, pat it gently dry with a towel, and arrange them side by side on a cake rack before you refrigerate them. The remaining strawberries can be dispatched more easily: Hull them, wash them in a sieve, spread them out on paper towelling, and pat dry. Cut the berries into quarters if they are large, or halves if small, and place them in a large mixing bowl while you prepare the pineapple.

To peel the pineapple, snap off the stem at the point where it joins the fruit. Slice about an inch off its base, and stand the pineapple upright on a chopping board. Hold the fruit securely and, with a sharp heavy knife, cut down through the peel perpendicularly, making sure to cut deeply enough so that all the little tufted "eyes" are removed with the peel at the same time. Lay the peeled pineapple on its side, and cut it as carefully as you can into thin even slices, a little less than a quarter of an inch thick.

Choose 12 of the most perfect and symmetrical of these slices, and cut off a half-moon-shaped piece from either side of the cores. This should give you 24 pieces—approximately half slices—when you finish. All should be exactly the same size; trim them if they aren't. Place the pineapple slices in a shallow glass baking dish, sprinkle them with a little sugar if they seem too tart, and moisten with ¼ cup of the kirsch. Refrigerate, and turn the fruit in the kirsch from time to time.

Gather up the remaining pineapple slices and scraps, cut out and throw away the cores, and chop the pulp coarsely. Add this to the cut-up strawberries in the mixing bowl, sprinkle with sugar, if necessary, and pour in the remaining ¼ cup of kirsch. Mix gently together and refrigerate until you are ready to assemble the dessert. All these preparations may be made hours before dinner if you wish; in fact, the longer the fruits marinate in the kirsch, the better.

✳ *It is a simple matter to make the apricot sauce at this time too. Merely combine in a small heavy saucepan the 1 cup of apricot preserves, ½ cup of cold water, and 1 tablespoon of sugar. Bring this to a boil, stirring constantly, and then simmer over low heat for about 8 minutes. Pour the hot sauce into a fine sieve set over a small bowl and, with a large metal spoon, rub it through. Stir in the lemon juice and kirsch. The sauce will thicken as it cools; if it seems unmanageably thick when you are about to use it, thin it to spreading consistency with a little more lemon juice or kirsch.*

To present this dessert most effectively, use a large round platter with a slightly indented well which should be 9 to 10 inches in diameter. Ideally, Pineapple Alexandra should be assembled just before you serve it, but you may safely put it together an hour before dinner. Much before that you will be courting disaster, for the whole edifice may collapse.

Begin by turning the cut-up strawberries and pineapple into a sieve set over a small bowl. Let the mixture drain. Meanwhile, whip the chilled cream in a chilled bowl until it thickens slightly; sprinkle over it 1 tablespoon of powdered sugar and 1 teaspoon of vanilla extract, and continue to beat until the cream is very stiff.

Remove the drained fruit from the sieve and spoon it into the center of the serving platter. Gently pat and shape the fruit into a small circular mound, leaving about 2 inches between it and the edge of the well. If any fruit juice accumulates on the dish, sponge it up with a paper towel before you proceed. Now coat the mound of fruit with the whipped cream, applying it with a spatula as thickly and evenly as you can. The fruit should be completely covered, and the cream should extend almost to the edge of the well.

"Fence" in this dome of whipped cream with the marinated pineapple slices, standing each one upright on one point and overlapping them slightly all around the center mound. Press them lightly into the cream to make them stick. When you finish, the cream-covered fruit should be completely ringed with overlapping slices of pineapple, leaving the whipped cream on top exposed.

Fill a large spoon with apricot sauce, thinned if necessary, and, holding it above each slice of pineapple in turn, let it drip slowly down the side of the fruit until it is thoroughly glazed. You can let as much sauce drip down into the side of the well as you like, but make sure you hold back enough to cover all the pineapple slices. The last step is to decorate the platter with the whole strawberries, arranging them as your fancy dictates, perhaps a few on top of the whipped cream and the remainder around the ring of glazed pineapple slices. Refrigerate until ready to serve.

AFTERTHOUGHTS:

✳ To serve the dessert, for each portion remove two slices of pineapple

314

from the platter with a large serving fork and spoon. Reach into the whipped-cream-covered mound through this opening and scoop out a spoonful of fruit. Place it between the pineapple slices and garnish the plate with two whole strawberries.

✳ If you have a pastry bag with a medium plain or fancy tip, use it in place of the spatula to coat the fruit with whipped cream. It will take less time and make your dessert look even more professional. Pipe the cream around the mound of fruit, starting at the base and working upward. Finish it on top with decorative swirls. After setting the pineapple slices in place and glazing them, make small whipped-cream rosettes around the base of the dessert with any left-over cream.

PÊCHES CARDINAL

AN INSPIRED French notion of what to do with a ripe peach is to poach it in vanilla-flavored syrup, chill it, then mask it with a raspberry purée as red as the cardinal's hat from which the dessert gets its name. In this version, a delicate Chantilly cream is piped around the peach, and the raspberry purée is sprinkled with coarsely chopped pistachio nuts.

] To serve eight [

8 large ripe peaches

2½ cups sugar
5 cups cold water
4-inch piece of vanilla bean
    or 3 tablespoons vanilla extract

2 packages frozen raspberries, defrosted
2 tablespoons sugar, "instant" or "verifine"
1 tablespoon kirsch

¾ cup heavy cream

315

2 tablespoons powdered sugar
1 tablespoon vanilla extract
¼ cup coarsely chopped pistachio nuts

So that they may have time to chill properly, poach the peaches at least 6 hours or preferably the day before you plan to serve them. Peel them first by dropping them, two at a time, into a pan of boiling water. After about 30 seconds, scoop them out with a slotted spoon, run cold water over them briefly and, while they are still warm, remove their skins with a small sharp knife. If any of the skins are resistant, return the peaches to the boiling water for a few more seconds.

When all the peaches are peeled, combine in a 2½- or 3-quart saucepan the 5 cups of water and 2½ cups of sugar. Stir until the sugar dissolves, then bring the syrup to a boil and let it boil vigorously for about 3 minutes before turning the heat down to a simmer.

Drop in the peaches and poach them slowly from 10 to 20 minutes, depending on how large and how ripe they are. They should be tender yet retain a hint of firmness when you remove them from the syrup. Chill until icy cold.

In the meantime, prepare the raspberry purée: Drain the thoroughly defrosted raspberries of all their syrup, and either discard it or use it for another purpose. With the back of a large spoon, rub the raspberries through a fine sieve into a small mixing bowl. Beat into this purée the 2 tablespoons of sugar (preferably the "instant" or "verifine" variety), then stir in the tablespoon of kirsch. Cover tightly with Saran wrap and refrigerate with the peaches.

No more than an hour or so before you plan to serve them, arrange the peaches either in individual dessert dishes or together in a large shallow serving dish. Mask each peach completely with the raspberry purée. In a chilled stainless-steel or unlined copper bowl, beat the chilled cream (preferably with a wire whisk), until it begins to thicken. Sprinkle over it then 2 tablespoons of powdered sugar, add 1 tablespoon of vanilla extract, and continue to beat the cream until it is stiff.

If you own a pastry bag with a small star or other decorative tip, with it pipe a thick ring of the whipped cream around each peach. Or, simply drop small mounds of whipped cream from a teaspoon all around each peach, then gently flatten the mounds into a ring with a rubber spatula. Sprinkle the top of each peach with a few chopped pistachio nuts, and chill until ready to serve.

AFTERTHOUGHTS:

✳ You may substitute fresh ripe apricots, two or three per serving, for the peaches in this recipe. They do not need to be peeled.

✳ Naturally, fresh raspberries, when you can get them, should be used in place of the frozen ones. However, their season is brief and their price prohibitive. Purée them as you do the frozen berries, but use twice as much sugar and perhaps another tablespoon of kirsch.

✳ The vanilla poaching syrup may be refrigerated or frozen and used again.

CASSATA ALLA SICILIANA

MOST Sicilian cakes are so elaborate that even Sicilian housewives, excellent cooks as they are, seldom attempt them and buy them from their local bakeries. The *cassata,* one of the most original and appealing of their cakes is fortunately one of the simplest and can be made easily in your own kitchen. Thin layers of pound cake are spread with a sweet creamy filling of ricotta cheese, orange liqueur, candied fruits, and bits of chocolate, then reshaped into a box, or *cassata,* and richly frosted with a chocolate butter cream. And a veritable treasure chest it is when you slice into it twelve hours later. The *ricotta* cream and layers of cake will have merged into a moist mélange, not quite cake and not quite cream, but a mellow combination of both.

317

] To serve eight [

A fresh pound cake, about 9 inches long and 3 inches wide

1 pound ricotta cheese
2 tablespoons heavy cream
4 tablespoons granulated sugar ("instant" or "verifine," if possible)
3 tablespoons orange liqueur (Grand Marnier, Curaçao, Triple Sec, etc.)
2 tablespoons candied orange peel, coarsely chopped
1 tablespoon candied lemon peel, coarsely chopped
2 squares, or 2 ounces, semisweet chocolate, coarsely chopped

CHOCOLATE BUTTER CREAM:

6 squares, or 6 ounces, semisweet chocolate
3 tablespoons cold water
4 egg yolks
1 cup granulated sugar
¼ teaspoon cream of tartar
½ cup cold water
½ pound unsalted butter, cut into 1-inch pieces
2 tablespoons orange liqueur

1 cup chopped toasted almonds (canned)

Short of baking one yourself, buy or order a pound cake at the best bakery you know. At all costs avoid the cellophane-wrapped cake euphemistically called a pound cake that in reality bears not the faintest resemblance to one.

With a long serrated knife, slice the end crusts off the cake if they seem thick and coarse, and level the top of the cake if it is sharply mounded. Slice the cake itself horizontally into slices ½- to ¾-inch thick, and don't worry too much if they are uneven.

Force the ricotta cheese through a not-too-fine sieve into a mixing bowl, and then beat it either in an electric mixer or by hand until it is perfectly smooth. Still beating, add to the cheese the 2 tablespoons of cream, 4 tablespoons of sugar, and the orange liqueur. With a rubber spatula, gently fold in the candied orange and lemon peels and the chopped chocolate.

Lay a double sheet of waxed paper on a flat 12-inch platter or board. On this place the base of the cake. Spread it with a substantial layer of the cheese mixture, and then reconstruct the cake layer by layer with the cheese between them, ending finally with the top layer of cake. Pressing the cake and cheese together gently, shape it into as compact a box shape as you can. Although it may seem soft and precariously constructed, the cheese mixture will firm up when it is cold and hold the cake together. Smooth the sides of the cake with a rubber spatula and refrigerate it for an hour or so before frosting it.

✳ *For the classic chocolate butter cream, an electric mixer is useful but not indispensible; a candy thermometer, however, is imperative. First, break up the 6 ounces of chocolate, and combine it in a small pan with the 3 tablespoons of water. Stirring constantly over low heat, let the chocolate melt until it is absolutely smooth. Put it aside to cool.*

In the mixer, or by hand with a rotary beater or wire whisk, beat the 4 egg yolks for 2 or 3 minutes, or long enough to thicken them and lighten them somewhat in color.

Dissolve the 1 cup of sugar and 1/4 teaspoon of cream of tartar in 1/2 cup of water, stirring them together thoroughly with a metal spoon in a small pan. Bring this syrup to a boil with the tip of the candy thermometer resting in it; don't stir, but tip the pan from side to side occasionally so that the sugar cooks evenly. When the thermometer reads **236° F.,** *the "soft-ball" stage, remove the pan from the heat immediately.*

Start beating the eggs again and, as you beat, pour in the hot syrup in a slow steady stream. With the mixer, beat at medium speed until the mixture cools to room temperature and changes

319

miraculously to a thick, smooth, white cream; this may take 10 to 15 minutes. By hand, to hasten the cooling as you beat, set the mixing bowl in a pan of cold water, and add the syrup a little at a time. Continue to beat until the cream is cool, thick and smooth.

Now beat in the butter, adding it piece by piece until it is all absorbed. Follow this with the cool dissolved chocolate and the 2 tablespoons of orange liqueur. If the mixture seems too fluid to spread, chill it in the refrigerator for as long as it takes to reach spreading consistency.

To frost the *cassata*, lay on the butter cream thickly and evenly until not a bit of the cake shows through. You may swirl the surface with a spatula, or put some of the cream in a pastry bag fitted with a star tube and decorate the cake with rosettes and anything else to your heart's content. Sprinkle the top of the cake with the chopped toasted almonds, and chill it overnight, at least, before serving. Transfer the cake to a cake plate with a large spatula.

AFTERTHOUGHT:

✳ If the frosting seems too formidable an undertaking, omit it and dust the cake instead with powdered sugar just before you serve it. It must be said, however, that without the butter-cream frosting—or some other frosting—the *cassata* misses that final touch of extravagance which makes it so characteristically Italian.

CHOCOLATE TORRONE LOAF

HERE IS a rich dessert in the most extravagant Italian tradition. It is prepared with a base of creamed butter, rum-flavored chocolate, ground almonds, and eggs, with small pieces of Petits Beurre biscuits scattered at random throughout it. Chilled into a firm but velvety loaf, it is reminiscent of the celebrated French *turinoise* with which it has, in fact, a close historical kinship. For some palates, however, the chocolate *torrone* has a more interesting and unusual texture.

] To serve eight [

½ pound semisweet chocolate
4 tablespoons dark rum
½ pound unsalted butter
2 tablespoons sugar, "instant" or "verifine"
1½ cups grated almonds (about 5 ounces)
10–12 Petits Beurre biscuits, or Social Tea Biscuits,
    cut into 1- by ½-inch pieces
1 teaspoon vegetable oil
Powdered sugar
½ cup heavy cream (optional)

Break the chocolate into small pieces and combine it with the 4 tablespoons of dark rum in a small heavy saucepan. Stir over moderate heat until the chocolate melts. To avoid having the rum boil, remove the pan from the heat before the chocolate is fully dissolved, and continue to stir; the heat remaining in the pan will be sufficient to melt the chocolate completely. Let it cool to room temperature.

Cream the softened butter with the 2 tablespoons of sugar in the electric mixer, beating at medium speed until the butter is smooth and satiny. To do this by hand, use a mixing bowl and wooden spoon, and mash the butter against the sides of the bowl until it is pliable enough to beat easily. Still beating, slowly add the sugar, then incorporate the 2 egg yolks, adding them one at a time and mixing until not a trace of them shows. Follow this with the grated almonds (pulverized dry in the electric blender, or grated by hand with a Mouli grater), and the cooled chocolate—and the chocolate must be cool or the butter will melt and become oily.

Now, with a rotary beater or a wire whisk, beat together the 2 egg whites and a pinch of salt until the whites are thick enough to cling solidly to the beater without drooping. With a rubber spatula, fold them into the chocolate mixture until streaks of white no longer show. (If you are doubtful about beating and folding techniques, see page 337.)

Scatter the cut-up biscuits over the top of the *torrone* mixture (it doesn't matter if the biscuits are ragged and uneven, but don't use the crumbs) and, with a large spoon and gentle hand, mix them in, distributing the pieces evenly. Be careful not to break them.

With a pastry brush or a crumpled paper towel, lightly coat the inside of a 1½-quart loaf pan with vegetable oil, and turn it upside down on a paper towel to allow any excess oil to run off. Spoon the *torrone* into the pan, and rap the pan sharply once or twice on the table to make sure the mixture settles evenly without air bubbles. Cover it tightly with Saran wrap or waxed paper, and refrigerate for at least 4 hours, or preferably overnight, until it is firm.

To unmold the *torrone*, carefully run a small sharp knife around the sides of the pan, cutting all the way down to the bottom. Then, for about 15 seconds, dip the bottom of the pan in a shallow pan filled with hot water. Unmold the *torrone* by placing a chilled platter upside down over it, and, gripping the pan and platter together, quickly reversing them. Still holding them together tightly, rap the platter sharply on the table and the *torrone* should emerge without any difficulty. If it doesn't (this has been known to happen), repeat the dipping process.

Smooth the top and sides of the unmolded loaf with a spatula, and return it to the refrigerator until ready to serve; because of its high butter content, the *torrone* tends to soften rapidly. Just before serving, sieve a little powdered sugar over the top; do not do this in advance or the sugar will dissolve. Serve the *torrone* cut in the thinnest of slices, accompanied, if you wish, by a bowl of whipped cream.

AFTERTHOUGHT:

❋ Don't attempt to chill the *torrone* in an ornamental mold. Dipping it in hot water to unmold it inevitably softens the surface and the *torrone* won't retain any of the designs.

COCONUT BLANCMANGE WITH STRAWBERRIES

BLANCMANGE is usually associated in our minds with a rather depressingly wholesome dessert composed of milk, cornstarch, and anonymous flavoring. But the classical blancmange, or "white eating" in literal translation, is something else again—a dessert delicate beyond description and the pride of great French chefs for centuries.

Made with the milk of sweet and bitter almonds blanched to a snowy whiteness and thickened ever so lightly with gelatine and cream, the original of this superb creation is almost impossible to make properly in the United States. Bitter almonds are poisonous when consumed in any appreciable quantity and can be purchased here only with a doctor's prescription. Without them, plain almond blancmange is a pallid imitation of the real thing and simply not worth the effort it takes to prepare. However, substituting fresh coconut and coconut milk for the almonds produces a blancmange in every way comparable to the original with an added distinction particularly its own. And with the electric blender, the procedures are simplified considerably.

] To serve eight [

2 fresh coconuts, about 2½ pounds each
2 cups coconut milk, about
3 cups light cream, plus 1 more cup if needed
1½ tablespoons (1½ envelopes) unflavored gelatine
1/3 cup kirsch (imported if possible)
½ cup plus 1 tablespoon confectioners' sugar
¼ teaspoon almond extract

1 pint fresh or frozen whole strawberries
Sugar and kirsch to taste
2 tablespoons toasted coconut

323

Shake the coconuts before you buy them to make sure they are full of "milk." There are two "eyes" in a coconut, one soft and the other hard. Puncture them both with an icepick or screwdriver forced through with a hammer, and drain the coconut milk into a measuring cup. If you have less than the 2 cups specified (the amount of milk in a coconut is quite unpredictable), don't worry about it. Just be sure to drain the coconuts dry.

Preheat the oven to **400° F.** and bake the empty coconuts for about 15 minutes. Remove them from the oven and, while they are still hot, split the shells with a hammer. If you are lucky, the shells will come off in one piece; if they don't, pry them from the meat with a small sharp knife. With a swivel-bladed peeler, while the coconut is still warm, pare off the brown inner skin. Cut the meat into ½-inch cubes. You should have about 6 cups and a little extra; save the extra to be toasted later.

Strain the coconut milk through a fine sieve into a 2-quart bowl, and add the light cream to it. If you have less than 2 cups of coconut milk, make up the difference with more cream; if you have more than 2 cups of the milk, use less cream. In all you should have exactly 5 cups of liquid.

The next step is rather an athletic one, but be consoled that the earlier mortar-and-pestle method was infinitely more so. Pour into the container of the electric blender a little more than ¾ cup of the combined coconut milk and cream. Add 1 cup of the diced coconut, and purée it at high speed until it has almost liquified; turn off the machine and scrape down the sides of the jar if necessary. Pour the blended coconut into a sieve set over a 2-quart bowl and, with a large metal spoon, press down hard on the pulp so that every bit of its moisture is drained through the sieve. Throw away the dry pulp.

Continue this operation, cupful by cupful, using ¾ cup of liquid each time, until all the coconut has been puréed and its cream extracted. Strain it all once more, pressing down again on whatever pulp is left in the sieve. When you finish, you should have only 3 2/3 cups of coconut cream. If your pressing of the pulp hasn't been vigorous enough and you have less (you won't have more), use more light cream to make up the difference.

The rest is simple. Stir the confectioners' sugar into the coconut cream, mix thoroughly until no trace of it remains, and add the almond extract. Measure the gelatine precisely and sprinkle it into 1/3 cup of kirsch, right in the measuring cup. Set the cup in a shallow pan of simmering water and, with a metal spoon, stir the gelatine until it dissolves and the kirsch is clear. While this is still warm, pour it in a steady stream into the coconut cream, stirring persistently until you are sure it is well combined.

Now dip a 1-quart ring mold in cold water, shake out the excess water and, without drying it, fill the mold with the blancmange. Cover tightly with Saran wrap or waxed paper, and refrigerate for at least 4 hours, or until the cream has set. It's a good idea to chill the platter you plan to serve it on at the same time.

Unmold the blancmange about an hour before serving it: First run a sharp knife around both inside rims of the mold. Then dip the mold quickly—no more than a second or two—into a shallow pan of hot water. Wipe the dripping bottom dry, and place the chilled platter upside down on top of the mold. Hold them tightly together and turn them over. The blancmange should come out easily. If it doesn't, rap the platter sharply on the table once. That will do it.

Just before serving, fill the center of the ring with the strawberries, sweetened to taste and moistened, if you like, with a couple of tablespoons of kirsch. Sprinkle the ring with toasted coconut.

To toast the coconut, shred dry in the blender the extra diced coconut you saved earlier. Spread it out thinly on a cooky sheet and bake it in a preheated **325° F.** oven for about 20 minutes, turning it with a spatula every now and then so that it browns evenly.

*

ORANGE GINGER BAVARIAN CREAM

A TRUE *crème bavaroise,* to give it its original name, illustrates precisely a sequence of classic techniques: the preparation of *crème à l'anglaise*—a simple egg-and-milk custard—and the addition to it of softened gelatine which transforms it into a *crème à l'anglaise collée.* For a *bavaroise,* this is then flavored and folded into whipped cream. The process is in fact as simple as it sounds, but there are insidious culinary traps awaiting the unwary which can turn this supposedly light, evanescent cream into a lumpy, unattractive pudding. However, the following recipe is so explicit that it is foolproof in almost every respect.

] To serve six or eight [

1 envelope (1 tablespoon) plus 1 teaspoon unflavored
    gelatine
1/3 cup strained orange juice.

1 cup milk
5 large egg yolks
4 tablespoons sugar

3 tablespoons preserved-ginger syrup
3 tablespoons finely chopped preserved ginger
1 tablespoon grated orange rind

1½ cups chilled heavy cream

Sections of 2 large navel oranges
1 tablespoon sugar
2 tablespoons Grand Marnier or Cointreau

With a pastry brush and a little vegetable oil, lightly film the inside of a quart-size charlotte or ring mold. Invert the mold on a piece of paper towelling until you are ready to use it.

Sprinkle the unflavored gelatine into the 1/3 cup of strained orange juice, right in the measuring cup. Let the gelatine soften for a couple of minutes, then set the cup in a shallow pan of simmering water and stir the orange juice over low heat for a few minutes until the gelatine is thoroughly dissolved. Turn off the heat but leave the cup in the hot water while you prepare the custard, or *crème anglaise*.

✻ *Slowly bring the cup of milk almost to the boil in a small enamel or stainless-steel saucepan. Meanwhile, with an electric mixer, rotary beater, or wire whisk, beat together the 5 egg yolks and 4 tablespoons of sugar for 3 or 4 minutes, or until the eggs are pale yellow and have thickened enough to fall lazily off the beater in ribbonlike strands.*

Now, beating slowly, pour the hot milk over the eggs in a thin steady stream (or a little at a time if you are beating by hand), and when they are well combined pour the mixture back into the saucepan. Cook over moderate heat, stirring constantly and deeply into the sides of the pan with a wooden spoon, until the mixture begins to thicken into a light custard that barely coats the spoon. Now lower the heat and don't in any circumstances allow the custard to boil or it will curdle irretrievably; continue to cook and stir it, raising the pan away from the heat every now and then if it seems to be getting too hot.

When the crème à l'anglaise *is thick enough to cling tenaciously to the spoon, remove it from the heat and at once stir the dissolved gelatine into it. Continue to stir until no trace of the orange juice shows, then strain the custard through a fine sieve into a 2- or 3-quart mixing bowl. You now have a* crème à l'anglaise collée.

Add the 3 tablespoons of ginger syrup, the chopped ginger and grated orange rind, and mix together thoroughly. Let the custard cool a bit while you whip the 1½ cups of chilled heavy cream in a chilled 2-quart mixing bowl. You may, if you like, beat the cream until it is stiff, but the texture of the Bavarian cream will be creamier and less spongy if the cream is whipped only to the point where it has doubled in volume and barely holds its shape.

Working now as quickly as you can, set the bowl of custard in another, larger bowl filled with either crushed ice or ice cubes half immersed in water. With a rubber spatula, stir the custard over the ice until it becomes quite cold and the gelatine begins to thicken. This will happen faster than you think—perhaps in 5 minutes or less—, so don't be taken by surprise and allow the custard to become a solid gelatinous mass. (If it does, however, simply reheat it, stirring constantly, until it regains its former consistency.)

While the custard is still fluid but cold and thick, pour it over the whipped cream, and, with a rubber spatula, carefully but thoroughly fold them together. In other words, using the flat of the spatula like a shovel, alternately turn the cream over the custard and the custard over the cream, and every so often run the edge of the spatula around the sides of the bowl. Continue to fold until the cream and custard are one.

If, by some mischance, the custard was too firm when it was folded into the whipped cream, the Bavarian cream at this point will have a decidedly lumpy appearance. Beat the entire mixture then with a rotary beater until the lumps disappear. In fact, even if you see no lumps, beat the Bavarian cream if you have the slightest misgivings about its smoothness.

Pour the cream into the prepared mold, cover it tightly with Saran wrap, and chill it for a couple of hours, until it is firm. Or, if you wish, by simply burying the mold in crushed ice you can have the Bavarian cream firm enough to serve half an hour after you make it.

Whether you have chilled the cream for half an hour or overnight, the unmolding procedure is the same: Half an hour or so before serving, run a sharp knife around the inside edge of the mold (if it is a ring mold, run the knife around the inside cone also), dip the bottom of the mold in hot water for 2 or 3 seconds, and wipe

328

it dry with a towel. Place a chilled platter upside down over the cream, then grasp the mold and platter together firmly, and invert them. Still holding them together, rap the platter sharply on the table; the cream should slide out easily. If it doesn't, either rub the mold with a towel wrung out in hot water, or turn the mold and platter back to their original positions and repeat the entire process.

In either event, once the Bavarian cream is unmolded, decorate it as fancifully as you like with the peeled orange sections which have first been sprinkled with a little sugar and Grand Marnier or Cointreau. Refrigerate the Bavarian cream until you serve it.

AFTERTHOUGHTS:

✳ *To section an orange, with a small very sharp knife cut deeply into the peel near the stem end. With short sawing motions, cut the peel and all the white membrane away from the orange in a spiral, leaving the flesh of the orange entirely exposed. Cut in on either side of each membrane division to the core of the orange and, as each section is freed, carefully lift it out.*

✳ You may garnish the Bavarian cream more elaborately: Whip ½ cup of chilled cream until slightly thickened, then add 1 tablespoon of powdered sugar and 1 teaspoon of vanilla extract, and continue whipping until stiff. Put this in a pastry bag fitted with a small star tip, and pipe small rosettes around the Bavarian cream between the orange sections.

✳ Preserved ginger in syrup is available in specialty food stores. Chinese grocers, particularly, always have it in stock.

✳ If you object to the solid bits of chopped ginger in the Bavarian cream, omit it, and mix into the *crème à l'anglaise collée* 2 extra tablespoons of ginger syrup.

*

CRÊPES SUZETTE

FOR GENERATIONS crêpes Suzette, like caviar and champagne, have been associated in the popular imagination with the unattainable luxury of the *haut monde*. Even now, in our equalitarian age, over-awed home cooks still do not realize how easily and inexpensively this glamorous dessert can be made. Naturally, a copper crêpe pan and an alcohol burner are impressive accessories if you can afford them, but a chafing dish, or even an electric skillet, managed with dexterity can be quite as effective. The crêpes themselves are the least of the problem and can be made at any time at your leisure. The customary routine of dipping them in orange butter, folding, and flaming them does take practice—you should not contemplate a tableside performance until you have the technique well in hand. But, for the timid, be assured that the crêpes may be dipped, folded, and flamed in the privacy of your kitchen and presented, less dramatically to be sure, but impressively nonetheless.

] To serve eight [

CRÊPES:

¾ cup milk
¾ cup cold water
4 large eggs
3 egg yolks
1½ cups flour
½ teaspoon salt
2 tablespoons sugar
3 tablespoons cognac
1 teaspoon grated lemon rind
8 tablespoons butter, clarified, in all

CRÊPES SUZETTE

ORANGE BUTTER:

½ pound softened unsalted butter
½ cup sugar
2 tablespoons grated orange rind
1 teaspoon lemon juice
½ cup orange juice
4 tablespoons Grand Marnier, or any other type of
   orange liqueur

Granulated sugar
½ cup or more cognac

Before you make the crêpe batter, clarify 8 tablespoons (one stick) of unsalted butter. Cut it into 1-inch pieces, and melt it slowly in a small pan without letting it brown. Off the heat, skim all the foam from the top and let the butter rest for a couple of minutes. Then tilt the pan and, with a large spoon, ladle off the clear butter without picking up any of the milky solids, or whey, which will have settled at the bottom of the pan. Put aside 4 tablespoons of the butter for the batter and use the rest to fry the crêpes.

❋ *If you have an electric blender, put in the jar all the crêpe ingredients in the order listed, and don't bother to sift the flour. Blend at high speed for about 10 seconds, then turn off the machine and, with a rubber spatula, scrape down the flour patches which will have collected on the sides of the jar. Blend at high speed again, this time for about a minute, or until the batter is smooth. Refrigerate (in the covered jar is easiest, otherwise in a covered bowl) for about 2 hours or as long as you like.*

If you make the batter by hand, sift the flour into a large mixing bowl, and with a spoon rub into it, one at a time, the whole eggs and the egg yolks. Add the salt and sugar, and then, little by little, the milk and water. When the batter is fairly fluid, beat it with a rotary beater or in an electric mixer until most of the floury lumps disappear. Strain it then through a fine sieve, and stir in the cognac, 4 tablespoons of clarified butter, and the lemon rind. Refrigerate for 2 hours or more.

331

Cook the crêpes hours ahead if you like. Give the batter a whirl or two in the blender, then pour it into a bowl; or beat it with a whisk for a few seconds. The batter should be as thick as heavy cream; if it seems much thicker, beat teaspoons of cold water into it, one at a time, until it thins to the proper consistency.

To make perfect crêpes—delicately brown, paper-thin, tender, and almost transparent—your crêpe pan, ideally, should be made of heavy cast aluminum or iron and measure 5 inches across the bottom. And if the pan has sloping sides, so much the better. Have ready a pastry brush, the 4 remaining tablespoons of clarified butter in a small bowl, a small (2- or 3-tablespoon, if possible) ladle, and a platter to receive the crêpes as you finish them.

Heat the pan until a drop of cold water flicked across its surface skitters off and evaporates instantly. With the pastry brush, lightly butter the bottom and sides of the pan, then lift the pan off the heat and hold it over the bowl of batter. Ladle 2 tablespoons of batter, more or less, into the pan, and rotate it slowly until the batter covers its entire surface. The pan should be hot enough so that the batter grips and sets almost upon contact. At once, tilt the pan back over the bowl and let the excess batter, no matter how little, run back into it. Don't be too upset if the crêpe slides out also; you may have to consider a few crêpes expendable until you perfect your technique. This is the only precarious part of the procedure; the rest is simple.

Cook the crêpe over fairly high heat until the faintest rim of brown shows around the edge. Turn it, either with a spatula or by grasping the edges on either side with your fingers and quickly flipping it over. Cook the crêpe only briefly on the second side; this will be the inside of the crêpe when it is folded and should be lightly speckled rather than too brown. Slide the finished crêpe onto the platter awaiting it, and continue in the same fashion with the remaining batter, piling the crêpes on top of each other.

With a small sharp knife or a pair of scissors, trim their un-

332

even edges and, if you don't intend to use them immediately, cover them tightly with Saran wrap so that they won't dry out.

When you have learned to make crêpes easily, try using two pans at once to save time: The second frying pan should be an inch or two larger, but this is not absolutely essential. Heat both pans simultaneously, then butter them. Leave the larger pan over the heat while you start one crêpe in the small pan. When the first side is cooked, flip it over into the second pan. The few seconds necessary for it to finish cooking will give you time to start another crêpe in the small pan. By then, your original crêpe will be cooked through and can be turned out onto the platter—and so on, indefinitely. After a little practice, you can establish a rhythm which will enable you to cook over forty crêpes in about twenty-five minutes. This recipe makes a minimum of twenty-four.

Make the orange butter in an electric mixer if you have one, otherwise use a mixing bowl and a large spoon. In either case, beat together the softened (not melted) butter with the ½ cup of sugar until it turns pale yellow and is smooth and creamy. Still beating, add the orange rind and then, literally drop by drop, the lemon juice, orange juice, and orange liqueur. Refrigerate the orange butter until you are ready to use it.

Whether you prepare the crêpes at the dinner table or in the kitchen, be sure that everything you need is within easy reach. Have directly in front of you the pan and heating unit you are going to use—be it crêpe pan and alcohol burner, a chafing dish, or an electric skillet. Whatever the pan, it is imperative that your source of heat be an intense one or the success of your performance will be seriously jeopardized. Check the other items: a large fork and spoon, a bowl of granulated sugar, the cognac, orange butter and, finally the platter of crêpes, warm or at room temperature. Have your dessert plates hot if you can, and a platter, too, if you are doing this in the kitchen.

Prepare the *crêpes Suzette* in small or large batches, depending upon the size of your pan, and divide the orange butter accordingly. The amount of butter specified here is easily enough for 8 portions, assuming that each portion consists of three crêpes, an average serving. Therefore, if you make the crêpes in two batches of twelve (a reasonable number), place approximately half the orange butter in the crêpe pan to start.

––––––––––––––

With the pan as hot as possible, heat the butter until it comes to a boil, and let it bubble vigorously for about a minute. Then lift up a crêpe with your fork and spoon, and lay it in the pan, speckled side up. Spoon the hot orange butter over it until it is thoroughly basted, then with your fork fold it in half, and in half again, to form a small neat triangle. Move the folded crêpe gently to the edge of the pan. Continue basting and folding more crêpes until your first batch of twelve is lined up around the edge of the pan.

Sprinkle each crêpe with a little sugar, and pour into the pan half the ½ cup of cognac. Step back and, with a long kitchen match, set the cognac alight. As the cognac flames (and, if the pan is really hot, it will immediately), shake the pan gently with one hand to keep the flame going and, with the other hand, spoon the flaming cognac over each crêpe in turn. When the cognac finally burns itself out, apportion three crêpes to a serving plate, and moisten them with the sauce left in the pan. Insist that your guests wait for no one; the crêpes must be eaten as soon as they are served, while you proceed with the second batch.

––––––––––––––

Or, in the kitchen, you may arrange the first batch of crêpes on a very hot serving platter, go on to the second batch, and bring them all to the table still piping hot to be served onto the heated dessert plates. Heat the platter and plates well in advance in a **250° F.** oven.

AFTERTHOUGHT:

✳ Good liqueurs are not inexpensive, but the miniature bottles of good brands that many liquor stores carry all cost well under a dollar. Check the ounce content on the labels; for this recipe, to serve eight, you need 2 ounces of orange liqueur and 4 ounces of cognac.

*

LEMON SOUFFLÉ WITH VANILLA CUSTARD SAUCE

THIS IS an extraordinary soufflé which not only rises, and falls, as all good soufflés are supposed to do, but also rises again when it is reheated! It is not difficult to prepare and, if proper attention is given to every detail, the soufflé should emerge light, moist, and flavorful. Reheating not only makes it puff again but in no way affects its delicate texture.

] To serve six [

1 tablespoon softened sweet butter
2 tablespoons granulated sugar

4 tablespoons sweet butter
2/3 cup sifted flour
1 cup milk
6 egg yolks

5 tablespoons granulated sugar
6 tablespoons lemon juice
2 tablespoons grated lemon rind

6 egg whites
Pinch of salt
1 tablespoon sugar

VANILLA CUSTARD SAUCE:

3 egg yolks
¼ cup granulated sugar
1 1/3 cups milk
2-inch piece vanilla bean
    or 1 teaspoon vanilla extract
Freshly grated nutmeg

335

In most baking procedures, accuracy is of the greatest importance and this soufflé is no exception. When you measure the flour, don't pack it down but let it fall gently into the cup; some cooks like to sift it directly into an exact-capacity measuring cup and level off the surface by scraping across it with a knife. Do it either way. When you separate the eggs, keep the yolks intact in a small bowl. Leave the whites resting in a large mixing bowl until they reach room temperature; they will beat to greater volume that way and make a lighter, more delicate soufflé.

Before you start any actual cooking, preheat the oven to **350° F.** and set a kettle of water to boiling on the stove. Heavily grease a 2-quart ring mold with a tablespoon or more of softened butter. Sprinkle 2 tablespoons of sugar into the mold, tilt it to one side and revolve it slowly so that the sugar clings to every part of the buttered surface. Knock out the excess sugar by turning the mold over and tapping it lightly on the table.

✳ *In a small heavy pan, melt the 4 tablespoons of butter. When it has melted, without browning, remove it from the heat and add the 2/3 cup of flour. Mix together thoroughly until you have a thick, smooth paste, or roux. Pour into this, all at once, the 1 cup of milk and, stirring constantly with a wire whisk, cook over moderate heat until the mixture begins to thicken and comes to a boil; don't be distressed if it seems a bit lumpy, it will smooth out as it continues to cook. Lower the heat and switch from the whisk to a large, wooden spoon. With this beat the mixture constantly and continue to cook it slowly until it thickens to an almost dough-like consistency and no longer clings to the bottom and sides of the pan. Transfer it at once to a 2-quart mixing bowl.*

While the doughy mixture is still hot, beat in the 6 egg yolks, one at a time, making sure each yolk is thoroughly incorporated before adding another. This soufflé base will have thinned considerably by the time you have beaten in the last yolk, so you can relax for the moment and stir in the other in-

gredients: 5 tablespoons of sugar, one at a time, 6 tablespoons of lemon juice, one at a time, and finally the 2 tablespoons of grated lemon rind.

Now add a pinch of salt to the 6 egg whites, and, with a new surge of energy, beat them with a large wire whisk or, lacking that—or the energy—with a rotary beater. The whisk is the best by far, for it will incorporate more air into the whites and expand them to greater volume; and for even greater volume beat them, as professional chefs have done for centuries, in an unlined copper bowl. Though the reasons may seem mysterious to us (scientists know exactly why), egg whites beaten in this fashion expand to seven or eight times their volume as opposed to about five times their volume beaten in glass, porcelain, stainless steel, or plastic bowls.

No matter with what or in what you beat the whites, when they have stiffened sufficiently to begin to cling to the beater, sprinkle over them 1 tablespoon of sugar, and beat with renewed vigor until they become quite stiff; in other words, until they no longer slide around the bowl and the small points of the stiffened whites remain upright when the beater is lifted out. If you are dubious about any of this, remember that it is better to overbeat the whites than to underbeat them.

✳ Note that the cutting and folding process here of mixing a soufflé batter is the prototype of any mixing procedure involving a light and a heavier element.

When the whites are stiff, don't let them stand around any longer than you have to. Fold them into the lemon soufflé base immediately. Naturally, this is more easily said than done, but if you remember to use a light hand and avoid any energetic stirring motion, you're on safe ground. However, it's a good idea first to stir in well two large spoonfuls of the whites before you fold in the rest. This will lighten the soufflé base and make it more manageable. Then scrape the remaining whites over this, and cut them in with a rubber scraper, the indispensable instrument for all folding operations: Cut across the mixture *with the scraper, pushing it down to the bottom of the bowl, and, with a lifting movement, draw up some of the heavy mixture below and turn or fold it over the white; then run the scraper around the inside edge of the bowl to gather up any whites which may have lodged there. Repeat these cutting, folding, and scraping movements until the whites are thoroughly incorporated into the soufflé base. There should be no white streaks showing when you finish.*

Immediately spoon—don't pour—this batter into the buttered and sugared ring mold. Fill it only three quarters of the way to the top. If there is any batter left in the bowl, regard it merely as a testimonial to your egg-white-beating ability and don't use it; if you do, the soufflé will rise too high above the mold as it cooks and will topple over.

Set the mold in a shallow pan, place it on the center shelf of the **350° F.** oven and, from your boiling kettle, fill the pan with hot water—halfway up the side of the mold should be enough. Bake the soufflé for 45 to 50 minutes. To be on the safe side, after 40 minutes insert a cake tester into the side of the risen soufflé; if it comes out dry, the soufflé is done; any moist batter on the tester indicates that another 5 or 10 minutes of baking are needed.

Remove the soufflé from the oven, and either serve it at once or let it cool. The cooled soufflé will fall, of course.

To serve at once, unmold the soufflé: Run a sharp knife around both inside rims of the mold. Place a round platter upside down over the soufflé and, grasping mold and platter together firmly, invert them. Tap the platter sharply on the table, then lift the mold off. Spoon over the soufflé the warm vanilla custard which you will have made while it was baking, sprinkle lightly with freshly grated nutmeg, and serve.

If you plan to make the soufflé ahead of time and reheat it, do not unmold it. Let it cool, but don't refrigerate it. Forty-five minutes before you want to serve it, preheat the oven to **350° F.** Place

LEMON SOUFFLÉ WITH VANILLA CUSTARD SAUCE

the mold in a pan filled with boiling water on the center shelf of the oven, as before, but now, to prevent the top of the soufflé from browning any more, drape over it loosely a piece of buttered aluminum foil. Bake the soufflé for about half an hour, or until it has puffed once more—and it will! Unmold and serve as described before.

VANILLA CUSTARD SAUCE:

This is the classic *crème à l'anglaise,* one of the basic dessert sauces of French cooking. It is worth knowing for its many uses besides the present one. Since it must be served warm with the soufflé, prepare it while the soufflé is baking or reheating.

In the electric mixer, or with a rotary beater, beat the yolks of 3 large eggs until they thicken slightly. Continue to beat as you pour in gradually ¼ cup of granulated sugar. After a few minutes the mixture will really thicken, turn a light yellow, and fall back upon itself in a heavy strand when the beater is lifted out. In the meantime, heat just to the boiling point 1 1/3 cups of milk with a 2-inch piece of vanilla bean.

Pour the hot milk little by little into the thickened egg yolks, beating all the while. When they are thoroughly combined, transfer the mixture back to the hot-milk pan. Cook the custard over moderate heat until it begins to thicken. In no circumstances allow it to come anywhere near the boil or it will most assuredly curdle. Of course, this whole procedure can be carried out more safely in a double boiler, but this takes so long and is quite unnecessary if you are reasonably careful not to let the custard get too hot.

When the sauce has thickened sufficiently to form a light but definite coating on the spoon, it is done. Remove it at once from the heat, stir in the vanilla extract if you haven't used the vanilla bean, and strain the custard through a fine sieve into a small bowl. To keep the sauce warm for a short while, place the bowl, tightly covered with Saran wrap, in a shallow pan of lukewarm water.

*

CRÊPES SOUFFLÉES

WHOEVER first thought of enclosing a soufflé in a crêpe was not only brilliantly original but daring besides; for this dessert can be so unpredictable that, except in the hands of a skillful chef, it almost always ends in disaster. This version, however, is literally foolproof. All of it may be prepared ahead except for the final baking, a matter of ten minutes or so.

] To serve ten or twelve [

One recipe for CRÊPES, pp. 330-333
One recipe for LEMON SOUFFLÉ, pp. 335-338
½ cup granulated sugar
Optional: Apricot Sauce, p. 313

To spare yourself frantic last-minute preparations, make the crêpes hours ahead, and stack and wrap them as the recipe describes. And, if you like, cook the lemon soufflé base ahead also, but do not beat and fold in the egg whites until just before you are ready to fill and bake the crêpes.

———————————————

Preheat the oven to **400° F.** Butter two large porcelain or Pyrex baking dishes 1½ to 2 inches deep and 10 to 12 inches long; or butter instead as many ramekins or small ovenproof dessert dishes as you will need for individual service.

Beat the egg whites for the soufflé mixture and fold them into the prepared base as the recipe describes. Carefully separate the stacked crêpes and lay them out, speckled side up, on a large sheet of waxed paper. Now place a tablespoon or so of the soufflé mixture on the upper half of each crêpe, and carefully lift the lower half up over it. Then gently fold the halves into quarters so that the filled crêpes become small triangles.

———————————————

Transfer the crêpes to the baking dishes, leaving about an inch of space between them so that they will have room to expand as they cook, and sprinkle each crêpe with ½ teaspoon or so of sugar. Bake them on the center shelf of the hot oven for about 10 minutes, or until they have fully puffed and the sugar has melted and glazed them lightly.

Serve them at once, either alone or with a bowl of warm apricot sauce flavored to taste with kirsch.

AFTERTHOUGHTS:

❉ If you are really the do-it-ahead type, you may safely fold the beaten egg whites into the cooled soufflé base an hour or so before the crêpes are filled and baked, provided you cover the bowl of soufflé batter tightly with Saran wrap (waxed paper will *not* do). It might be interesting to note here that almost all uncooked soufflé mixtures may be prepared ahead in this way. The trick is to seal the mixing bowl literally airtight with the Saran, which will keep the beaten whites intact.

❉ And remember always to cover a cooled soufflé base in similar fashion if you are going to put it aside for some time; otherwise a skin will form on the base that will spoil your soufflé. Lastly, you may also beat the egg whites and put them aside tightly covered for about an hour before you fold them into the base.

PROFITEROLES AU CHOCOLAT

PÂTE À CHOU appears again here after its debut in the GOUGÈRE BOURGUIGNONNE on page 17. But this time, it becomes a dessert. With sugar and orange extract replacing the cheese and seasonings of the *gougère,* exactly the same simple dough is shaped into little puffs, baked, cooled, then filled with a coffee-flavored cream, and coated with a hot chocolate sauce.

] To serve eight or ten [

PROFITEROLES:

¼ pound butter, cut into small pieces
1 cup water
1 cup unsifted flour
4 large eggs

Pinch of salt
2 teaspoons sugar
¼ teaspoon orange extract

2 tablespoons soft butter
1 egg yolk and 1 tablespoon heavy cream
  (optional)

FILLING:

1 cup heavy cream
3 tablespoons confectioners' sugar
1 tablespoon instant coffee
  or 1 tablespoon vanilla extract

CHOCOLATE SAUCE:

½ pound semisweet chocolate
8 tablespoons strong coffee

Confectioners' sugar

Follow the directions on page 17 precisely, preparing the *pâte à chou* with the water, butter, flour, and eggs listed. In place of the cheese and seasonings of the GOUGÈRE, beat into the dough the pinch of salt, 2 teaspoons of sugar, and ¼ teaspoon of orange extract, and the *chou* paste is ready. Preheat the oven to **450° F.**

With a pastry brush, spread a light film of soft butter over the entire surfaces of two large jelly-roll pans or cooky sheets, then wipe them almost but not quite clean.

If you own a pastry bag with a ¼- or ½-inch plain tip, fill it half

342

full with the *pâte à chou,* and press out on the pans even mounds of dough about 1 inch in diameter and ¾ inch high. Place the puffs 1½ inches apart. Don't be tempted to crowd them; they will literally double in size as they bake. If you have no pastry bag, drop small mounds of the dough on the pans with a teaspoon and don't fuss with them too much. Their disparate shapes will be part of their charm.

If the puffs are now allowed to remain at room temperature for about half an hour, they will have a slight sheen after they are baked. But, if you prefer to bake them at once, you may paint them ever so lightly with a pastry brush dipped into an egg yolk mixed with 1 tablespoon of heavy cream and the glaze on each puff will be even brighter.

Bake the puffs in the **450° F.** oven for 5 minutes, then turn the heat down to **425° F.,** and bake them 10 to 15 minutes longer. When the *choux* are done, they should be twice their original size, a light golden brown, and free from any external moisture. Break one puff open to make sure it is done; if the inside is at all doughy, bake them all a few minutes longer.

Turn off the oven when the puffs are done, and pierce the sides of each one once with the point of a small sharp knife to release the steam. Return the *choux* to the turned-off oven to dry for about 5 minutes before cooling them on a cake rack.

Prepare the coffee-cream filling about an hour before you plan to serve the *profiteroles.* The cream cannot wait too long and, filled much before that, the puffs will become soggy and lose all their delicate lightness. In a chilled bowl, with a chilled beater, whip the cold cream until it begins to thicken; sprinkle over it then the 2 tablespoons of confectioners' sugar, and continue to beat until the cream is stiff. With a rubber spatula, gently fold in the instant coffee (or a tablespoon of vanilla extract).

Either break the tops off each puff gently, or slit each one in half with a small sharp knife. Fill the lower half with a generous spoonful of the whipped cream. Replace the tops, pressing the halves together gently. Or you may, if you prefer, pipe the cream through slits cut in the bottoms or sides of the puffs with a pastry bag fitted with a ¼-inch plain tip. But splitting the puffs is less trouble, and when they are coated with the chocolate sauce they are just as effective. Refrigerate the filled puffs until you are ready to serve them.

The chocolate sauce may be made at any time and reheated over hot water when you need it. In the top of a double boiler, over moderate direct heat, dissolve the 8 squares of semisweet chocolate in 8 tablespoons of strong coffee, stirring constantly until the sauce is absolutely smooth. Don't allow it to come anywhere near a boil, and keep it warm over hot, not boiling water.

Profiteroles may be served in any number of ways. The most usual is to arrange three or four *choux* on each plate and to cover them liberally with the hot chocolate sauce. Or they may be arranged on a large serving platter, sprinkled copiously with confectioners' sugar, and served thus at the table with the sauce passed separately. More unusual would be to fill a shallow silver platter with the hot chocolate sauce (you may need more sauce in this case), and to float the puffs on top, each one first sprinkled lightly with confectioners' sugar.

AFTERTHOUGHTS:

✳ Don't be beguiled into making these puffs with commercial mixes, unfortunately available almost everywhere. They are much too sweet and usually have the texture of wet papier-mâché. With a little more effort and much less expense you can make your own. And if you are so fortunate as to own an electric mixer with a pastry-arm attachment, the *pâte à chou* can be whipped up in a matter of minutes; but not, alas, with an ordinary beater attachment—that simply won't work.

✳ You may double or triple the recipe and freeze the baked puffs for as long as you like. And they needn't be defrosted. Just heat them in a 400° F. oven for a few minutes, then let them cool before you fill them. Unfrozen puffs which have been stored for a day or two are much improved if they are reheated in a moderate oven and cooled before filling.

✳ In place of the coffee in the melted chocolate sauce, you may use rum or any orange liqueur.

344

Menus

*

RARELY, if ever, does anyone follow exactly a menu set down by someone else, and it is not suggested that you should use these menus without making changes to suit your own needs. Their purpose is, rather, to illustrate how a fine recipe can be given a correct setting, how the same dish can often be a part of either a very simple or a more formal meal, and to indicate in a most general way what type of wine would be appropriate. Needless to say, one should not attempt the elaborate menus suggested without competent help in the kitchen.

These menus are composed almost entirely of recipes in this book; the recipe titles are printed in CAPITAL LETTERS and can be located in the Index.

*

HOT GOUGÈRE BOURGUIGNONNE; escarole, FRENCH DRESSING
Raspberries and cream
California Pinot Noir

Scrambled eggs with TOMATO FONDUE; SPINACH SALAD; toasted
buttered French bread
Sliced navel oranges
California Grenache rosé

CHICKEN BROTH
KASHA WITH SAUTEÉD MUSHROOMS, sour cream
Strawberries with their hulls, powdered sugar
Beer

SPIEDINO ALLA ROMANA; SPINACH SALAD
Fresh fruit
White Chianti

Tureen of s'CHEE with diced BOILED BEEF; black bread,
sweet butter
Caraway cheese
Stewed fruit, cream
Beer

S'CHEE with sour cream; black bread or pumpernickel, sweet butter
Sliced BOILED BEEF; KASHA
Raspberry sherbet
Beer

Prosciutto and melon
PASTA with TOMATO SAUCE; GREEN SALAD; hot Italian bread
Red Chianti

SPAGHETTI with CHEESE AND BUTTER SAUCE
SALADE NIÇOISE
Gorgonzola, French bread, seedless grapes
Rosé de Provence

SPINACH SOUP WITH SPRING ONIONS
PASTA with CHEESE AND BUTTER SAUCE; TOMATOES NIÇOISE
STRAWBERRIES NARCISSE
Cabernet Sauvignon

Prosciutto and fresh figs
PASTA with PESTO GENOVESE; broiled tomatoes
Italian almond rusks, espresso coffee with lemon peel
Soave

CLAMS ROCKEFELLER
CAESAR SALAD; hot Italian bread
Fresh fruit, or CHOCOLATE TORRONE
California Pinot Blanc

BROILED SHRIMP WITH TARRATON AND GARLIC; hot French bread
CAESAR SALAD
Cheese and fruit
Dry Orvieto

CONSOMMÉ BELLEVIEW
BROILED SHRIMP WITH TARRAGON AND GARLIC; RICE PILAF;
hot Italian bread
Sliced fresh pineapple
California Chablis

CHILLED LEMON SOUP
SAUTÉED SEA SQUAB (or SCALLOPS) PROVENÇALE WITH TOMATO
FONDUE; BOILED RICE
Arugala, field salad, or romaine, FRENCH DRESSING
Bel Paese, Italian bread, fresh fruit
Corton-Charlemagne

MARINATED ANCHOVIES WITH HERBS, PIMIENTOS, AND OLIVES
BOURRIDE OF SOLE WITH AÏOLI SAUCE; BOILED NEW POTATOES
Curly chicory, FRENCH DRESSING
Italian bread and cheeses, or CASSATA ALLA SICILIANA
Pouilly-Fuissé

SPINACH SOUP WITH SPRING ONIONS
BROILED SWORDFISH WITH COLD CUCUMBER AND DILL SAUCE;
BOILED NEW POTATOES
Imported Swiss cheese, French bread, McIntosh apples
Riesling

CHICKEN BROTH with chopped fresh tarragon
HALIBUT MOUSSE WITH SHRIMP SAUCE; BOILED NEW POTATOES;
MIMOSA SALAD FIFI
Coffee ice cream, CHOCOLATE SAUCE, petits fours
Chablis

LOBSTER À L'AMÉRICAINE; BOILED RICE
GREEN SALAD
French bread and cheese
Strawberries marinated in light rum and sugar
California Chablis

MUSHROOM CROUSTADES
LOBSTER À L'AMÉRICAINE; RICE PILAF
Cold asparagus, FRENCH DRESSING
Assorted cheeses, French bread
Sliced navel oranges with Curaçao
Montrachet

CHICKEN FRICASSEE; BOILED RICE; BRAISED PEAS À LA FRANÇAISE
GREEN SALAD
Fresh cut-up fruit
Bordeaux Graves

HOT CHICKEN BROTH
COLD POACHED CHICKEN WITH AÏOLI; VEGETABLES À LA GRECQUE
Blue cheese, Italian bread, ripe pears
Red or white Chianti

CONSOMMÉ BELLEVIEW
SAUTÉED CHICKEN WITH SHALLOTS AND ARTICHOKE HEARTS;
BOILED RICE
COCONUT BLANCMANGE
White Côtes-du-Rhône or Burgundy

AMERICAN FRIED CHICKEN; MASHED POTATOES; corn on the cob;
buttered string beans
Berries and cream
California Pinot Chardonnay

MUSHROOM CROUSTADES
CHICKEN VALLÉE D'AUGE; BOILED RICE
Bibb lettuce, FRENCH DRESSING; French bread and butter
STRAWBERRIES NARCISSE
Vouvray

BROILED CHICKEN WITH LEMON GARLIC BUTTER; BOILED RICE or
NEW POTATOES; whole baby string beans
Cantaloupe with vanilla ice cream
Corton-Charlemagne

COQ AU VIN À LA BOURGUIGNONNE; BOILED NEW POTATOES;
GREEN SALAD
Assorted cheeses, French bread, fresh fruit
California Pinot Noir

CHICKEN LIVER PÂTÉ, hot toast; sliced cucumbers with chives,
FRENCH DRESSING
COQ AU VIN À LA BOURGUIGNONNE; SAUTÉED POTATOES or
POTATOES ANNA
Ripe Brie or Camembert, French bread
PÊCHES CARDINAL
La Tâche or Vosne-Romanée

BREAST OF CHICKEN CURRY WITH NINE CONDIMENTS; BOILED RICE
GREEN SALAD or SPINACH SALAD
ORANGE GINGER BAVARIAN CREAM
Beer

351

Sliced tomatoes with parsley and chives, FRENCH DRESSING;
imported sardines, lemon; sliced salami, Italian black olives;
radishes, French bread, sweet butter
CHICKEN IN A COCOTTE BONNE FEMME
Cheese and fresh fruit, or an apricot tart from a good pastry shop
Meursault

CHICKEN CUTLETS KIEV; KASHA with sautéed mushrooms; MIMOSA
SALAD FIFI
PINEAPPLE ALEXANDRA
Pouilly Fumé

Plain BROILED DUCKLING garnished with water cress; MASHED
POTATOES; BRAISED TURNIPS
Liederkranz, French bread, fresh fruit
California Burgundy

BLINI WITH BUTTER, CAVIAR, AND SOUR CREAM
PLAIN BROILED DUCKLING; KASHA; endive, FRENCH DRESSING
Honeydew melon, quartered lime
California Riesling or Pinot Chardonnay

CRÈME DU BARRY
BROILED DUCKLING WITH ORANGES; SAUTÉED POTATOES CHÂTEAU
Imported white asparagus, mustard French dressing (see SPINACH
SALAD); hot French rolls, sweet butter
Sliced pineapple, petits fours
Alsatian Traminer

TRUFFLED ROAST TURKEY WITH SAUSAGE AND CHESTNUT STUFFING;
buttered Brussels sprouts
Water cress and endive, FRENCH DRESSING; French rolls,
sweet butter
ORANGE GINGER BAVARIAN CREAM
California Pinot Chardonnay

Clams or oysters on the half shell, lemon
Chablis
Truffled roast turkey with sausage and chestnut stuffing;
braised onions; spinach purée
Chambolle-Musigny
Vermont white Cheddar, hot French rolls
Chocolate torrone
Fresh fruit

Chlodnik
Cold rare roast beef; kasha with sautéed mushrooms;
spinach salad
Black bread, sweet butter
Cut-up fruit with kirsch
Tavel or California rosé

Cheese fondue jurassienne
Salad of cold beef vinaigrette garnished with sliced
tomatoes and water cress
Apple tart from a good pastry shop
Riesling

Carbonnade of beef flamande; pasta shells with cheese and
butter sauce; green salad or spinach salad; hot French bread
Fresh fruit
Beer or California Pinot Noir

Pan-fried steak with sauce marchand de vins; boiled new
potatoes; green salad
Cheese, French bread, fruit
Cabernet-Sauvignon

Pan-fried steak garnished with water cress, béarnaise sauce;
sautéed potatoes château; broiled tomatoes; French rolls
Sliced fresh pineapple with kirsch
Beaujolais

MUSHROOM CROUSTADES
PAN-FRIED STEAK WITH BORDELAISE SAUCE; POTATOES ANNA;
broiled tomatoes or TOMATOES NIÇOISE
Assorted French cheeses, French bread
PÊCHES CARDINAL
St. Estèphe, Château Clos d'Estournel

CLAMS ROCKEFELLER or smoked salmon with lemon
PAN-FRIED STEAK with SAUCE MARCHAND DE VINS; BOILED NEW
POTATOES or POTATOES ANNA; CARROTS VICHY
Château Smith-Hant-Lafite or Moulin-à-Vent
CRÊPES SOUFFLÉES
Château d'Yquem

Artichokes, FRENCH DRESSING
HOT BEEF À LA MODE; buttered NOODLES or BOILED POTATOES
Assorted cheeses, hard rolls
Fresh fruit or French pastries
Côtes-du-Rhône

COLD BEEF À LA MODE IN ASPIC garnished with water cress; FRENCH
POTATO SALAD; hot buttered French bread
LEMON SOUFFLÉ WITH VANILLA CUSTARD SAUCE
French Burgundy or California Pinot Noir

BEEF BOURGUIGNON; BOILED NEW POTATOES; GREEN SALAD
Roquefort, French bread, ripe pears or figs
California Burgundy

BEEF BOURGUIGNON; buttered NOODLES or BOILED RICE
Mixed GREEN SALAD, hot GOUGÈRE BOURGUIGNONNE
Fresh strawberries, CRÈME CHANTILLY
Musigny or Gevrey-Chambertin

354

Veal scaloppine marsala with prosciutto; boiled rice;
tomatoes niçoise
Green salad
Italian bread, cheese, and fruit
Bardolino

Bagna cauda
Veal scaloppine Marsala with prosciutto; rice pilaf; arugala
or escarole, French dressing
Cassatta alla siciliana
Valpolicella

Vitello tonnato; hot Italian garlic bread
Chocolate torrone
Fresh fruit
Soave or dry Orvieto

Veal marengo; pasta shells with cheese and butter sauce;
braised onions
Green salad with chopped fennel; Gorgonzola, Italian bread
Sliced navel oranges with orange liqueur
Valpolicella

Herring fillets in oil, celery hearts, radishes, black olives,
French bread, sweet butter
Blanquette of veal à l'ancienne; boiled rice; braised peas
à la française
Strawberries Narcisse
Château Margaux or Château Lascombes

Marinated anchovies with herbs, pimientos and olives
Osso buco; risotto milanese; arugala or escarole,
French dressing
Chocolate torrone, or cheese and fruit
Chianti Classico

355

ROAST LARDED RACK OF VEAL; buttered NOODLES; BRAISED ENDIVES
Assorted French cheeses, French bread
Fresh fruit
California Pinot Noir

COLD CREAM OF CHICKEN SOUP SENEGALESE
ROAST LARDED RACK OF VEAL; SAUTÉED POTATOES CHÂTEAU;
TOMATOES NIÇOISE or broiled tomatoes
CRÊPES SOUFFLÉES
St. Julien, Château Léoville-Poyferré

CONSOMMÉ BELLEVIEW
GALANTINE OF VEAL with CHAUD-FROID SAUCE; FRENCH POTATO
SALAD; VEGETABLES À LA GRECQUE or SPINACH SALAD
CRÊPES SUZETTE
Tavel

Hot GALANTINE OF VEAL; RICE PILAF; CARROTS VICHY; buttered
hot French bread
PÊCHES CARDINAL
Pauillac, Château Mouton-Rothchild

BRAISED LEG OF LAMB À LA CUILLÈRE; SIMMERED DRIED BEANS
Boston lettuce and water cress, FRENCH DRESSING
Assorted cheeses, French bread
Apricot purée, CRÈME CHANTILLY
Muscadet

NAVARIN OF LAMB; hot buttered French bread
Fresh raspberries and cream
Pomerol

NOISETTES OF LAMB ON CROUTONS WITH BÉARNAISE SAUCE; SAUTÉED
POTATO BALLS; whole baby string beans
COCONUT BLANCMANGE
St. Emilion, Château Cheval Blanc

GAZPACHO
BROILED LEG OF LAMB WITH AVGOLEMONO SAUCE; FRENCH POTATO
SALAD; hot Italian bread
Pineapple sherbet or fresh fruit
California Grenache rosé

ROAST SADDLE OF LAMB PERSILLÉ; BOILED NEW POTATOES; CARROTS
VICHY; French rolls, sweet butter
STRAWBERRIES NARCISSE
California Pinot Noir

ROAST SADDLE OF LAMB PERSILLÉ; POTATOES ANNA; buttered peas in
artichoke hearts
Boston lettuce, FRENCH DRESSING
PROFITEROLES AU CHOCOLAT
Pauillac, Château Latour

GLAZED HAM; BAKED POTATOES; CARROTS VICHY
GREEN SALAD
Vanilla ice cream, CHOCOLATE SAUCE
Cider, or a dry white wine

CHICKEN LIVER PÂTE, toast
JAMBON, SAUCE MADÈRE; spinach purée
Ripe Brie or Camembert, French bread
Fresh peaches
Bordeaux Graves

MUSHROOM CROUSTADES
BRAISED SMOKED HAM WITH TARRAGON CREAM; POTATOES ANNA;
spinach purée
COCONUT BLANCMANGE, or strawberries and cream
Beaujolais

CHICKEN BROTH with chopped fresh herbs
ROAST LOIN OF PORK À LA BOULANGÈRE; endive, FRENCH DRESSING
ORANGE GINGER BAVARIAN CREAM
Beer, cider, or a chilled rosé

BRAISED PORK CHOPS WITH MUSTARD CREAM; SAUTÉED POTATO BALLS
or BOILED RICE; BRAISED ENDIVES
Lemon sherbet, RASPBERRY SAUCE
New York State Riesling

Oysters on the half shell, lemon
TRIPE À LA MODE DE CAEN; BOILED POTATOES; GREEN SALAD
Assorted French cheeses, French bread
Fresh strawberries in their hulls, powdered sugar
Cider or beer

Smoked salmon, toast, lemon, freshly ground pepper
SWEDISH MEAT BALLS; buttered NOODLES; SPINACH SALAD with
oranges
Fresh fruit, or CHOCOLATE TORRONE
California Burgundy

FILLETS OF MACKEREL EN ESCABECHE
PAELLA VALENCIANA; curly chicory, FRENCH DRESSING; hot
Italian bread
Sliced navel oranges with Curaçao
Spanish Rioja, or California Grenache rosé

CASSOULET; GREEN SALAD
Roquefort, hot French bread, ripe pears
Côtes-du-Rhône

Index

*

Navarin of Lamb, 219
Noisettes of Lamb on Croutons
    with Béarnaise Sauce, 211
noodles, *see* pasta

onions, *see* vegetables
orange, to section, 329
orange butter, 331, 333
Orange Ginger Bavarian
    Cream, 326
Osso Buco, 187

Paella Valenciana, 244, 252
Pasta, 287
    to cook, 287
    noodles, 288
    Pesto Genovese, 290
    spaghetti, 288
pâte à chou, 17, 309, 341
Pâté, Chicken Liver, 12
peaches: Pêches Cardinal, 315
Peas, Braised, à la Française,
    269
Pesto Genovese, 290
Pilaf, Rice, 285
pineapple: to buy, 312
    to peel, 312
Pineapple Alexandra, 311

PORK & HAM, 230; *see also*
    casseroles
Ham
    Smoked, Braised, with
        Tarragon Cream, 238
    whole, braised, 242
Pork
        how long to cook, 237
    Chops, Braised, with Mus-
        tard Cream, 231

Loin of: Roast, à la Bou-
    langère, 233
    to buy, 234
salt pork, to blanch and
    render, 159

pot roast, à la flamande, 157
potatoes, *see* vegetables, salads

POULTRY, 104; *see also* cas-
    seroles
chicken
    to disjoint, 106
    to truss, 125
    à la provençale, 184
    Breast of, Curry, with
        Nine Condiments, 128
    breasts, to bone, 137
    Broiled, with Lemon-Gar-
        lic Butter and Coarse
        Salt, 121
    in a Cocotte Bonne Fem-
        me, 124
    Coq au Vin à Bourgui-
        gnonne, 109
    Cutlets Kiev, with
        Herbed Lemon Butter,
        133
    fricassee, 35
    Fried, American, with
        Cream Gravy, 117
    hen, poached, for curry,
        133
    Liver Pâté, 12
    Paella Valenciana, 244,
        252
    poached, hot, 35
    Sautéed, with Whole Shal-
        lots and Artichoke
        Hearts, 106

✳